HYPNOSIS

Is It for You?

OTHER BOOKS BY LEWIS R. WOLBERG

The Psychology of Eating

Hypnoanalysis

Medical Hypnosis

The Technique of Psychotherapy

Short-term Psychotherapy

Psychotherapy and the Behavioral Sciences

The Dynamics of Personality
(WITH JOHN KILDAHL)

Micro-Art: Art Images in a Hidden World

Group Therapy: An Overview
(EDITOR, WITH E. K. SCHWARTZ; 1973)

Group Therapy: An Overview
(EDITOR, WITH M. L. ARONSON; ANNUAL SERIES, 1974–79)

Group and Family Therapy
(EDITOR, WITH M. L. ARONSON; ANNUAL SERIES, 1980–82)

Art Forms from Photomicrography

The Practice of Psychotherapy

HYPNOSIS
Is It for You?

SECOND EDITION, REVISED AND ENLARGED

Lewis R. Wolberg, M.D.

DEMBNER BOOKS NEW YORK

Printed in the United States of America

Dembner Books
Published by Red Dembner Enterprises Corp.,
1841 Broadway, New York, N.Y. 10023
Distributed by W. W. Norton & Company, Inc.,
500 Fifth Avenue, New York, N.Y. 10110

LIBRARY OF CONGRESS CATALOGING IN PUBLICATION DATA

Wolberg, Lewis Robert, 1905-
Hypnosis is it for you?
Bibliograhy, p.
Includes index.
1. Hypnotism -- Therapeutic use. I. Title.
RC495.W63 1982 615.8′512 82-2491
ISBN 0-934878-15-3 AACR2
ISBN 0-934878-16-1 (pbk.)

Contents

Preface ix

PART ONE

1. Is Hypnosis Effective? 3

Experimental and Teaching Uses of Hypnosis 8
Medical Applications 12
Rehabilitative Uses 14
Pain Control 15
Diagnostic Uses 17
Psychiatric Uses 18

2. Who Can Be Hypnotized and How Deeply? 22

Is Compliance Always Necessary? 24
The Problem of Hypnotic Susceptibility 26
Factors in Susceptibility 30
The Importance of Depth of Trance 32

3. What Does It Feel Like to Be Hypnotized? 36

Behavioral Patterns 40
Postinduction Reactions 42

4. The Induction of Hypnosis 47

Operator Differences 49
Suggestibility Test 51
Trance Induction 54
The Deeper States of Hypnosis 64
Preferred Methods of Induction 76

5. The Happenings in Hypnosis 77

Rapport 79
Catalepsy and Other Muscular Phenomena 80
Hypersuggestibility 81
Physiological Happenings 83
Effect on Sensations of Touch and Pain 90
Effect on Vision, Hearing, Taste, and Smell 91
Intellectual Functions 93
Time Sense 96
Regression 98
Posthypnotic Suggestions 103
Can Hypnosis Improve Performance? 112

6. How People Become Emotionally Ill and Get Well Again 114

7. How Does Hypnosis Work? 127

Reduction of Tension 128
The Placebo Factor 129
The Relationship Factor 134
The Factor of Verbal Unburdening 136

8. How Hypnosis Influences Psychotherapy 138

9. Pain Control in Hypnosis 156

Effect of Hypnosis on Pain Perceptions 157
Hypnosis as an Anesthetic in Surgery 159
Hypnosis in Childbirth 161
Hypnosis and Dentistry 164
Hypnosis for the General Relief of Pain 166

10. Relieving Symptoms Through Hypnosis 169

Emergency Use of Hypnosis 176
Hypnosis and Behavior Therapy 180
Analytical Techniques for Symptom Relief 186

11. The Recovery of Buried Memories 190

12. When Is Hypnosis Not Effective? 201

13. Can Hypnosis Be Dangerous? 214

Untoward Reactions in Hypnosis 219
Sexual Seduction Through Hypnosis 221
Dangers of Dependency 222

14. Who Should Do Hypnosis 224

Can Paraprofessionals Be Trained To Do Hypnosis? 226
Stage Hypnosis 228
The Professional Person as a Hypnotist 231

PART TWO

15. Common Questions and Misconceptions 237

16. The Nature of Hypnosis 257

How Can One Tell if a Person is Hypnotized? 258
Physiological Theories 262
Psychological Theories 267
Applications of Theory to Practice 271

17. The History of Hypnosis 272

The Impact of Mesmer 275
The Post-Mesmeric Period of Animal Magnetism 278
Contribution of James Braid 282
Pre-Freudian Period 283
Freud and Hypnosis 285
The Revival of Hypnosis 291
Present-Day Trends 294

Bibliography 297
Glossary 299
Index 303

Preface

The presentation of an introductory book seems especially timely in view of the current interest in therapeutic and investigatory potentials of the trance state. As an introduction, I have styled the writing popularly to avoid complex phraseology, without deleting authoritative data regarding the present-day status of hypnosis—its values, limitations, uses, and misuses.

The mighty influence of hypnosis is not simply legendary; it has been attested to by some of the greatest minds of this century. Some years ago Aldous Huxley, during a conversation, told me with great conviction that in his opinion hypnosis was destined to become one of mankind's major means of solving its problems. I doubted his prediction then, and I still do, since it is obvious that agencies far beyond hypnosis will be required to rectify most of humanity's ills. But in the fifty-odd years that I have employed hypnosis as a clinical tool, I have become increasingly impressed with its values as a healing vehicle, as well as a research instrument, when it is used conservatively with an understanding of its limitations.

Unfortunately, hypnosis has been associated with charlatanry for so many centuries that it is still shrouded with superstition and magic. In the minds of some people it continues to be associated with the occult and supernatural. In the opinions of others it is a futile and sometimes dangerous device. These attitudes flourish not only among the population at large but also among some segments of the professional community. Such misconceptions may be the reason why hypnosis fluctuates so in popularity.

What are the true facts about hypnosis? What are its values in the practice of medicine? Can it help solve emotional problems, and, if so, what kinds of problems? Can it enhance learning, memory, and athletic performance? Can it eliminate the smoking habit, nail biting, bed wetting, and overeating? Can it improve sexual competence and enjoyment? What about its pain-relieving potentials? Can it enhance telepathic communication? What are its true merits as an adjunct in surgery, childbirth, and dentistry? Exactly what is hypnosis, and how does it work? Can everybody be hypnotized? Who are the most susceptible subjects? What risks accompany its use? These and other questions will concern us in succeeding chapters.

The purpose of this book, then, is to present a factual account of what we know and speculate about hypnosis. Of its therapeutic merit, there is little question in my mind. I have employed it all through my practice, even after my formal training as a psychoanalyst. In my opinion, hypnosis is a remarkably valid adjunct in practically all forms of psychotherapy, enabling patients to hurdle resistances to change that would otherwise obstruct their progress. I have detailed some of the reasons why it periodically falls into neglect and why some members of the medical and psychological calling continue to regard it with suspicion. Some of these professionals not only fail to endorse hypnosis but tend to discredit it as well. Because its principles appear to run counter to their cherished theoretical and methodological schemes, they regard it as an outmoded form of treatment. It is my hope that with the publication of this book I shall succeed in illuminating some areas of misunderstanding.

Acknowledgment is made to the Postgraduate Center for Mental Health who sponsored and supported the research and writing of this volume.

Lewis R. Wolberg, M.D.

PART ONE

1

Is Hypnosis Effective?

- A baby is born without pain. Lovingly, dispassionately, a hypnotized mother watches the miracle of emerging life.
- A man lies quietly on an operating table, casually chatting with surgeons while they repair an ugly, disabling hernia without administering any anesthetic whatsoever.
- An amnesia victim bewilderedly wanders into the emergency department of a public hospital. A few words by a skilled intern who has induced hypnosis, and he resumes the broken thread of his existence.
- Bloated, unhappy, frantic with fruitless efforts to diet, even with appetite-suppressing drugs, an obese girl is spurred into the pursuit of a successful weight-reducing regime.
- A mouse phobia continues to possess a housewife despite years of psychiatric treatment. In a trance she discovers its forgotten source in childish fears and misinterpretations. Result: liberation from her distressing handicap.
- Crippled by his inebriety and clutching at straws, an alcoholic takes refuge in hypnotic treatments, which cause a physical revulsion at the very sight or thought of alcohol.

- Because of a terror of dentists since childhood, an adolescent has neglected his rotting teeth. In a trance state fear is overcome, and his teeth are drilled with comfort and celerity.

These are some startling accounts of hypnosis that have recently cropped up in the press. The accounts, however, popularized though they may be, are true. The scientific facts about hypnosis, although less dramatic, are even more interesting. Unfortunately, the ubiquitous wish for magic often colors some newspaper accounts and tends to exaggerate the power of hypnosis.

Consider some of the following reports:

1. a famous baseball player with a paralyzing air phobia is hypnotized, and in the company of his hypnotist flies comfortably to a destination, never again to complain of fear;
2. a woman driven to a suicide attempt by an unfaithful lover and desperate beyond reason easily learns to overcome her depression in two trance sessions;
3. a well-known actress paralyzed by stage fright on opening night is put into a state of hypnosis and through posthypnotic suggestion delivers the greatest performance of her career;
4. a three-hundred-pound woman achieves sylphlike proportions with no drugs and little inconvenience;
5. a man who has been impotent for years is happily quoted, after a series of hypnotic sessions, as considering renting himself out as a stud.

To this day, articles appear in the press attesting to the "miracles" of hypnosis. Numerous sensational stories are counterbalanced only partially by a few factual, responsible articles that have appeared in a small number of well-known reputable magazines.

It is little wonder that most people, who are, after all, in no position to evaluate the validity of newspaper and magazine stories and advertisements, are under the impression that hypnosis can achieve the impossible. This is particularly true when articles comment on the work of physicians. For example, were a layman to read the conclusion of an article called "Terminal Cancer Pain Reduced by Hypnosis," he would obtain a mistaken idea of the painkilling virtues of hypnosis: "Because there are no side effects, hypnosis is the only real practical approach to the patient with terminal cancer." Now hypnosis may help *some* patients, but it certainly is by no means the "only practical approach" to this fatal malady. Nor can hypnosis cure all phobias rapidly, which is the implication of certain case reports. It is true that some phobias are the product of simple conditioning to a traumatic incident, the revival of which may be of therapeutic value in or out of hypnosis. But that is not the case in the majority of fears that become highly organized and widely ramified, requiring a considerable period of treatment for relief or cure.

The sensational claims made for hypnosis are fabricated not only by writers and reporters. Sometimes, professional persons claim that it can do the impossible. A number of self-appointed spokesmen for hypnosis, some writing extensively, unfortunately help discredit it by overdramatizing the process, by exaggerating its virtues, by participating in and publishing results of poorly conceived experiments, by engaging in naïvely organized therapeutic schemes, and by offering theoretic formulations that violate the most elementary precepts of dynamic psychology. At an opposite pole to these drum beaters are skeptics, including some psychiatrists and physicians, who not only depreciate the potentialities of hypnosis but tend to run it into the ground. The most vociferous of these doubting Thomases are those who not only have never done hypnosis themselves but have never even witnessed an induction. There are some psychotherapists who are so entrenched in their own passive methods that they find a variant, active approach like hypnosis unacceptable. Some are still swayed by Freud's rejection of hypnosis at the turn of the century, misinterpreting this as an indelible stamp of infamy. Some consider hypnosis a revival of an archaic, esoteric method and classify it in the category of cupping and blood letting. Finally, there are therapists whose personalities and inner problems are totally unsuited for the technique and whose efforts with hypnosis go unrewarded. Competence in bringing about hypnosis and proficiency in guiding the trance toward therapeutic goals are mandatory for success. After all, a scalpel is no better than the surgeon behind it.

In my own experience I have found hypnosis an invaluable aid in my work with patients. Some samples of the initial complaints of a series of patients who come to me for consultation, and with whom I employed hypnosis, are the following:

"I can't stop smoking, and my doctor tells me I must."

"I have tried everything to lose weight, and nothing works."

"My marriage is breaking up because I am impotent."

"I can't study, and when I do my mind goes blank as soon as I look at the examination papers."

"Airplanes scare me, but my job demands that I travel extensively all the time."

"I am totally frigid and have never had an orgasm."

"I feel depressed and hopeless; I pray every night that I won't get up; I hope tomorrow morning I will die; I've struggled sixteen years and never got over it."

"I have very bad insomnia."

"I find I am drinking too much."

To some readers many of these complaints may sound trivial. And in the bounteous catalogue of human maladies, they do seem to occupy a minor place. To the patients who presented them to me at the initial consultation, however, these symptoms were irritants which, like a speck of dirt that could not be dislodged from the cornea, plagued their very existence.

The man with the smoking problem, for example, was in a state of despair. Warned by his doctor to give up tobacco, he had tried the usual expedients. He rationed himself, allotting one cigarette an hour. Then he found himself watching the clock, scarcely able to wait until his reward was forthcoming. He futilely popped into his mouth various tablets and lozenges that were advertised to kill the smoking habit. He asked his wife to conceal his cigarettes, only to rush out to the drugstore for new supplies when he discovered that she had disposed of them instead. He chewed gum and walked around with an empty cigarette holder dangling from his lips. All measures failed. Not only did he feel defeated, but he was crushed by the thought that logic and common sense were no longer able to halt a plunge into what his physician had warned him would ultimately result in a serious lung illness.

The overweight lady was also in a state of desperation. She too had exhausted every measure known to her friends and her doctors. The abundant current literature on how to lose weight started her off enthusiastically on one dietary regime after another. Banana diet, protein diet, rice diet—nothing worked. She was not able to endure the empty ache in her stomach. A retreat to a milk farm for two weeks took off six pounds, which were regained with interest in a matter of ten days.

The man with a sexual disorder was convinced that he would never again function in "marital responsibility." He kept emphasizing this phrase, as if sex had more to do with performance that with pleasure. Each contact with his wife left him shaken, embarrassed, disillusioned with himself, and guilt-ridden at having frustrated his mate.

The student in a study slump had used all the props suggested by his colleagues, from benzedrine ("speed") to a rapid-reading course. An honor student at high school, his marks at college plunged to the lowest class percentile. Failure and the draft stared him in the face.

Only a person with claustrophobia could appreciate the terror of *the man grounded by his anxiety*. To add to his discomfort he would rationalize train travel to his colleagues, only to have them retort with not too subtle barbs about "being chicken." After three years of concentrated depth therapy, his personality had benefited, but he still could not get himself into a plane.

The lady with frigidity was no happier. Excited and eager at the beginning of her marriage, she gradually experienced a dwindling of feeling. Sex had become a bore; her gynecologist could find no organic reason for impoverishment of sensation. The thing that brought her to therapy was the realization that in warding off her husband, he was likely to stray.

A massive depression that responded only temporarily to anti-depressant drugs and electrical treatments prompted *the melancholy patient* to consult me. A thin, smiling façade concealed her deep desperation, which threatened to lead to suicide.

Counting sheep and devising countless other means to bring on slumber had little impact on *my insomniac patient*. He had had the good sense to use drugs sparingly, but he was sorely tempted to give up and make sleeping pills a way of life.

The man with the yen for triple martinis was on his way to becoming a secret drinker. He had enough insight to realize that he was using drink as a tranquilizer, and he decided that he had to do something about his shaking hands and his tension rather than drowning them in alcohol.

In all of these cases the outcome was successful. What contributed to the results was a series of hypnotic sessions without which, in my opinion, therapy would have been much more prolonged, and in some cases, probably unsuccessful.

This does not mean that all patients respond equally well to hypnotic treatments. Failures occur, as they do in any other form of therapy; a special chapter in this book is devoted to this topic. The complexity of the human mind is so great, its defenses against health often so elaborate, that the most expert practitioner may be confounded with stubborn resistance. His skill will then be challenged in outwitting an enemy that has defied correction for years. He may discover that other kinds of treatment are needed in addition to or instead of hypnosis.

Hypnosis is not a bludgeon that can shatter all psychological and physical symptoms. It is not the most reliable penetrating instrument to dissect the unconscious in a short-cut psychoanalysis. It is not a universal way of forcing people to a good adaptation and the acceptance of more constructive philosophical and spiritual precepts. What values does it then possess? Does it have real validity in medicine? What are its limitiations?

After an extensive investigation, both the British and American Medical Associations have endorsed hypnosis, properly utilized, as an effective treatment method within the limitations that bound any good medical techique. After all, even penicillin has little or no value in some bacterial and viral infections. Insulin is helpful in diabetes, but it offers no benefit whatsoever in other metabolic disorders. And hypnosis can score successes in certain kinds of problems and little or none in others.

Experimental And Teaching Uses Of Hypnosis

Let us now consider some specific situations in which hypnosis may be employed. First, hypnosis is an extremely interesting and useful tool to explore and teach aspects of human behavior. To illustrate, I shall describe an experiment I once devised to see if psychosomatic symptoms could be produced by artificial conflicts created in hypnosis.

I selected a group of volunteer subjects who were able to achieve a trance state deep enough to produce amnesia for the suggestions given them before they were aroused. In other words, the suggestions would be tucked away into unconscious recesses not easily available to the conscious flashlight of attention, although these suggestions might nevertheless influence a subject without his knowing why. If two emotionally charged, contradictory suggestions were given to the subject, he would then be at the mercy of diametrically opposed impulses that, it was hoped, would set up a conflict. We would then study the effect, if any, of the induced conflict on the subject in the waking state.

While in hypnosis, all the subjects were given the following suggestions: "When you awaken, you will notice at your side a table on which there is a bar of chocolate. You will have a desire to eat this chocolate, a desire so strong you will not be able to resist it. Yet you will not want to take the chocolate because it is wrong for you to do so; it does not belong to you. You will have an uncontrollable urge to eat the chocolate and an uncontrollable need to resist the temptation."

What are we doing here? First, we are stimulating in the subject one of his most fundamental impulses—the need to eat, to get oral gratification. Second, we are stimulating a fundamental moral prohibition, a "thou shall not." In our culture, conflict between a fundamental impulse and a moral prohibition is extremely common. It is, in fact, at the basis of a good deal of psychopathology.

Here are some of the results obtained with my voluntary subjects. The first, a male medical student, upon awakening, professed not to remember what had occurred in the trance. He complained, however, of "feeling cold." His arms were covered with goose pimples, and his face was extremely pale. He looked straight ahead while he fidgeted in his chair. When asked if he wanted some chocolate, he started to shiver. He then broke into a cold sweat. I finally suggested that he look at the chocolate, the sight of which sent him into an even greater spasm of shaking. He stood up to go to the bathroom, but he could not make it, collapsing in his chair. I felt it best to rehypnotize him, suggesting that he would no longer have a desire for chocolate, but that if he did, it would be perfetly all right for him to eat it. In other words, I removed the conflict. The subject recovered his physiological balance almost immediately. In this instance, we had produced a conflict that was unresolvable for the subject. He responded with tension and anxiety, which in turn overwhelmed his nervous system with excitations, disorganizing his physiological equilibrium. Why did this man show this particular kind of reaction? I learned from his history that several times a year he developed what his physicians diagnosed as "afebrile influenza," which had very much the same symptoms that he showed in our experiment. We might postulate that these illnesses were really psychological, brought on by a conflict similar to that which we had artificially produced. His personality resources did not enable him to resolve his conflict readily, and so he was under the influence of a kind of psychological tug-of-war.

The second subject was given the same suggestions in hypnosis, but he responded differently. Upon lifting his eyes, he appeared to be quite at ease. He immediately switched the conversation to the topic of entertaining and the duties of guests and hosts. "When you go visiting," he said, "your host always expects that you will partake of any food that is offered you." With this pronouncement, he turned to the chocolate on the table, pulled off the layer of paper, and started to eat it with satisfaction. When he had eaten three-quarters of the bar, he turned to me and asked, "Say, what is wrong with this chocolate? It tastes bitter. It's awful." He put the candy down, got up from the chair, and walked to the bathroom, where he disgorged the contents of his stomach. He then calmly returned to his chair, not appearing to be particularly upset. What this man had apparently done with his conflict was to gratify the oral impulse in part and the moral prohibition in part. He had swallowed a portion of the chocolate, and then had rid himself of the crime by bringing it up. The vomiting was the psychosomatic gastrointestinal symptom he had developed to solve his conflict. His personal history revealed that he often got attacks of dyspepsia. He lived on Tums. His stomach obviously was the organ through which he experienced and dealt with conflict.

The third subject was a psychopathic personality with whose antisocial history I was familiar. He was a young "ne'er-do-well" whose career of alcoholism and gambling was a great concern to his conservative and well-established family. It is an accepted theory that the psychopath possesses as uneven conscience; he is generally concerned with the immediate gratification of his impulses irrespective of the consequences. Because of this, I predicted that he would not be upset by the conflict, if one could be induced. Instead, he would probably become defiant. When he came out of the trance, the subject started laughing gleefully. He reached for the chocolate and tore off the wrapper, which he crumpled and threw at the wall. He then proceeded to eat the chocolate, smacking with delight and gazing at me furtively during the proceedings. This obviously was a characteristic way of solving his conflicts—defying authority and indulging his impulses.

I will describe one other case in this experiment in which there was a peculiar reaction. The subject was an alcoholic patient who periodically developed a numbness and lack of sensation in his right hand, a condition known as hysterical "glove anesthesia." When he came out of hypnosis, there was no apparent response, either in his behavior or conversation. He talked easily and with no emotional upset. I finally asked him, "Don't you want the chocolate?" He replied, "What chocolate?" "Why, the chocolate over at your side," I responded. He looked at the table casually and remarked, "I don't see any chocolate." I picked up the bar of chocolate. He could see my hand, but not the chocolate! I dropped the chocolate, and he said, "My God, I heard something land, but I don't see anything." He had developed a "negative hallucination" for the chocolate, that is, he had eliminated it from his perceptual range. Why had he manifested this reaction? *To avoid conflict*. Hysterics quite characteristically repond to conflict by acting as if factors that stimulate it do not exist, often by deadening their senses. Hysterical symptoms—not feeling, not seeing, not hearing, not tasting, not smelling—are defenses against perceptions that, if acknowledged, would touch off anxiety. By temporarily not seeing the chocolate, this man avoided trouble at the expense of total awareness.

Hypnosis, therefore, may sometimes be valuable in demonstrating the workings of the human mind in its everyday functioning. The chief value of hypnosis, however, is in treatment.

Medical Applications

An important use of hypnosis is in the abatement of tension. The significance of stress is known to every physician and dentist, for it has a deleterious influence on the individual, both physically and psychologically. Hypnosis helps lower tension in two ways. First, its induction can have a profoundly relaxing influence on the subject. Muscles loosen; breathing becomes deep and regular; the pulse slows; somatic processes apparently quiet down. Second, suggestions that the subject deliberately acquire the habit of tension control reinforce the spontaneous relaxing effect of the hypnotic state. Since tension exaggerates both organic and functional symptoms, its reduction permits the person to mobilize forces which diminish symptoms and bring into operation elements that help to induce cure.

An experiment was done with a group of chronic ulcer patients. Half the patients in the group were taken off all medications and given hypnotic treatments organized solely around relaxation and tension control. The other half continued with the traditional medicinal treatments. After a period of several months the results were reviewed. The patients who received hypnotic treatments had improved much more than had those on the usual regimen of drugs and diet. This is not as surprising as it seems, since we now know that gastric ulcers are often induced and sustained by emotional factors operating through tension.

What holds true for gastric ulcers applies also to many other physical maladies. It seems reasonable to assume that any organ of the body can be disrupted by a glandular upset or by undue nerve stimulation, which occur in long-standing states of tension. Any residual weakness in an organ system will certainly show up under this kind of nerve stimulation. Eventually, organic pathology may result. There is no more dramatic example of this than in certain obstinate chronic skin conditions. A number of years ago I discussed with a London physician experiences he had had with so-called "incurable" skin cases. He had treated over one hundred patients with chronic skin disorders that had persisted for more than ten years, in spite of the most expert diagnosis and treatment. The sole therapy administered was relaxing suggestions under hypnosis. The majority of his intractable cases were cured and remained cured over the ensuing years.

The tremendous influence of tension on all the body organs can be demonstrated experimentally as well as clinically. Of great importance is the detrimental effect that tension has on the healing process in both acute and chronic maladies. One should not get the impression that hypnosis is a specific remedy for tension. There are many ways through which tension may be controlled, for instance through tranquilizers, relaxing, exercises, biofeedback, or the simple reassuring bedside manner of a compassionate physician. But hypnosis is one of the most effective means of helping to relieve a person who is undergoing extreme stress. Relaxation through hypnosis may, therefore, exert a beneficial effect on any medical, orthopedic, or neurological ailment. The extent of this effect is dependent upon the degree to which the ailment is being influenced by tension.

In my casebook, patients with the following conditions and diagnostic categories were definitively helped by hypnosis: *"irritable colon," spasm of the stomach outlet (pylorospasm), constipation, mucous colitis, gastric irritation (chronic gastritis), peptic ulcer, "heartburn," hiccuping, postoperative complications after a stomach operation (dumping syndrome), pseudoangina, generalized physical exhaustion (neurocirculatory asthenia), extraordinarily rapid heart rate (paroxysmal tachycardia), fluctuating hypertension, impotence, frigidity, enuresis, urinary discomfort (dysuria), menstrual difficulties, allergic reactions, skin irritations, (urticaria), unexplainable skin eruptions (neurodermatitis), psoriasis, eczema, asthma, migraine, arthritic pains, neuralgias, muscle pains (myalgia), insomnia, stammering, nail biting, tics, reactive depression, obesity, fatigue and faintness due to low blood sugar (hypoglycaemia), and intractable pain.*

The list seems impressive, but it must not be assumed that hypnosis was the only or even the chief therapeutic instrumentality. In practically all cases some kind of co-ordinate medical or psychological treatment was used along with hypnosis, which functioned as a means of reducing tension or as a catalyst for psychotherapeutic techniques.

Hypnotic relief of tension is also helpful as a principal therapy in some emotional problems, especially where there is not too pathological an underlay, that is, where the provocative psychodynamic factors do not require more extensive treatments. In cases where those factors do indicate the need for more extensive treatment, psychotherapy may be essential, in the course of which hypnosis, utilized as an exploratory or reinforcing instrument, may still be valuable.

Rehabilitative Uses

Another use of hypnosis is in the field of rehabilitation. The effect of hypnosis here is principally to increase motivation. In malnutrition, accompanying organic or psychological illnesses of various sorts, for example, hypnotic encouragement of the appetite may dramatically improve nutrition. At the opposite pole is obesity, in which food acts as a prop to relieve tension and to supply gratifications otherwise lacking in the individual's life. Obese people virtually drown themselves in excess poundage that undermines their health, damages their appearance, and reduces their chances for longevity. Appeal to common sense and will power merely serves to depress the person, causes him to lose repect for himself, and prompts him to turn for relief to more food with an oral voracity that overwhelms his reason. Approximately 50 percent of obese persons can benefit from hypnosis, which may help motivate them to follow a diet and to control the tensions that previously were appeased through overeating. In the remaining 50 per cent, overeating is a product of a deep personality disorder, and more intensive psychotherapeutic procedures will be required, which may or may not be successful.

Similarly, smoking may be controlled or eliminated in a considerable number of people through suggestions made under hypnosis. In cases where cancer of the lung and upper respiratory system threaten, in emphysema, in cardiac or blood-vessel illness, such as Buerger's and Raynaud's disease, the giving up of tobacco is mandatory. Here again the victim clings to his destructive habit with frightening tenacity. He seems to be helpless in the face of an urgent need to suck on a cigarette and to fill his breathing passages with clouds of burnt tobacco. Tension is a formidable master, and the habitual smoker is helpless under the whiplash of his compulsion for relief of distress through smoking. A certain number of smokers, not all, can be helped to give up their habit by hypnosis and self-hypnosis. Suggestions seem to divert their tensions and enable them to function without the need for tobacco. The relief the individual soon experiences physically and in terms of bolstered morale produced by his conquest of smoking helps him in his determination to rid himself of his cigarette compulsion. This process is not as easy as it sounds, and in a number of cases, where smoking has acted as a safety valve for neurotic tensions, supplementary psychotherapy will be required in order to deal with underlying personality and emotional factors.

Other rehabilitative uses for hypnosis include reducing stress and overactivity in cardiac conditions, facilitating speech retraining in aphasic speech disorders, exercising a limb that has been immobilized by a cast or arthritis, obtaining essential sleep in insomnia, and inspiring the "will to live" in chronic debilitating illness.

Pain Control

The use of hypnosis for pain control in surgery, dentistry, obstetrics, and various illnesses has come into prominence in recent years, and it is important to clarify its values and limitations. By promoting relaxation and raising the pain threshold through suggestion, hypnosis has been employed as an adjunct in anesthesia. It is *only* an adjunct. It is no substitute for chemical anesthesia. The dramatic cases one reads about in the press, in which patients have undergone major surgery with hypnosis as the sole anesthetic, are exceptional. These are the persons in the 10 per cent range who go into the deepest, somnambulistic trances with almost any type of trance induction. The average person requires chemical anesthesia for any operative procedure, surgical or dental. But hypnosis, in lowering excitement and tension, can lessen the amounts of chemical anesthetic required, thereby reducing postoperative toxemia and shock. When the individual is sensitive to or intolerant of a chemical anesthetic that depresses the respiration and lowers the oxygen level of the blood, the use of hypnosis reduces the risk. In heart and lung operations, the joint measures of hypnosis and chemical anesthesia are particularly valuable.

The use of hypnosis in dentistry has expanded in recent years. Here, too, hypnosis is no substitute for chemical anesthetics like procaine. But it is a helpful adjunct in relaxing a frightened patient who feels, mostly as a result of unfortunate childhood dental experiences, nameless terrors at the sight, the sound, and even the thought of dental procedures. It can also enable a person who gags easily to co-operate better with the dentist. It may permit an individual intolerant of dentures to master his discomfort. Carefully employed, with proper precautions, it helps control teeth grinding.

Hypnosis has some use also in general pain control—in both functional and organic cases—by enabling a person to detach himself from his suffering. Obviously, the employment of hypnosis here must be prescribed by a physician after careful diagnosis and evaluation of proper interventions. In some cases, medicine and surgery may remedy an underlying organic condition, but may not relieve the accompanying pain. Here, hypnosis, executed by a skillful physician, may help alleviate the painful state, with the co-ordinate use of psychotherapy, if required. In real organic pain, such as in neurological ailments and cancer, a deep hypnotic state is essential for a productive measure of pain control. For the few subjects who are able to achieve a very deep trance, hypnosis may be more effective than medication. At the same time that pain-relieving suggestions are given, suggestions may be made to relieve tension and to motivate the person to adopt a wholesome and realistic outlook about his situation.

In certain extreme conditions, such as extensive burns, hypnosis has been used with great benefit, reducing the existing shock reaction and pain, enabling the surgeon to change dressings more easily, motivating the patient to drink water for the replenishing of his exhausted fluids, and helping him to eat in spite of his nausea. Because of the prevailing toxemia in extensive burns, chemical anesthetics are not as safe as is hypnotic analgesia. Hypnosis has also been employed in plastic surgery and has made it possible for the patient to remain comfortable during the convalescent period. In examination of the various orifices, such as in bronchoscopy, sigmoidoscopy, and proctoscopy, hypnosis has been applied with benefit.

Diagnostic Uses

Advantage is sometimes taken of the symptom-removing ability of hypnotic suggestion in the case of people with physical symptoms of psychological origin. This is important, particularly when the symptom warns of an organic malady that necessitates surgical intervention. It would be hazardous to operate on a person with a complaint of psychological origin, since his symptoms would probably continue with even greater force after the operation. Hypnosis can help, in some cases, to identify the psychological condition by temporarily removing the symptom.

An example of how hypnosis may be employed for diagnostic purposes is provided by the case of a woman who complained of persistent abdominal pain that did not yield to medications or physiotherapy. Periodically the pain became so severe that she had to be rushed to the emergency room of a nearby hospital. Here physicians were reluctant to perform abdominal surgery despite insistent demands for this by the patient and her family. During one of her attacks, I was enjoined by a consultant surgeon to see her to rule out the possible presence of a psychiatric factor. During hypnosis, I was able by suggestion to shift her pain from her abdomen to other parts of her body and then by posthypnotic suggestion to remove the pain completely for several days after our visit. In subsequent sessions, we explored the psychological conflicts behind her complaints of pain, and we were able to embark thereafter on a successful program of psychotherapy. Pain syndromes are not too uncommonly caused by or complicated with psychological forces, and a determination and treatment of these through adequate psychotherapeutic measures is the only reasonable way of dealing with such problems.

In addition to pain, there are other conditions in which hypnosis may prove diagnostically useful. These include headaches, paralysis, tics, spasms, gait disturbances, vomiting, hiccuping, urinary retention, enuresis, sexual dysfunctions, anesthesias, paresthesias, and disturbances of hearing and vision. It must not be assumed that hypnosis is an infallable diagnostic instrument. A patient motivated to retain a symptom because it serves an important psychological need may successfully resist suggestions aimed at symptom alleviation. But even in these stubborn cases, a trained therapist who establishes a good working relationship with a patient may often succeed in circumventing such resistances toward making a proper diagnosis.

Psychiatric Uses

Perhaps the most extensive application of hypnosis is in the field of psychiatry. Here hypnosis can be valuable, not only because of its ability to produce physiological relaxation and alleviate tension, but also because it can enhance the effectiveness of psychotherapeutic techniques. Hypnosis alone has only a partial value in psychiatry; it must always be combined with some form of psychotherapy, functioning as a catalyst. One must not assume that hypnosis is always necessary or effective. Indeed, patients can be helped in psychotherapy without resorting to hypnosis. But hypnosis is valuable as an adjunct, particularly when there is resistance that interferes with the therapeutic process.

Experience has shown that it is not a particular theoretical premise or special technique that produces improvement or cure in psychotherapy. Rather, it is the degree of constructive use the individual makes of the therapeutic relationship that is the key to his progress. The therapeutic relationship is occasionally helped by employing hypnosis. In many instances, hypnosis initiates in the patient a feeling of trust, confidence, and faith in the therapist that is conducive to the development of a good therapeutic climate. This is particularly true when overwhelming anxiety affects the individual's ability to cope with his problems.

In short-term psychotherapy, where the objective is to restore the individual to an optimal level of functioning rather than to bring about a structural change in the personality organization, hypnosis may be selected as treatment of choice. Patients with symptoms that are destructive to them may be restored to an equilibrium. For example, articles appear in the newspapers from time to time about amnesia victims admitted to hospital emergency rooms. Through the use of hypnosis their memory and self-identification are improved. No great change is brought about in the basic personality structure. Under the impact of extreme stress or conflict the person may later break down again and develop amnesia, which is only one of the symptoms that he may exhibit when his capacity for adaptation collapses. However, at least for the time being, short-term hypnotic therapy has advanced him to a point where he can function in society. Enabling the individual to master his symptoms permits him to live more comfortably, but it is generally necessary to employ some form of psychotherapy over a period of time before a corrective change can be accomplished in the thinking, emotional, and behavioral patterns responsible for the maladjustment.

In selected cases hypnosis may help expedite this psychotherapeutic process. It is particularly suited to the patient who is paralyzed by resistance. Resistance often develops during psychotherapy in the form of overt or covert defensive maneuvers employed by the individual to preserve his neurotic adjustment. Usually the patient is unaware of such resistance. An example of subtle resistance is the patient's denial that there are things going on within him of which he is unaware. He is often certain that he knows all about his attitudes, prejudices, and conflicts, and he will stoutly resist the implication that he is under the influence of forces over which he has no control or recognition. If the patient is a fairly good hypnotic subject, he may be given a posthypnotic suggestion which he will not remember, but which he punctiliously follows. This may demonstrate to him that he has acted on impulses not determined by his conscious self. He may then be able to accept the fact that other subconscious drives are operating within him. Resistance may also develop toward the special techniques that are being used in psychotherapy or psychoanalysis. The person may block the free association of his thoughts or he may forget his dreams, which if recalled yield valuable clues to his inner fears and conflicts. The combined uses of hypnosis and psychoanalytic techniques is known as *hypnoanalysis*.

Dream interpretation is an important part of analytic therapy and a way of understanding the unconscious. During sleep the mind seems able to conceptualize its inner problems in dream structure better than when it is awake. If a trained professional translates these dreams, he may be able to bring the person to an awareness of some of the unconscious conflicts with which he is struggling.

A patient once came to me with symptoms of alcoholism, anxiety, backache, and painful stiffness of the right leg. We worked on his problem for a while, but we could find no explanation for his symptoms. He professed an inability to dream. Hypnosis was induced, and he was given a suggestion to dream that evening, and, if desired, to forget the dream. On his next visit his leg spasm was much greater and more painful than before. I induced hypnosis and asked him to dream the same dream he had had the evening of his last visit. In the trance state he appeared to be undergoing an emotional experience, which was accompanied by the jerking of his right leg. When he came out of hypnosis, he remembered his dream. In it he was driving his mother and father to my office. As he drove, he felt himself to be out of control of the car. An accident occurred and his father was killed, in spite of the fact that the patient tried to press his right foot on the brake with painful force. The dream was like a revelation to the patient. It appeared to explain the spasm in his right leg. It could be interpreted as a consequence of "applying the brake" to stop murderous hostility toward his father. It was possible then to explore with the patient his ambivalent relationship with his father and to bring him to an awareness of his inner conflicts and defenses. The tension, spasm, and pain in his leg rapidly went away.

Hypnosis is also helpful when there are blocks in executing the technique of free association because of a variety of resistances. Not only does hypnosis release verbalizations, but it opens up areas of psychic activity habitually under repressive control. Puzzling thoughts, fantasies, and impulses—derivatives of the unconscious—are made available to further examination.

Guided imagery is a means through which a patient is helped to recapture repressed thoughts that relate to problems for which help is sought. Such images are usually fragmentary, evanescent, and sometimes highly symbolized. This necessitates a decoding of fantasies before their meaning becomes clear. Hypnosis not only facilitates imagery but helps in this decoding.

To some extent, hypnosis is also valuable during therapy in bringing back forgotten memories, especially in cases where it is essential to trace a pattern of formative experiences and conditionings in childhood. Only rarely are such forgotten or repressed memories curative in themselves when revived. However, a reintegraton of significant experiences in the past permits the reevaluation of neurotic attitudes and helps the person to approach life from a new and constructive perspective. Occasionally, the recovery in hypnosis of an important traumatic experience in the past is followed by the giving up of a hysterical symptom.

In nonanalytic therapy, such as behavior therapy, hypnosis is useful by helping the patient relax, by increasing susceptibility to suggestions, by accelerating appropriate behavior, and by determining the rewards and reinforcements that encourage healthy relearning.

These are a few of the instances in which hypnosis may prove valuable during the course of psychotherapy. As explained before, hypnosis is not always useful or necessary. Only an experienced therapist who is trained in the skills of hypnosis and psychotherapy can evaluate whether or not hypnosis can be helpful in a particular case. Hypnosis should therefore be employed only by an ethical, competent, professional person who recognizes its limitations as well as its virtues and who uses hypnosis within the context of a structured therapeutic plan. Under these circumstances, hypnosis will prove to be an effective and in some cases an indispensable tool.

2

Who Can Be Hypnotized and How Deeply?

People who are convinced that they cannot be hypnotized often make the best subjects. Even though they express a conscious inability to let themselves go and relax, they may have an unconscious craving to be hypnotized and will readily comply with suggestions. But when a person is dead set against being hypnotized, it is usually impossible to induce a trance.

Hypnotizability is a normal trait, and everyone—healthy, neurotic, or psychotic—can be hypnotized if he is willing and able to focus his mind on the induction stimulus presented to him. In actual practice, however, we are successful in hypnotizing about 90 per cent of our subjects. The remaining 10 percent resist entering a trance for one reason or another. This resistance is a relative thing, because at certain times it may cease. A number of my patients, for example, were unsure of themselves at the start of therapy but were able to achieve hypnosis once they had arrived at the point where they could trust me.

Among the most common resistances to hypnosis are:

1. fluctuating attention and distractibility, which prevent concentration on the operator's suggestions,
2. a need to defy "commands," with an unverbalized challenge to and the desire to defeat the operator,

3. qualms about revealing repulsive inner secrets and impulses,
4. terror at yielding one's will and independence, with an intense desire to maintain constant control, and
5. a fear of failure and the conviction that hypnosis is a test of one's ability to perform. Often a combination of resistances is at work.

The normal trait of hypnotizability may therefore be counteracted by one or more motives to resist hypnosis. Such motives may be unconscious. The following experiment illustrates an example of this resistance. During a trance several well-trained somnambules were given the posthypnotic suggestion that they would not be susceptible to hypnotic induction by anyone but myself. Amnesia for this suggestion was then induced. An acquaintance of mine, adept at the art of hypnosis, and known also to the subjects since he was a witness to the experiments, informed them one afternoon that I was ill and would not be present. He asked the subjects whether they would be willing to continue if he carried on my work. They were eager to go on. However, his efforts to induce hypnosis were entirely unsuccessful, even though the subjects appeared to co-operate. Each subject remarked later that he could not seem to fix his attention on what the hypnotist said. "A million thoughts entered my mind," one of them told him. "I couldn't keep my thoughts on what you said. It suddenly occurred to me that I would be unable to fall asleep no matter how hard you tried. I thought this was strange because I really did want to be hypnotized." Another subject had been instructed that no one, including myself, would be able to hypnotize him thereafer. He had a similar experience, although his resistance lasted only a few days. Thus an unconscious motive to be unhypnotizable can be artifically induced or may arise spontaneously in the subject, blocking all attempts at hypnosis.

When the nature of the resistance motivation becomes known, it is sometimes possible to work toward its resolution or circumvent it by the appropriate phrasing of suggestions. For example, certain competitive patients who opposed my usual induction techniques entered a trance readily when challenged. The suggestion "See if you can make your arm stiff and rigid and, as I count from one to ten, see if you have the ability to make your arm so stiff that you will be unable to bend it" produced a muscular spasm unattainable before. By means of acceptably phrased suggestions, drowsiness and hypnosis were finally achieved.

Is Compliance Always Necessary?

As a general rule a prospective subject must be willing to enter a trance state. There are, however, exceptions to this rule. A surface fear or aversion may, as stated before, be subverted by a need to comply and to be guided and directed by a powerful authority figure. Some of the best subjects I have had were those who insisted that they could never be hypnotized because they could not allow themselves to be dominated by another person. But even when an individual has no latent impulse to comply and decides not to enter hypnosis, he may sometimes be persuaded to enter a trance state by a clever and skilled hypnotist who eventually wears the individual down. One of my professional friends is an accomplished hypnotist who refuses to accept defeat. He will persist for hours until he has exhausted his subjects to a point where they simply give in and enter hypnosis. Of course, the subject must be willing to expose himself to such prolonged grueling. If he refuses to do so, not even this master hypnotist could succeed.

The point is that the attention of the subject must always be engaged in some way by the operator. The idea that one can be seduced into hypnosis against his will and without attending to the pronouncements or gestures of the hypnotist makes good fiction; but it does not happen in real practice. However, a master hypnotist may trick a person into hypnosis by absorbing his interest in a roundabout way. I once observed a psychiatrist giving a lecture on hypnotic induction during which he concentrated on the body movements of a member of the audience who had expressed doubts that there was such a phenomenon as hypnosis. Illustrating how hypnosis could come about by focusing on the body movements of his unbelieving subject, he soon inducted him into a trance without the audience or subject being aware of what was happening until the person's eyes closed and his chin rested on his chest.

From a therapeutic standpoint, it is not good practice to deal with resistance to hypnosis by artifice. An attempt to break through resistances without analyzing them may create difficulties. An example of how upsetting this can be is illustrated by the case of a patient who was referred to me after two years of unsuccessful psychotherapy. The patient was a compulsive person who had built up a rigid system of detachment in which he maintained exaggerated, arrogant notions of his own abilities and a defiant attitude toward any type of persuasion. Psychotherapy seemed to be a threat to his neurotic personality structure, and he defended himself by a supercilious and hostile attitude toward the psychiatrist. This behavior interfered with all attempts to establish the type of relationship that might have brought about beneficial results.

As his therapy proceeded, he became more and more frustrated, finally insisting that his psychiatrist hypnotize him. Only through hypnosis, he claimed, would he be able to get to the bottom of his difficulty. The psychiatrist sent him to a number of hypnotists, whose efforts were unsuccessful. The patient strongly resisted the induction process, yet felt intense frustration and disappointment at his failure to be hypnotized.

The psychiatrist asked me to attempt hypnosis with the patient, believing that if induction were successful, it might be possible to get around his detached attitude. When the patient appeared for the initial visit, his first words to me were, "I'll bet you can't hypnotize me." He then smiled in an arrogant manner and remarked that four hypnotists considered skilled in their profession had failed. He had challenged each of them to put him into a trance, stating that he had made a bet with himself that nobody would be able to do this. I asked why he thought I might be successful when others had failed, and he replied that he was not sure that I would be successful, but that he had heard about sodium amytal as a catalyst in hypnosis. If I were to give him three capsules of the drug, his resistance might be removed. On my desk were blue placebo capsules of sodium bicarbonate. The patient pointed to the capsules and said, "Those are sodium amytal capsules, aren't they? Could I take them now?" I agreed that a powerful sedative often facilitated hypnosis and that the capsules on my desk might possibly put him into a state where he could not resist hypnosis.

To my surprise, shortly after he had swallowed the tablets, he began to complain of feeling drowsy. I then started trance induction and succeeded in putting him into a deep hypnotic state. When he awoke, he was very elated, but almost immediately thereafter he had an anxiety attack with severe heart palpitations, difficulty breathing, and a feeling that the walls were closing in on him. What had apparently happened was that he had cajoled himself into believing that he could be hypnotized through the agency of the blue capsules, and he had permitted himself to relax his vigilance to a point where he could enter a trance state. The feeling that he had yielded his defenses even temporarily was enough to create panic.

The psychiatrist reported to me that the anxiety attack lasted the greater part of one week. He believed the experience was valuable because it allowed him to bring to the patient's attention in a dramatic way the realization that anxiety was associated with closeness in his relationships with people, and a yielding of his controls.

Even though the induction of hypnosis was probably justified by its results, the case illustrates how an abrupt breakdown of an individual's defenses can produce severe anxiety.

The Problem of Hypnotic Susceptibility

Even though most people are easily inducted into hypnosis, the problem of why only approximately 10 per cent are capable of entering into the deepest stages (somnabulism) still persists. There are also a number of auxiliary questions. Does susceptibility to hypnotic induction vary with different hypnotists? Is it different, for example, with beginning hypnotists in contrast to experienced ones? Are there differences in susceptibility with various kinds of induction methods? Can subjects who usually experience only a light trance sometimes achieve a deep hypnotic state? If so, what are the best ways to doing this? Do "deep trancers" have a special kind of personality?

Two skilled researchers, Ernest R. Hilgard and A. M. Weitzenhoffer, of Stanford University, developed a scale of responses that indicated different levels of depth in the hypnotic state. This scale provides a gauge in which variations in the trance depth of a subject exposed to different induction procedures can be studied. Hilgard's and Weitzenhoffer's findings seem to indicate that a subject's hypnotic susceptibility under ordinary laboratory conditions is fairly consistent, even with different hypnotists. Indeed, subjects did as well with beginners as with experienced hypnotists and even responded well to an unfamiliar voice recorded on tape.

Another finding reported by the researchers is that the level of depth achievable with successive inductions is relatively stable, and that unless an individual goes into a fairly deep trance at the beginning, he will not make gains with practice. In other words, a person who is capable of achieving only a light trance will probably go no deeper; a subject who shows a facility for some depth can be helped to go deeper. Since the data on which these conclusions are based was gathered from experiments with volunteer subjects, the experimenters caution against generalizing from their results to the responses of another sample, for instance, clinical subjects.

G. R. Pascal and H. C. Salzberg of the University of Tennessee, using techniques based on learning theory, have published the results of an experiment which indicate that 52 per cent of fifty-six subjects were brought to a somnambulistic trance state in one session. The techniques used, they state, can be taught and learned by any operator. Whether or not this fact is true, the point suggested by the experiment is that hypnotic susceptibility is not a fixed quantity. It can shift under certain circumstances. A skilled hypnotist who alerts himself to the subject's reactions and adapts his techniques to take advantage of any latent capacities for learning trance behavior will score the greatest success.

In my own work, I have found that patients vary from day to day in their susceptibility, depending on how upset they are, the nature of their immediate attitudes and feeling toward me, and the specific material with which we are dealing at the time. Moreover, I have been able to ascertain, both from the personal reports of patients and from their former hypnotists, that some subjects who could not enter a trance with a previous therapist did so with me. Nevertheless, universal conclusions cannot be reached on the basis of my experience alone. I tend to think that the susceptibility of persons who apply to a therapist for help because of an emotional problem depends on the degree to which they invest the figure of the therapist with symbolic meaning and the extent to which they are willing to accept the hypnotic interaction.

This is not an extraordinary statement, since patients will respond in varying ways to the personalities and actions of the therapists working with them. Much of this reaction is of course a projection (transference), but it nevertheless has an effect on how the patients react. Resistance toward one therapist-hypnotist may differ from that directed at another, and this will affect the susceptibility to induction, the depth of trance, the activity or passivity displayed by the subject, the intensity of liberated anxiety, and various trance phenomena.

For example, a subject with great unconscious fears of authority, which he masks by a façade of toughness, may defer to a hypnotist of imposing bearing and reputation, whom he feels he cannot resist. He will submit to him by assuming a deep, passive trance. With a hypnotist he judges to be weak, he may resist, be defiant, or actively control the depth of trance. With a "strong" female hypnotist, who represents a mother figure with whom he was too close, he may respond with sexual fantasies and fears of mutilation, which will prevent him from succumbing to deep hypnosis. With a weaker woman figure whom he does not fear, he may become seductive and respond with a deep trance as a means of getting into her good graces. With any one hypnotist, the subject's level of trance, as well as the phenomena in the trance, will continually change with transferential ebbs and flows, and these will shift and distort the image of the hypnotist in kaleidoscopic ways. The hypnotic state is subject to many vicissitudes. Fluctuations and varying levels are common in the same subject from day to day or even during a single trance state.

In my work with clinical subjects, I have found that with practice many can reach progressively deeper trance levels. Overcoming their own resistance is an important factor, as is the *conviction* that they have entered a trance. I have found that when I can *convince* a patient that he has experienced genuine glove anesthesia—a suggested anesthesia of a hand—he finds it easier to achieve a somewhat deeper level of hypnosis. However, those patients who could not reach somnambulism early in the game, either in the first or second session, rarely have been able to develop into somnambules later on. In several instances, patients who were habitually "light trancers" developed somnambulism after a catastrophic event in their lives shattered their security. But they returned to light levels after the crisis was over and they had regained a sense of security and stability.

There is no such thing as a permanent inability to be hypnotized. There may be a temporary unwillingness to enter a trance state. Hypnosis can be resisted successfully much as a person can force himself to stay awake after his customary bedtime. A subject's fear can block the efforts of the hypnotist as will a competition with the operator and a need to fail.

One interesting circumstance that can lead to hypnotic susceptibility is "sensory deprivation." If a person is completely sealed off from stimuli in a darkened room that is comfortably heated and ventilated, a number of interesting things may happen to him. After a short period, feeling cut off from the world, he will experience anxiety, disturbances in physical sensations, and feelings of depression. Soon he will be unable to orient himself, and he will show "stimulus hunger" and reach for stabilizing cues. He may even begin to have hallucinations in which he hears voices and then will carry on a conversation with imaginary people.

In an experiment at Michigan State University, Raymond S. Sanders and Joseph Reyher placed ten subjects who had been resistant to hypnosis in a cubicle for a maximum of six hours or until sensory-deprivation phenomena occurred. Hypnotic induction was undertaken by way of a communication system, the subjects remaining in the cubicle. The gain in the hypnotic susceptibility of this group was statistically significant compared with a control group.

Another means of increasing susceptibility is a group setting for hypnosis. Once, while I was speaking at a meeting of physicians, the question of nonhypnotizability came up. Several physicians said that they had tried a number of hypnotists but could not be inducted into a trance. When I asked for volunteers who had failed at being hypnotized, five physicians consented to sit on the platform and participate in an experiment. I then proceeded to suggest glove anesthesia without going through the formality of induction. Four of the five subjects admitted a diminution of sensations in the hand chosen for the experiment. Immediately thereafter, with their consent, I asked them to *put themselves into a trance* while I counted slowly from one to twenty. The results were so rewarding that two of the four physicians refused to come out of hypnosis until several minutes after the signal for termination was given.

Factors in Susceptibility

A question often asked is whether there are correlations between the physical and psychological characteristics of subjects and their susceptibility to hypnosis. Here again there is some difference of opinion. However, the following conclusions are generally accepted:

Sex: males and females are equally hypnotizable.

Physique: there is no difference among people of different stature and body build.

Age: young children make excellent subjects and are generally more susceptible than adults.

Intelligence: no correlation has been found between the intelligence quotient and hypnotizability.

Personality and projective psychological tests: no tests that are reliable in predicting susceptibility have yet been devised.

Degree of Anxiety: the greater the anxiety level and the more in need of help the individual believes himself to be, the more susceptible he is. For example, soldiers go more readily into deep trance states when in battle fatigue than after the shock of combat has subsided. Yet subjects with little anxiety can easily be hypnotized if they are willing to co-operate.

Motivation: lack of motivation for hypnosis will lessen the attention given to induction suggestions and hence reduce susceptibility.

Religion: people brought up under a strict religious code, and having more or less accepted its precepts at one time, tend to make good hypnotic subjects even though they may have moved away from orthodoxy.

Personality characteristics and neurotic syndromes: no correlation between susceptibility and any standard personality or neurotic classifications has been found. However, people who sleepwalk or who report lapses of memory may turn out to be somnambules. Individuals who relish sensory experiences, or who are able to project themselves into roles, like actors, show a greater aptitude for hypnosis than others. In Dr. Hilgard's laboratory, individuals who had imaginary companions in childhood, who read a good deal, and who had a capacity for immersing themselves in adventure or nature were most susceptible. I have found that suspicious, withdrawn, and hostile people tend to resist hypnosis. Dependent personalities and hysterical individuals are not necessarily the most hypnotizable; some may actually be difficult to induct into a trance, even though the literature alludes to their easy susceptibility. Psychotic persons, difficult to hypnotize, may respond if their attention is gained and sustained, and if the relationship with the operator is a reassuring one.

Suggestibility: there is some evidence that people who are highly suggestible make the best subjects. An experiment to test this hypothesis was designed by G. Wilson Shaffer of Johns Hopkins University. Twenty-five subjects were divided into five groups. Group 1 consisted of mental patients; in Group 2 there were physicians and professors; in Group 3, nurses; in Group 4, business executives; in Group 5, college students. In exposing the subjects to tests for suggestibility, Shaffer discovered that 77 per cent of all the subjects accepted false suggestions given by a single experimenter. The records of students, nurses, and patients were almost identical, and only slightly lower in the other two groups. A sample of suggestible subjects revealed that all were hypnotized in less than ten minutes and some in less that five minutes. Among the subjects who refused suggestions, only one was capable of being hypnotized and then only after a long period of time. When Shaffer repeated the same experiment but with different experimenters, he found the level of suggestibility and hypnotizability was reduced considerably. Especially interesting was the fact that the level of suggestibility changed with different experimenters. It is apparent from this experiment that people tend to be open to suggestion with some individuals and react negatively to others.

The Importance of Depth of Trance

From the results of some experiments it would be reasonable to assume that a very deep trance is more effective than a light trance and the effectiveness of therapeutic suggestions is greatest in somnambulism. This assumption is not supported in clinical practice. Other factors besides how deeply hypnotizable a person may be enter into the picture when we are dealing with the resolution of an emotional problem. There are many reasons why a person will not give up his neurotic illness or his crippling symptoms, no matter how distressing these may be, and suggestions made for him to do so, even in the deepest somnambulistic state, may have little corrective impact. Such resistance must be dealt with through the conscious layers of the psyche before the individual begins to show any sign of improvement.

Recall phenomena in hypnosis, released by suggesting that the subject return to a previous period in his life (regression), are extremely exciting. So are the revelations of experimental conflicts, automatic writing, mirror and crystal gazing, sculpting under hypnosis (hypnoplasty), time distortion, and other hypnoanalytic techniques, all of which require a deep trance. Were we so naïve as to conclude that such divulgences in themselves are therapeutic, we would be in for disillusionment.

When dealing with emotional difficulties, we are wrestling with a powerful adversary—resistance. This often takes the form of a refusal and an inability to profit from insight. Residues of obsolete childish needs, attitudes, and values continue to operate beyond the reach of reason; they seem to have an existence of their own. Even though they bring only misery, they continue to maneuver the individual into self-defeating pursuits. The sources of these infantile drives are generally barricaded against awareness by a group of defenses that are difficult to counteract. In hypnosis these repressive defenses may be temporarily swept aside. But this measure will not eliminate the impulses or the defenses that support them. Before the individual can even begin to challenge them, he must analyze and deal with the subversive gratifications he gets from his childish drives and the guilt feelings that prevent him from acting in his own best interests.

For example, one of my first patients, a successful businesswoman, was suffering from harsh emotional difficulties when she came to me seeking help. She had been three years old at the time her sister was born, and when her parents paid more attention to the new baby, she felt destructive emotions and impulses toward her younger sister, whom she looked upon as a competitor. She was angry at her parents for removing her from the center of the stage and for giving her sister the attention and love that she wanted exclusively for herself. Punished for cruel behavior toward her sibling, she learned to control and repress her rage. Later in life, as a buyer in a large department store, she was thrown into competition with younger women who were also hired as buyers.

Competitive jealousy is not unusual in our society. However, because of our patient's early experience of competition in the family, her business situation infantriggered an excessive reaction of rage. Automatically, she invoked defenses of control and repression and on the surface was pleasant to and genial with the younger, prettier, and more aggressive buyers. But underneath this congenial exterior I believed there was resentment. The repression of anger and hostility, I hypothesized, encouraged depression and migraine attacks, which led her to seek help.

In therapy, she was inducted into a deep trance and was able to recall her earlier experience with her sister and parents, which released feelings of murderous rage. I therefore postulated that these emotions were responsible for the symptoms that brought her into therapy. I hoped that the release of her repressed attitudes and liberation of the associated emotions would eliminate her troubles. Actually, when she came out of the trance, the patient had complete amnesia for the trance events. But I had recorded the transactions, which I then played back, hoping to convince the patient that she had divulged her experiences, even though she could not remember having done so. The patient listened to the episode with detached interest, intellectually acknowledging my interpretations. Emotionally, she was unmoved by the revelations. She continued to be depressed and to suffer from headaches. She seemed to be insulating herself against help.

With the laborious "working through" of her resentment in the waking state, her guilt feelings were eventually resolved, and she accepted her right to feel hostile. This enabled her emotionally to understand the source of her feelings and their manifestations. Eventually, she resolved her need to repress hostility; she found it unnecessary to feel hostile in competitive situations. Her depression and migraines were greatly relieved.

Situations like this have led many therapists to the conclusion that a deep trance does not necessarily lead to a shortening of therapy. Indeed, some believe that a light trance, in which resistances and defenses continue to operate, is more effective in the long run, since one can deal directly with the mechanisms that support repression.

Generally, we may say that there is no correlation between the depth of trance and the effectiveness of therapeutic suggestions. This is because a variety of circumstances occur that significantly counteract or reinforce each other, promoting or negating the influence of suggestions.

First, the degree of suggestibility varies from subject to subject. For some this degree is greater in a light trance than it is for others in deep hypnosis. It can also vary in the same subject according to his current emotional state, the intensity of his anxiety, and the kind of defensive mechanisms he has. It varies with his attitudes toward the operator. Sometimes a patient will resist apparently innocuous suggestions from some hypnotists, while he will accept from others suggestions that cause much conflict and require him to exercise extraordinary mental and physical effort. Interestingly, while it is possible that a patient may accept more and more complicated suggestions as he descends into a deeper and deeper trance, this does not always happen. For while he may be capable of following suggestions that necessitate complex internal readjustments, he may resist them or awaken if they create anxiety. Indeed, he may perceive a threat to his defenses as he enters a deep trance. As a result, the moment he senses even minimal anxiety, he may block further suggestions in order to ward off dangers that he fears he will be unable to master later. Because he feels protected by his defenses in a light trance, he may allow himself to follow suggestions that stir up considerably more anxiety that he will tolerate in a deeper trance.

Second, there are some therapeutic procedures that are better achieved in a light rather than in a deep hypnosis, mainly because there is no need to cut through the patient's defenses or to penetrate into areas of deep conflict. Thus, when the therapeutic goal is to promote relaxation, achieve relief from tension, control symptoms, intensify motivation, give reassurance, challenge the validity of defensive behavior, and direct one's understanding toward change, a light or medium trance will serve best.

When amnesia is essential, as in the creation of experimental conflicts for research purposes, or for elaborate posthypnotic suggestions, a somnambulistic trance may be required. It may also occasionally be beneficial in the probing of an incident that has been obdurately repressed and sealed off from memory. Here certain hypnoanalytic procedures, such as regression and revivification, and automatic writing, will require very deep hypnosis. Deep hypnosis may also be necessary for diagnostic purposes, such as distinguishing an organic from a psychological symptom, for the relief of dangerous hysterical symptoms in emergencies, or the elimination of organic pain. These occasions for a deep trance, however, are not too frequently encountered in professional practice.

3

What Does It Feel Like to Be Hypnotized?

No two people react the same way to their first hypnotic induction. The experience elicits a variety of responses. It has been described by some people as similar to "floating on a cloud," "being dipped into a healing pool," or "being covered with a nice warm blanket." Others have found it less reassuring. "It scared me," said one patient. "I got the idea that my body had swelled up and filled the room." Another experienced disturbing physical symptoms. "There was a muscular tightness across my chest. My fear of a heart attack brought about by this muscular change made me come out of it just as you were telling me to relax more." For others it was an exotic sensation. "A strange experience; I was actually in another world." One person felt she had been transported to "the middle of a scene in which there was an extremely beautiful pavilion made of straw and rush combining Haitian and South Sea elements in a vivid and pleasing image."

Yet no matter how varied the descriptions, there is often a common reaction to induction—a sense of letdown or disappointment. People expect to experience something extraordinary in a trance, without realizing that the early stages of hypnosis are very much like certain other states familiar to everyone. For example, we have all had the experience of drifting into distraction when our attention is supposed to be fixed on an unchanging focal point. Our thoughts stray far away from the immediate situation and surroundings. So, too, in falling asleep, one often enters into a dreamy, drowsy state of partial awareness, a kind of suspended "not-awake-not-asleep" condition. If the telephone rings, one wonders whether it is a dream or whether the phone is actually ringing. It is not clear whether one is awake or asleep. This is the normal "hypnoidal" state, a kind of intermediate station en route to sleep. The average trance, induced by traditional techniques, is very much like this.

In this state a person can hear, feel, smell, understand, reason, imagine, and remember quite actively, as readily and effectively as when he has full consciousness. He is fully aware of what is going on around him. He may be either critical and antagonistic or accepting and co-operative, and he may arouse himself if he does not desire to continue in the hypnotic phase.

This may puzzle the person who is being hypnotized, because he usually has the idea that in hypnosis he becomes an automaton, completely at the mercy of the hypnotist. He believes he will simply follow commands and not engage in independent activities. He also has the idea that he is supposed to be "unconscious," as if he were asleep or anesthetized.

It is important to understand that these are misconceptions about hypnosis. A persons is never in a condition of unconsciousness during this state; the mind always functions actively.

Yet, during the trance the subject undergoes psychological and physiological experiences that are characteristic of both waking and sleeping. The number of waking or sleep characteristics will depend upon how close to either state the person in hypnosis actually is. At one end of the hypnotic spectrum he is close to wakefulness, and his behavior—the quality and content of thinking and the physiological manifestations—is very similar to the waking condition. This is a light trance.

As the person goes into a deeper trance and approaches sleep, the thinking processes and the physiological manifestations begin to take on some of the properties of sleep. They are never quite the same as in sleep, because hypnosis is not sleep. One individual, therefore, may be in a very light trance that is phenomenologically indistinguishable from waking; another may be in a deep trance and appear as if he were asleep. But both are in a hypnotic state.

The question of what determines whether a person reaches a light, a medium, or a deep hypnotic state is still controversial. A combination of factors is probably responsible. We can draw an analogy from sleep phenomena. There are some people who are habitually deep sleepers, who practically fall into a stupor when they drift off. An alarm clock can blast away next to their ear without interrupting their slumber. Other people are very light sleepers, and the slightest movement or sound in the room will arouse them. But there are times, during physical and psychological exhaustion, for instance, when light sleepers drop off into a profound slumber. And there are times when deep sleepers doze fitfully and lightly, for example, during periods of emotional upset. In hypnosis the situation is similar. "Light trancers" may periodically go into deep states; there may be a tendency to do so when they are extremely exhausted physically and psychologically. "Deep trancers" may resist going into more than a light hypnosis for many reasons, for instance, when they defy or do not trust the hypnotist.

The nature of the subject's thought processes often depends upon his attitude toward the hypnotist and toward hypnosis itself. If he interprets hypnosis as an invasion of his privacy or as a potentially dangerous adventure, he may have fearful or hostile thoughts. If he feels contempt toward or animosity for the hypnotist, he may inwardly defy him and resist his suggestions. If he has great expectations concerning the benefits he will derive from hypnosis and from the hypnotist, he may symbolize these by appropriate ideas or fantasies.

When an induction technique uses a fixation object, a few subjects experience a variety of visual illusions and even hallucinations. Streaks of light, kaleidoscopic patterns, fantastic shapes, or abstract forms apparently symbolize the repeated rhythm of the induction process. One patient described himself as an egg-shaped disk over which I was suspended in the form of an embracing luminous crescent. The hypnotizer's voice may be symbolized as the sound of a drum or orchestral instrument. Feelings of relaxation and sleepiness are occasionally represented as "descending into a shaft" or "rising up in an elevator." A subject visualized himself on a magic carpet "soaring up into the clouds." There may be illusions of the room widening or shrinking, of the furniture warping, of the physiognomy of the hypnotist changing. An art student described her surroundings as a surrealistic painting. Skin warmth or coldness, and sensations of tingling or feelings of electricity (paresthesias) are occasionally experienced. These sensations are probably due to alterations in apperception and body image.

Illusions of strangeness are sporadic, and the individual may develop ideas that his body or identity has changed. One subject saw himself as a mechanical man whose limbs moved without his participation. Other reports: "My mind and body were disjointed"; "I felt as if I couldn't recognize myself apart from you"; "My body seemed strange, as if it didn't belong to me"; "I felt like several different people all at the same time"; "My body seemed to be made of rubber"; "I seemed to be standing in a corner of the room looking at myself on the couch"; "I had a sensation that my whole body, except the right side of my face, was swollen. I saw a blinding light. I felt sensations that my left hand was rising and my body moving. A pounding in my head, not too uncomfortable." Some subjects have ideas of rebirth. These impressions of depersonalization and unreality closely resemble the subjective experiences that take place during the onset of normal sleep or upon awakening. They are probably the psychologic components of the withdrawal from the reality cues of the external world that occurs during sleep.

During the induction phase the subject may have feelings and inclinations that are due in part to an automatic release of inhibitions and repressed emotions. They may also be in part the product of the subject's own interpretation of the trance experience. The mood may vary from joy to fear, depending on the person's associations. In most cases, the experience is a pleasurable one with feelings of lightness and relaxation. But in cases where the hypnotist is associated with a frightening or destructive figure of authority the emotion may be somewhat unpleasant or intimidating. In some instances, the subject may look upon hypnosis as a seduction and have vivid sexual fantasies about the hypnotist. These emotions and fantasies are in no way abnormal. They also occur in other close interpersonal relationships.

In rare cases, a few adverse reactions are encountered during trance induction. Occasionally, for example, a person who has had a bad experience with anesthesia during surgery may develop anxiety or a choking sensation. He will then open his eyes and refuse to continue with the hypnosis. Sometimes a subject may complain of a headache before hypnosis ends. I have usually avoided this reaction in the following sessions by insisting that he take a longer time coming out of the trance.

For the most part the average person experiences no unusual sensations or feelings such as have been described above, apart from reactions of pleasant relaxation or responses suggested by the hypnotist that the subject decides to accept.

Behavioral Patterns

There are no set patterns of how people behave under hypnosis. In many cases, a subject's behavior is determined by his ideas of the way people are supposed to act. Should he have witnessed a hypnotic session or received certain impressions from his reading about how hypnotized people act and look, he may readily incorporate these ideas into his own behavior. Moreover, a subject's fantasies about hypnosis may influence his own reaction. Thus the subject may act sleepy or display muscular movement, even convulsions, if he models himself after persons who were presumably hypnotized and acted this way.

In our culture, the most common idea of a person undergoing hypnosis involves a pose similar to that of dozing. If the subject is sitting, he slumps in his chair, his chin approaching the chest, or his head tilted to the side. Facial muscles are relaxed; breathing is slow and relatively deep; and he remains immobile even though he may be somewhat uncomfortable. Spontaneity is lacking, and he usually responds slowly and mechanically to commands. If asked to talk, his voice is low, comments are scattered, and his speech is slow. In our society this sterotype would represent most people's idea of a hypnotized person.

In other cultures, however, the stereotype is not the same, and the individual in a trance will display an entirely different kind of behavior. An example of ecstatic and even violent reactions in the trance state may be observed in some religious revival meetings. During these gatherings a few are propelled into convulsive states, sometimes speaking in "unknown tongues," and exhibiting other unusual manifestations, which are often interpreted as evidence of spiritual possession. Studies of these "possessed" souls reveal that they are indulging in behavior not habitual for them in the waking state. For instance, they demonstrate an ability to maintain awkward postures for incredibly long intervals; they endure painful stimuli without flinching, and they experience intense hallucinations of hearing, sight, and touch.

Cultural factors often influence other behavioral stereotypes. Among the Malays a hypnosislike syndrome, *latah,* has been observed, in which the person in a trance gives bizarre imitations of the actions and manners of those within his perceptual range, and does not appear to be able to restrain himself. The "jumpers" in Canada, of French-Canadian extraction, who suddenly break out in jumping and hopping behavior, are also known to indulge in a similar imitativeness, as do tribes in some areas of Siberia. In the culture of many primitive peoples hypnotic postures often constitute a routine aspect of religious and ceremonial customs. For example, through dancing and whirling to the monotonous beating of drums, the dervishes of Algiers and the religious devotees of Tibet enter into a condition of trance, becoming insensitive to pain. The Yogis of India are well known for their ability to induce self-hypnosis through meditation and prolonged fixation of the eyes, or by assuming strained positions during which they learn to control vital body functions.

These examples offer ample evidence of how a culture may influence the nature and quality of trances. They indicate also the wide variety of responses that are possible in hypnosis. Although as a general rule in our society the concept of hypnosis is linked with passivity and a sleeplike condition, there are exceptions to be found among subjects.

A limited number show dramatic reactions during trance induction. These responses sometimes take the form of the release of emotions, such as crying or intense fantasies that give rise to descriptions of childhood experiences and memories, or utterances of such extraordinary content that they could be interpreted by some as communications from the spirit world (the trance-speaking of spiritualists falls into this category), or from a previous existence (as in *The Search for Bridey Murphy**). These

* *The Search for Bridey Murphy,* which enjoyed great popularity upon its publica-

unusual reactions are generally found in persons who possess a rare ability to enter the twilight zone of consciousness, with altered awareness, even in the waking state. When this occurs, they may experience thoughts and engage in actions that interest, amuse, or even frighten them.

Such dreamlike reveries suggest the vast scope of thinking and feeling processes operating beyond the narrow beam of conscious awareness that exist in everyone, but to which only a few have ready access. The achievement of this heightened awareness may be brought about by meditation, concentration on a monotonous stimulus like blinking lights, or certain drugs (psychotomimetic drugs or hallucinogens) like LSD and mescaline. Under such circumstances a curtain is drawn on outer stimuli and inner processes take over.

There are some people who have a unique talent for delving into the pool of their unconscious. They readily fish out dormant needs and drives, which come to the fore during trance states in direct or symbolic forms. A highly repressed person, whose ordinary life is drab and grey, may, for instance, be transported into a world of color. Within the limited time span of the trance, he may have fantasies and even act out compulsions that could have become conscious had he taken drugs or indulged in meditation practices. Such a person may be inclined to sleepwalk, and to be subject to lapses of memory or to certain physiological reactions like temporary numbness, anesthesia, and other disturbances of the sensory and body organs (hysterical symptoms).

Postinduction Reactions

Immediately after the first induction, most subjects—even those who have gone into a somnambulistic trance—will deny having been hypnotized. This may be a defensive reaction against the idea of having given up some control. It may be an expression of a habitual lack of confidence in their ability to perform an important task. It usually is the product of a mistaken notion about the

tion, purportedly established the fact of reincarnation by describing how through hypnosis a woman was brought back in her memory to a previous existence. Shortly after the book was published, a rash of articles and booklets appeared, further attempting to substantiate hypnotic evidence for reincarnation.

nature of hypnosis, the expectation of something extraordinary, like being in the nose cone of a rocket. When they find themselves merely pleasantly relaxed and capable of controlling their thinking and reactions, they believe that they have failed to achieve a state of hypnosis.

The individual's response to induction and to the events in the trance can be of great diagnostic value to a trained clinician. The hypnotic state liberates some samples of the subject's customary behavior in a strange situation and yields important clues to his inner impulses, conflicts, and defenses. Sometimes a person may verbalize or act out a drama that portrays his attitudes toward authority. These expressions may indicate defiance, aggression, excessive submission, or other characteristics that began in the early formative periods of his life. I have found this a most important facet in my work with patients in hypnosis, and I believe it can cut down the prolonged time ordinarily spent on an exploration of the less conscious elements of personality. The style of the response thus serves the purpose of a projective test and tells something about the subject's attitudes toward yielding control, complying, trusting, and taking risks. The trance imposes on the subject a situation to which he must react with his customary defensive maneuvers. I have on occasion found the reactions so revealing that after a certain point, sometimes even following the first induction, I could proceed to work psychotherapeutically with patients without further recourse to hypnosis.

The reactions may also give a therapist clues about how to deal with resistances that are being developed to withstand further trance induction and the psychotherapeutic process itself. When the first hypnotic experience has been a pleasant one and has not caused too much anxiety, a patient will be motivated to enter into further and perhaps deeper trances, in which he will come to grips with his problems and thus be able to deal progressively with his fears and conflicts. If, on the other hand, the trance has proved to be an uncomfortable or frightening physical or emotional experience, in which the subject feels his defensive props have been threatened, he will interpret hypnosis as a force that can crush or control him against his will, and resistance may develop. This is often characterized by a refusal to expose oneself to further induction attempts, an inability to enter a trance even though there is a conscious desire to do so, or the maintaining of a hypnotic level so light that it permits awakening at the slightest threat. Hypnosis can thus take on a variety of meanings to a person. The most important factor of all in creating resistance is the formation of an untrue or unrealistic image of the therapist, whereby he is given the attributes of punitive or seductive authorities in the patient's past.

Such reactions may appear solely in dreams that follow upon the first or subsequent induction experiences. The dreams often include many obscure symbols and require an analytically trained psychotherapist to be interpreted. For example, a patient who was in a state of depression the evening after her first trance related this dream to me: "I was standing on something that appeared to be a boardwalk, watching men and women pass by together. They were holding hands, laughing, and enjoying themselves tremendously, but I wasn't a part of it. Several times I dropped my keys and couldn't find them, and each time a man would come over and find the keys for me and then continue walking with the woman he was with. I was sad and went home by myself. I then dreamed I was in a very deep sleep, and I heard someone unlock the door and open the latch and the next thing I knew (in my dream), because he couldn't open the latch (it was closed from the inside), he was terribly, terribly angry. He stormed over to the bed trying to wake me. I made a tremendous effort to get up when he did this. I guess I did awaken at this point, and may have cried out in my sleep, since my eyes were wet and I was shaking all over."

The first part of her dream symbolized her feelings of "being lost and an outsider," and the second part reflected, as she herself expressed it, "terrible guilt combined with fear of punishment and reprisals." The dream was a manifestation of her feelings of isolation from and rejection by men and her resistance to my "unlocking the door," which could lead to a cure of her illness. When she understood and accepted the meaning of her dream, I was able to work through her defensive reaction.

Another patient had this dream after her first trance: "I am in a cave. There is room to go back and forth. There is a desire to go out, but I am afraid. I have never before left the cave. Whenever I get close to the mouth of the cave, I go back. I wake up disturbed." It was not difficult to help the patient see that getting well imposed on her threats of rejection in love, failure in her career, and challenges to which she could never respond. Being ill was actually less of a threat. Her previous psychotherapeutic failures resulted from her dread of normality. She never left the "cave" of her isolation because of her fear.

A young man recalled this dream: "I am in a fort surrounded by troops. Out of it come men, including me, who are taken as prisoners with the head prisoner on a motorized cart. I talk to the guard, who then hypnotizes the two men with me. I say to him, 'You are not going to do that to me.' We fight with ropes, flaying at each other, while he is trying to hypnotize me. I escape and climb down a huge metal erection." The guard in the dream represented me, and as this authority figure I symbolized for the patient his punitive, domineering father. It was necessary to work out with the patient his transference reaction to me, before our therapeutic efforts could succeed.

A woman who was disappointed in our first hypnotic session had this dream: "I get into a strange elevator. I see a salesman there. I tell him I have lost my bag, but he refuses to help me." Her dream revealed that she assumed salesmen were always broke and who, therefore, went out with women for money. The patient, although married, had strong inclinations toward infidelity, which she felt was dangerous. Hypnosis posed the threat of possible seduction, and she was afraid of being hurt by it (the dangerous elevator). She felt that I would exploit her (as a salesman in need of money), and would ultimately "refuse to help her" or restore her femininity (her lost bag).

In contrast to these reactions there may be a strong positive reaction to hypnosis. This note was written immediately after a trance: "It is strange, but my body is not tense. I don't know what it is, but I am not rigid, which I was when I came in; I felt like jumping out of my skin. I have the feeling of the calm of the ocean after the fierce turbulent storm when the waters are churning. Now I'm like the calm sea. I just don't understand, it's so strange. I think my faith in your ability to help me get well is greater by far than the doubts I might have. I do feel in control and relaxed even as I write this. I don't know how to explain it."

4

The Induction of Hypnosis

Stage hypnotists and quack operators like to give the impression that one must be profoundly gifted and possess great powers of influence in order to hypnotize people. This is not true. Hypnosis is a fantastically easy phenomenon to bring about; the technique is so simple that even a talented child can learn it in a few minutes. I remember an amusing incident that occurred some years ago when I was working in a state institution. My next-door neighbor was a psychiatrist whose eleven-year-old daughter had learned to induce hypnosis from seeing the movie *Kim*, in which a storekeeper put Sabu, the hero, into a trance by enjoining him to stare fixedly at the fragments of a shattered vase on the floor. The child, impressed by the movie, painted a vase on a piece of cardboard, cut it up into jigsaw pieces, and proceeded to hypnotize the boys in her classroom, to the horror of the teacher. Her parents were requested by the school authorities to halt the activities of this child hypnotist, who, drunk with power, had begun to extend her talents into other classrooms. When I admonished the young lady, she looked me squarely in the eyes and retorted, "Do you want me to hypnotize you?" And she could have done so had I co-operated!

There are many ways of producing hypnosis. Experience shows that there is no one superior method. They all work. Most methods involve the fixing of attention on an object like a flashlight, a pencil, or a coin while the hypnotist suggests in a quiet monotonous tone that the eyes are getting heavy and the subject is getting drowsier and drowsier. Sometimes the hypnotist prefers to have the subject close his eyes while he utters sleep suggestions.

The operator usually proceeds from the simplest suggestions, which most subjects can accept, such as feeling drowsy and relaxed, to increasingly complex ones, such as arm rigidity, to uncommon ones, like hallucinations. The more suggestible the subject and the more skilled the hypnotist, the more the subject will be likely to achieve increasingly unusual responses by going more deeply into the trance state.

It is important to understand that the induction of hypnosis is the least significant part of the process. Anybody can learn induction techniques. What really matters is the way in which the hypnotic state is used, since its whole purpose is to help a subject. For this reason, the hypnotist must be a competent professional person with experience. Untrained persons, stage hypnotists, and amateurs can hypnotize people into doing amusing tricks, but they are unable to employ hypnosis as an effective therapeutic instrument.

Stage hypnotists know how to select susceptible subjects who will go into somnambulistic trances so deep that when they are aroused they believe themselves to have been asleep. They seem to have forgotten the events during the trance and apparently do not remember the instructions given them by the hypnotist, although they will execute these on a suggested signal. For instance, if a hypnotist tells a subject that at the word "Chicago" he will experience an extreme thirst, the subject will usually respond by drinking water, thinking only that his need is a spontaneous dryness of throat. This "posthypnotic suggestion" is an impressive phenomenon because it seems so bizarre. The person no longer seems to be master of his own destiny; he appears to be under the spell of the hypnotist. To the audience this is an awe-inspiring situation. The stage hypnotist capitalizes on the illusion of power he creates, although it is more imaginary than real. Actually, the hypnotized person is following a suggestion because he wants to do so. He can resist if he sets his mind against a specific injunction, although this may cause him some distress.

In therapeutic hypnosis no effort is made to impress or overwhelm the subject. And although a deep somnambulistic trance is possible in a few people (they have not been selected as in stage hypnosis) the majority of persons, as it has previously been shown, will go into a light or medium trance. This depth is entirely adequate for most purposes, since the susceptibility to therapeutic suggestions is present even in light hypnosis.

Operator Differences

Some hypnotists ask their subjects to gaze upward at the hypnotist's finger, or at a coin or pencil point held directly above the forehead. This is called eye fixation. Some use a spot or irregularity on the ceiling as a focus. Sometimes the subject is requested to roll his eyes up under the lids. Some hypnotists employ the subject's own hand and fingers, suggesting that the latter will soon move, spread, and proceed upward toward the face. This is called hand levitation. There are operators who stroke the subject's forehead and arms in a soothing, reassuring way. A light and soothing massage may have a hypnotic effect on some people, but physical touching is not necessary and is generally used only minimally at specific phases of induction. In certain cases, touching may actually interfere with induction since some subjects may interpret it as a disturbing sexual or infantilizing gesture. Some operators use impressive gadgets that are really not necessary but have suggestive effects on some gullible people. In this age of electronics one would expect hypnosis machines to be introduced. There are several of them on the market. Presumably, they influence the brain waves or are patterned after a "Russian sleep machine." There is no evidence that these instruments, or whirling disks, or other complicated paraphernalia are more effective than simple eye fixation or relaxation measures.

The hypnotist talks to the subject in a rhythmic and soothing way; the cadence of his speech often suggests the measures of a lullaby. Most people have a childish longing to be lulled to sleep, and the hypnotist takes advantage of this yearning. Although this is the most common method, hypnosis may be induced with the eyes open. However, it is more difficult to achieve this type of trance than induction through relaxing or sleep suggestions. Hence it is rarely used.

In treating difficult subjects, some hypnotists cope with such obstinacy by giving contradictory instructions that are both confusing and frustrating. The aim of this tactic is to interfere with the subject's control and mastery to a point where he will yield to the commands of the hypnotist. This works for some individuals, but its shock value may damage the patient-therapist relationship and interfere with constructive therapeutic work.

Usually, a series of gradated steps, involving progressively difficult suggestions, is followed. When the subject has successfully executed those that are easy to achieve, for example, deep breathing and imagining oneself in a relaxing place, he is then asked to try more difficult injunctions, such as hand anesthesia.

In therapy, the operator does not try to impress the subject or to overwhelm him by sinking him into a trance against his resistance. He emphasizes the fact that hypnosis is not a struggle for power. He attempts to help the subject achieve certain effects as marks of his own accomplishment. Failure is always minimized, since most patients with a devalued self-image believe failure is inevitable. The subject is not expected to respond to every suggestion. When he fails, he is encouraged to try again with the assurance that inevitably he can be successful.

Every operator develops a particular way for working hypnotically with his subjects, which to a slight degree will differ from that of other operators. I once submitted questionnaries to the best-known authorities in the field of hypnosis, asking them to describe their techniques. No two individuals used the same induction procedure. Each had obviously introduced modifications in technique that perhaps worked best for his own personality and proved to be most effective for him. An operator's confidence in his method seems to be an important factor in influencing his subjects and securing their co-operation. Subjects will respond well to hypnotists whose methods of working they find congenial. From a percentage standpoint there is little difference in the success ratios reported by experienced operators.

In giving suggestions under hypnosis operators usually build a word picture. Thus, if a hypnotist wishes to suggest that a subject prone to chilliness will feel warm, he might propose that the subject picture himself in a room with the windows closed and the heat turned on. The subject is not told that he will lose his tension and become relaxed. Instead, he may be asked to visualize himself lying on the beach in a comfortable position, inhaling deeply and feeling free from care. Some hypnotists avoid negative suggestions. Instead of saying, "You cannot open your eyes," they say, "Your eyes and lids are so heavy they will want to stay closed even though you try to open them."

A skilled operator observes the behavior of his subject in the trance and adapts his suggestions to the latter's responses. He is aware that his manner, rhythm of speech, and emphasis on words are as important as the content of his suggestions.

One cannot overemphasize the fact that hypnosis is no parlor game to be practiced by nonprofessional people. Even professionals who have had no special training with hypnosis can get into serious trouble if they hypnotize a person and then are unable to deal with trance behavior. The descriptions of hypnotic induction that follow in this chapter are given to explain the process of hypnosis and are not meant to be a set of instructions for the untrained to sally forth as amateur Svengalis.

Suggestibility Tests

Some operators give their subjects tests for suggestibility, usually proceeding from these directly into a trance state. If a subject resists the suggestibility test, the chances are that he will also resist hypnosis. There are many such tests; among the most common are the following:

1. The coin test

The subject is asked to extend his arm fully, with palm up at right angles to his body. A coin is placed on the palm. He is told, "Your hand will gradually turn over, and the coin will fall on the floor.

Watch it as it slowly begins to turn. Turning, turning, turning." Those suggestions are repeated until the coin drops.

2. *The postural-sway test*

The subject stands with his feet together, his body held rigid, and his eyes fixed on a spot on the ceiling directly overhead. The hypnotist stands behind the subject and asks him to close his eyes, but to remain rigid. The subject is then instructed as follows: "I want to test your capacity to relax. I am going to place my hands on your shoulder blades." The hands are placed on the medial part of the shoulder blades and the subject is told, "As I press my hands against your shoulders, you will feel a force pulling you back toward me. Do not resist. I will catch you when you fall. You are falling, falling, falling. You are being drawn back . . . falling . . . falling." The hands of the operator are then drawn back. Usually the subject will start swaying. If he does not, the hands are placed on his shoulders, and he is rocked back and forth with the comment that he is resisting and that he should loosen up. The same sugestions about falling back are then repeated, and the pressure of the hands suddenly released.

As soon as the subject starts swaying, suggestions become more forceful. "You are falling back, back, back—all the way—back, back, back. I shall catch you when you fall." The operator, of course, catches the subject before he falls.

3. *Hand levitation*

The subject is asked to sit at a table, his elbow resting on the surface, the palm of the hand down,. The operator says, "I am going to put my hand on yours, and I want you to pay attention to the feelings in your hand." The operator then presses the hand of the subject lightly and remarks, "Now you are going to feel your hand growing very light, as if it has no weight. It is growing lighter and lighter. It feels very light." This is repeated several times. "Do you feel it growing light?" If the subject replies in the negative, the suggestions are continued. If he has a sensation of lightness, the hand pressure is relaxed, and the subject is told, "Your hand is so light that it has no weight. It gets lighter and lighter. It gradually begins to leave the table, and it comes up right off the table as if it has no weight. It is rising higher and higher."

4. *Hand clasp*

The subject sits in a chair and is asked to clasp his hands firmly together. The hypnotist demonstrates this to the patient. Then he says, "I want you to close your eyes for a moment and picture a vise, a heavy metal vise whose jaws clamp together with a screw. Imagine that your hands are like the jaws of the vise, and as you press them together more tightly, they are just like the jaws of the vise tightening. I am going to count from one to five. As I count, your hands will press together tighter, and tighter, and tighter. When I reach the count of five, your hands will be pressed together so firmly that it will be difficult or impossible to separate them. One, tight; two, tighter, and tighter, and tighter; three very tight, tight, your hands feel glued together; four, your hands are clamped tight, tight; five, so tight that even though you try to separate them, they remain clasped together, until I give you the command to open them. Now open them slowly."

5. *Pendulum test*

A ring is attached to a string twelve inches long. The subject seated at a table holds the end of the string with his arm outstretched, the ring dangling above the level of the table. He is instructed as follows: "As you support the ring, imagine that you are looking at a large circle that is etched into the table top. Let your eyes travel around the circumference of the circle and keep your eyes moving around in a circle. The ring will begin going around in a circle even though you pay no attention to it." When the subject follows these suggestions, he is asked to concentrate on an imaginary line running directly in front of him, then on a line running directly across the table. The pendulum will swing in the direction his eyes travel.

Even if a subject follows suggestibility tests, this does not always mean that he will make a good hypnotic subject. However, when he resists suggestions, he will probably not be susceptible to hypnosis.

Trance Induction

An illustration of how a trance is conducted is given below in the transcription of a session I recorded with a voluntary subject, who consented to serve for a class demonstration. The techniques involved are those generally used by many operators, although there are always modifications in methods and numbers of techniques employed. Once again, a word of caution. A person who is not a trained psychotherapist must avoid inducing hypnosis in others no matter how urgently the latter demand it. Many unfortunate aftereffects may result that may not be immediately apparent. The following session is included in this volume, not as a training vehicle, but to point out how people respond to the induction of a trance.

Dr.: Won't you sit down in this chair to talk things over?

S.: Thank you very much.

Dr.: As you know, you're here to act as a voluntary subject for hypnosis. How do you feel about it? How do you feel about being hypnotized?

S.: Well, it's a funny feeling.

Dr.: What do you mean?

S.: I mean, well, I mean we've all heard a lot about it, but I've never been hypnotized myself, or course, and the only time I've ever seen it is on the stage.

Dr.: What did you see on the stage?

(It is important to determine what the subject knows about hypnosis or imagines hypnosis to be in order to correct misconceptions.)

S.: I saw the hypnotist take a group of people. A group, a lot of people, came up on the stage, and he hypnotized them. He hypnotized one man and just left him sitting there way over on the edge of the chair. (*Pause.*)

Dr.: On the edge of a chair?

S.: Yes, while he hypnotized other people.

Dr.: I see.

S.: And the people looked pretty droopy. As a matter of fact, they looked pretty silly. He had them doing foolish things.

Dr.: Uh huh. Are you afraid I may ask you to do foolish things?

S.: Well, I don't know. Are you going to?

Dr.: No, of course not.

S.: No?

Dr.: Hypnosis as it's used scientifically is not stage hypnosis.

S.: No.

Dr.: There is a lot of difference between the two. In stage hypnosis the hypnotist picks susceptible people, and then he causes them to do all sorts of fantastic things in order to get a laugh out of the audience.

S.: Yes.

Dr.: But in scientific or therapeutic hypnosis an entirely different attitude prevails. Of course, I will not ask you do do anything silly.

S.: No.

Dr.: Do you have any other feelings or notions about hypnosis?

S.: Well, I don't known whether it's possible to hypnotize me.

Dr.: What do you mean?

S.: Well, I—I can't imagine myself being hypnotized.

Dr.: Well, what do you think is going to happen? What are your ideas of what happens in hypnosis?

S.: I don't know. Is one completely unconscious?
(*This is a very common misconception.*)

Dr.: That is the idea most people have. As a matter of fact, you never go into a state where you lose contact with the hypnotist. During hypnosis, you're in complete control of your activities, except those that you want to feel are happening in spite of you. And you're in contact with me at all times. You do not lose consciousness. That's a fantastic notion that people have got out of observing the antics of a stage hypnotist.

S.: Well, I have a rather strong will. I don't—I don't know. I just don't feel that I will be likely to—to submit my will to another person.

Dr.: You feel then that you might possibly lose your will power in hypnosis? Is that what you mean?

S.: Yes.

Dr.: That is another idea that has to be clarified. As a matter of fact, in hypnosis people do not lose their capacity for independent action. You can resist any activity or group of activities that you do not desire, really desire, to perform. Hypnosis does not work on people with weak wills. Actually, people who are mentally defective or who have very severe intellectual problems cannot be hypnotized.

S.: Well, I—I wouldn't have thought of it that way.

Dr.: Do you have any other ideas on hypnosis?

S.: Yes. Well now, supposing, doctor, that I was hypnotized; how can I be sure that I'll wake up?

Dr.: You fear that you might possibly go to sleep and that I may not be able to wake you up?

S.: Yes.

Dr.: Hypnosis is not actually sleep. In deep forms of hypnosis, it is possible to suggest sleep to a person. But even when a person goes to sleep, deeply asleep, he will wake up after a short time. The idea that a person may be left in a trance for days or weeks is pure fiction. That just does not happen. Of course you'll wake up. You'll wake up very, very easily. It'll be much harder for you to fall asleep than to wake up, actually.

S.: Then all these things that we hear over the radio about people who have been made to do things—I mean sustained action for days and days—that couldn't really happen?

Dr.: No, of course it can't. That's nonsense. (*Pause.*) Now, you do have a desire to be hypnotized?

S.: Yes.

Dr.: That's very important, but the incentive of just coming here to be my subject may not be enough. You may have to have some other goal that we can shoot for. If you have any particular problems, such as sleep difficulties or the like, we may be able to help you with them. Is there anything you feel I might be able to do for you in a positive way?

S.: Well, I—I've been thinking of going to look for a new job.

Dr.: I see.

S.: And the very thought of just looking for a job is terrifying to me.

Dr.: Is that so?

S.: Yes. Once I have a job, I like it. I'm willing to work eighteen hours a day, and I enjoy everything I do; but looking for a job is very difficult.

Dr.: I may perhaps be able to help you.

(*It is not difficult to find out from the average patient what his or her motivation is in seeking therapy. They are usually aware of the symptoms that are causing distress.*)

S.: That would be wonderful, because this really is a fear of mine.

Dr.: I may be able to help you gain a certain feeling of relaxation in a job situation. And you may find that as a result of the work you do with me—perhaps not in this session, but in a later session, if you turn out to be a suitable subject—you may be able to master certain fears and trepidations in this particular situation.

S.: Yes.

Dr.: Then suppose we now begin to talk about what may actually be required of you during this first trance. I'd like to give you an idea, just in brief, of some of the general things that happen. First you'll notice that you begin to relax and that you feel just a little bit drowsy. It's not necessary to try too hard.

S.: No.

Dr.: Just let things happen as they will. Make your mind passive and relaxed, if possible. Now, you'll become aware of certain things that are happening as you relax. I'd like to have you concentrate on these. I may even bring them to your attention. You may not be able to follow all the suggestions that I give you, but don't let that bother you.

S.: O.K.

Dr.: You may be able to follow some and not others. You'll be in constant contact with me, and when you come out of it, you probably will remember everything that happened.

S.: Really?

Dr.: You may have only a vague idea about certain things and perhaps even have forgotten some; but in general you'll recall everything that happened.

S.: Yes.

Dr.: You'll probably even have a feeling, when you come out of it, that you might have resisted all of the things that I suggested to you. If you want to resist, you can resist.

S.: That's what I wanted to ask. Should I try to do everything that you tell me to do, or should I be passive?

Dr.: It's important not to do things voluntarily. Let things happen as they will.

S.: Yes.

Dr.: And don't force them. Don't push yourself too hard. If things just do not happen, well they just don't happen.

(*These preparatory suggestons are, unfortunately, too often neglected in routine inductions.*)

At this point I proceeded to give several of the susceptibiliy tests, previously described, to the patient. I began with the postural-sway experiment, to which she responded well. Next, we demonstrated the hand-clasp test and the hand-levitation test. The patient was becoming increasingly relaxed. After we had gone through all the susceptibility tests, the patient was asked to shut her eyes, and suggestions to deepen the trance were given.

Dr.: I'm going to stroke your arm. I'm going to stroke your arm and your hand. As I stroke your arm, you'll notice the heaviness sweep from the shoulder right down into your arm, into your elbow, into your fingers. Your whole arm will get very heavy as I stroke it; it will get very heavy as I stroke it; it will get very heavy, so heavy that as I stroke it, it will feel just like lead. It will get so heavy that when I reach the count of five, it'll be impossible for you to budge the arm. It'll feel so heavy it will be as if a hundred-pound weight is pressed down on the arm. One, heavy; two, heavier and heavier; three, as heavy as lead, as heavy as lead, as heavy as lead; four, heavier and heavier still; five, just as heavy as lead, as heavy as lead. It's impossible for you to budge your arm no matter how hard you try. It remains stiff, exactly as I have pressed it down, just resting comfortably, resting comfortably on your thigh, resting comfortably on your thigh, just like that. The next thing I'm going to do is to show you how stiff we can make the arm.

(*Arm catalepsy, a condition of muscular rigidity, is produced here.*)

I'm going to start stroking it, and as I stroke it, the whole arm becomes stiff and heavy and rigid, just as heavy and stiff and firm as a board. As I stroke it, it'll get heavier and heavier and heavier. The muscles will stiffen. They will be just as stiff and rigid as a board. I'm going to count from one to five. When I reach the count of five, the arm will have stiffened up, just as stiff and heavy as a board. One, stiff; two, stiffer and stiffer and stiffer; three, as stiff as a board, as stiff as a board, as stiff as a board; four, stiffer and stiffer and stiffer still; five, stiff, stiff. I'm going to let go, and when I let go, your arm will remain stuck out in front of you, just as stiff as a board, just as stiff as a board, just as stiff as a board, just like that. Stiff, stiff, stiff. No matter how hard you try to bend it now, it'll remain stiff and rigid. It'll be just like a board. It will not budge until I snap my finger. When I snap my finger, the arm will suddenly relax, and it will then be possible for you bring the arm down to your thigh. I snap my finger. Now, it relaxes; it comes down; it comes down, just like that. And you go into an even deeper, deeper, more relaxed state. Breathe in deeply and get more drowsy. Your breathing is becoming very deep now and very, very relaxed. Your breathing is deep and relaxed. And you're going into a deep, deep, relaxed and comfortable state. When I talk to you next, you'll be more deeply drowsy. You'll be more deeply drowsy. When I talk to you next, you will be more deeply drowsy, more deeply relaxed. Your eyes are closing, closing.

(*Long pause.*)

I am going now to stroke the other arm, and, as I stroke it, it's going to start feeling light, light, light, light; just as light as a feather. I'm going to count from one to five; at the count of five, it'll feel just like a feather. I'm going to grasp it by the wrist as I count. It'll float around in the breeze like a feather. One, light; two, lighter and lighter, just as light as a feather; three, as light as a feather, as light as a feather; four; five, just as light as a feather, floating around in the breeze, just like that, it will not come down; it will not come down. I'm going to let go now, and it's floating around in the breeze, floating around in the breeze.

(*Arm is extended in the air.*)

And you go into a deeper, deeper, more relaxed state. Go deeper now; go deeper. (*Pause.*) Now listen carefully to me. I'm going to put a book in your hand. You're going to grasp the book in your hand, in your right hand. I'm going to ask you to grasp it very, very tightly.

(*A book is placed in subject's hand.*)

You're going to grasp it very, very tightly. Just let it hang this way, just like that. You grasp it very tightly. Your hands are closed down on the book. It's impossible now for you to drop the book. You're glued to the book. You cannot let go; you cannot let go; you cannot let go, until I stroke your hand and remove the book, just like that. Your breathing gets deeper and more automatic, and, when I talk to you next, you will still be more deeply relaxed, more deeply drowsy, more deeply drowsy. (*Pause.*)

Listen carefully to me. I'm going to take your hands and start revolving them, one around the other.

(*This is for the purpose of inducing automatic movement.*)

They'll begin revolving, one around the other. They'll revolve faster and faster and faster and faster, faster and faster and faster, just like that, just like a wheel. Around and around and around they go. When I let go, it will be impossible for you to stop rotating your hands. When I let go, they'll keep going around faster and faster and faster. It's impossible to stop, it's impossible to stop, until I snap my fingers. When I snap my fingers, they'll suddenly stop, just like this.

(Fingers snap and revolutions cease.)
Now, bring them right down. You're going into a deeper and deeper and more relaxed, more comfortable state. When I talk to you next you'll be more deeply relaxed, more deeply drowsy.
(Pause.)
Now I want you to bring your left hand right down on your thigh here, like this. I'm going to stroke it, and it will be able to signal to me when I give you certain suggestions. By lifing a few inches, it will tell me you are responding positively. It'll be able to tell me when certain things are happening within you.
(This permits the subject to participate more actively and allows time to elapse while inner adjustments are made to suggestions before they are accepted. Often, lifting the index finger is used as the signal instead of the entire hand.)
For instance, I'd like to have you visualize yourself getting up out of the chair, walking through the door, going ouside, and walking outdoors. As soon as you visualize yourself walking outdoors, I want you to indicate that to me by your hand, this hand, rising up just about six inches. It'll come up to about six inches, just as soon as you visualize yourself walking outdoors.
(Pause, and hand rises.)
Up it comes. Now bring it down, straight down to the thigh. Now, you see yourself walking outdoors, and you see an alley between two houses. You walk along this alley. You notice that on the side, on the right hand side, there is a pail of steaming hot water. You see the steam issue from the surface of the water, and you realize that the water is extremely hot. You wonder how hot the water actually is, so you take this hand, the right hand, this hand, and you plunge it right into the water.
(The purpose of these suggestions is to produce hyperesthesia, a state of increased sensitivity.)
You notice that soon your hand begins to feel warm; it feels flushed. It may even begin to ache, and the muscles begin to contract; the skin begins to feel flushed. It may feel very, very tender, very, very tender, very tender and sensitive. I'm going to pinch it. When I pinch it, it will feel just as tender and sensitive as can be. I'm going to pinch it now.
(Hand is pinched, and subject withdraws hand. The withdrawal reaction indicates a susceptible subject. Absence of withdrawal is not too significant.)
You just draw your hand back. It feels very painful,

very painful, just like that. I'll show you the difference in comparison with the other hand. Your other hand is insensitive. There's no real pain when I pinch it.
(Left hand is pinched.)
But this other hand is sensitive when I pinch it.
(Right hand is pinched.)
Sensitive, just like that. And you go into deeper and deeper sleep. *(Pause.)*
Now, imagine that you're wearing a glove, a heavy leather glove on your left hand. Imagine that you're wearing a glove, a heavy leather glove. As soon as you get the sensation of wearing a thick leather glove on your hand—a sort of dullness in your hand—as soon as you see your hand in your mind's eye with a heavy leather glove, indicate it to me by raising your hand up a few inches. *(Pause.)* Your hand comes up; bring it down. Next, I want you to visualize yourself going into a doctor's office. You have a boil on your finger. You have a boil on your left finger. What I'm going to do is inject Novocaine all around the wrist. When I put my finger around the wrist, it'll feel as if I'm injecting Novocaine into the skin.
(Wrist is tapped with finger, circling it as if a Novocaine block is being made. The purpose of these suggestions is to induce hand anesthesia.)
Your hand will soon begin to feel dull; your hand feels very, very dull, dull, dull. It is going to lose all sense of pain. In a moment I'm going to prick the hand with a sterilized needle, and you're going to notice how insensitive it is, how free of pain it is. I'm going to count from one to five. It gets dull, dull, dull. One, there's no pain, no pain; two, it gets duller and duller; three, there's no pain, there's no pain, there's no pain; four, no pain, no pain; five, no pain, no pain, no pain, no pain. I'm going to show you the difference between this hand here, the sensitive one here on the right, and this hand here, the dull one on the left. I'm going to poke this right hand here with a needle, just like that, and it'll be very tender, even though I poke it very lightly.
(Hand is touched with a needle.)
But in the other hand, even though I poke it deeply, there will be no pain whatsoever, no pain in it whatsoever. When I poke it with a pin, you may feel a little pressure, but no real pain, even though I dig it in, just like that.
(Hand is touched with a needle.)
Do you notice the difference in the two hands?

(*Subject nods.*)
Yes, you do; good, good.
Now I'm going to stroke the hands again. I'm going to stroke both hands, and normal sensations will return in them.
(*Hands are stroked.*)
You'll feel yourself getting drowsier and drowsier and drowsier. Go in deep, deeply drowsy, deeply drowsy, deeply drowsy, as if you are asleep. You begin to feel yourself dozing off and going deeper; drowsier and drowsier and drowsier. You're getting very, very drowsy, drowsy, drowsy. Listen carefully to me. The next time we try this, you'll go in very deep, very soon after I give you the suggestion to sleep. You'll go in easily, with no effort, easily with no effort. (*Pause.*)
You're going to arouse yourself now, and I'm going to help you up in a minute or two. When you come out of it, you'll notice an extremely interesting thing. It'll be practically impossible for you to keep your eyes open when you come out of it. Your eyes will get heavier and heavier and heavier. They'll feel so heavy that they will want to shut; you may even begin dozing off until I snap my fingers, and then you will come out of it completely. You'll be completely awake.
(*The purpose here is to help convince the subject that she was actually drowsy as a result of the trance.*)
In other words, I'm going to count now from one to five, and when I reach the count of five, you'll open your eyes. But even though you are awake, your eyes will be so heavy that it'll be almost impossible for you to keep your eyes open, or they'll feel heavy, very heavy, so that you'll find it uncomfortable to keep your eyes open. Your eyes may even close, or they may remain open, but they'll blink. But then, when I snap my fingers, you'll wake up completely; you'll wake up completely.
One, slowly start awakening, slowly start awakening, slowly start awakening; two, more and more; three, more and more still more and more still; four, five. Open your eyes now, open your eyes, open your eyes. You notice how heavy they feel; they blink; they want to close, they want to close, until I snap my fingers, (*fingers are snapped*) and then you wake up completely. You wake up completely now; you wake up completely, just like that. Wake up, wake up.
(*Subject comes out of the trance.*)

Well, how do you feel?

S.: I still feel a little sleepy.

Dr.: Do you?

S.: Yes.

Dr.: Could you describe your feelings to me?

S.: I feel as if I've been an awfully long way away.

Dr.: Really?

S.: Yes.

Dr.: What do you remember?

S.: I think I . . . well, I . . . I . . . I . . . I think I remember what you said to me.

Dr.: You remember practically everything?

S.: I think so, yes.

Dr.: Do you have any thoughts or any ideas that you'd like to discuss with me? You seem to have something on your mind.

S.: I still feel sleepy.

Dr.: You still feel sleepy?

S.: Yes, I do.

Dr.: Did you resent waking up?

S.: (*Pause.*) Um, just a little.

Dr.: Your eyes are closing still.

S.: Yes.

Dr.: Well, you'll wake up in a moment; you'll wake up. In a moment you'll be completely awake. You'll feel relaxed.

(*In most instances the drowsiness produced by the trance does not persist as long as it has here.*)

Do you have a headache or any other sensation?

S.: No, I just feel as if I could sleep for forty-eight hours.

Dr.: Well, it may be a minute or two before you wake up completely. I think you'll make a fairly good subject. I think we will probably be able to train you to go into a very deep trance state.

S.: That sounds wonderful.

Dr.: Did you have an idea that you might be able to resist the suggestions? I mean, what was your reaction to the suggestions I gave you?

S.: I felt at first that I wasn't hypnotized at all. And then I realized that I was.

Dr.: What made you realize that?

S.: I thought I could resist any suggestions that you made.

Dr.: Yes.

S.: But I found that I couldn't.

Dr.: Did you actually try?

S.: Yes, I really tried.

(*If she really had had a strong desire to resist, she could have done so.*)

Dr.: Well, now, most people feel when they come out of a trance they haven't been hypnotized; they feel they could have resisted suggestions. Now, actually that's true; they could have.

S.: Yes.

Dr.: But in a trance state they usually don't want to.

S.: No.

Dr.: And the feeling that one wasn't really asleep isn't far from wrong, because a person really isn't asleep. He is just in a mild state of relaxation in which he feels that suggestions have an effect in spite of himself. Can you tell me how you felt about your hand? Did you feel things happening in spite of yourself, or what?

S.: Yes, I did, I did. When you . . . when you told me about my hand getting numb, I thought, well, now, that isn't going to really happen. And then I could feel it, just exactly like a shot of Novocaine, and that tingling numbness that you get if you have a shot of Novocaine, you know.

Dr.: Yes.

S.: Then it seemed like a heavy leather glove, no sensation in it at all.

Dr.: I see.

S.: Really, it surprised me.

Dr.: It did?

S.: Yes, it did.

Dr.: Good.

The Deeper States of Hypnosis

Hypnotherapy can often achieve the desired results with people who proceed no further than the voluntary subject above. Indeed, as explained in the last chapter, it may be preferable to keep the trance in a light or medium state. However, in some cases, a deeper trance may be required, particularly where exploratory techniques, such as the probing for forgotten memories, are used. This may be possible in roughly one-quarter of the subjects inducted, and even here only some (about 10 per cent of all subjects) will be able to enter the deepest somnambulistic states with the usual induction techniques.

It may be of help at this point to present a scale of hypnotic susceptibility illustrating the different stages of hypnosis. The types of therapy that are often successful at particular stages are printed in italics.

Stages of Hypnosis

(With a standard trance induction using a fixation object)

Waking State
- Smarting of eyes
- Watering of eyes
- Heaviness of eyes
- Fluttering of lids

Prehypnotic Stage (Hypnoidal State)
- Heavy sensation in extremities
- Drowsiness
- *Supportive therapy (reassurance, persuasion, reeducaton, confession and ventilation)*
- *Hypnoanalysis (free association, fantasy induction)*

Light trance
- Closing of eyes
- Physical relaxation
- Arm immobilization
- Arm rigidity
- Inhibition of voluntary movement
- *Supportive therapy*
- *Reeducational therapy*
- *Behavior therapy*

Medium Trance
- Disturbances in cutaneous sensibilities
- *Ability to learn technique of autohypnosis*
- Partial analgesia (glove anesthesia)
- Automatic obedience
- *Hypnoanalysis (dream induction)*
- Partial posthypnotic anesthesia
- Induced personality changes

Deep Trance
- Simple posthypnotic suggestions

Hypnoanalysis (automatic writing)
Extensive anesthesias
Emotional changes
Hallucinations
Regression
Symptom removal by prestige suggestion (extensive desensitization techniques)

Somnambulistic Trance
Ability to open eyes without awakening
Complex posthypnotic suggestions
Production of experimental conflicts
Profound amnesia for trance events

The above table must not be accepted literally. Various subjects may go through different processes at certain stages. Some subjects may dream vividly on command and follow posthypnotic suggestions even though they have never progressed beyond the light stages of hypnosis. Other subjects in somnambulistic states may not dream or follow particular posthypnotic suggestions. Emotional changes may take place in some patients in light stages of hypnosis, while they may not occur at all in other subjects, even in somnambulism. These exceptions are frequent enough to prohibit dogmatic statements about successive phenomena at different trance depths.

Ability to talk in hypnosis without coming out of the trance

It is sometimes desirable to get the subject to a point in hypnosis where he is able to carry on a conversation without waking from the trance. In a number of cases this ability can be developed in the subject through training, even though he may not have the aptitude of developing analgesia. Various suggestions are used: "Even though you are drowsy, you will be able to hear my voice distinctly and talk to me without awakening. You will talk back just like a person in his sleep. You will be able to answer my questions without awakening and without difficulty."

At this point, simple questions that do not arouse conflicts or fears are asked. Does he feel comfortable? Where does he live? How old is he? Then the operator will offer encouragement.

"Now, you see, you are able to talk to me, even though you are drowsy. Your eyes are still shut fast, you do not want to move your limbs, and you remain very drowsy, even though you talk to me. As you talk, you may want to open your eyes or move your limbs, but you will feel you do not desire to do this until I tell you to open your eyes and to move your limbs." Later on, as the subject becomes better trained in hypnosis, he is usually able to answer questions, even though they may invoke considerable anxiety.

Therapists who practice psychoanalysis may also train a subject for hypnotic free association. The patient is informed that he is to express every thought or feeling, no matter how insignificant or ridiculous these may seem, and to talk about anything that comes into his mind. In order to do this he must allow his mind to wander and keep nothing back. The patient may then be told, "Try to make your mind go blank for a moment, and then tell me the first thing that pops into it." The subject may not succeed very well at first, but with training he may become facile in talking about his associations.

Hallucinatory suggestions

To induce hallucinations, imaginative suggestions are made to the subject. The operator might begin this way: "As you sit there, I'm going to suggest to you that you imagine yourself walking outside. You enter an alley that takes you to a courtyard. As you look up, you see a church, the steeple, spire, and a bell. Picture this in your mind, and as soon as you see the church, indicate it to me by raising your left hand (or index finger)."

When the hand or finger rises, suggestions continue: "Now look at the church building and steeple and notice a bell, a large bell. As soon as you hear the bell ringing or get a sensation as if the bell is ringing, indicate it to me by raising your hand (or finger) again."

If the subject is responding readily, and if he seems to be in a hypnotic state, the following suggestions are given to him: "Now listen very intently. You will be able to hear the sound of the church bell tolling. It rings loud and clear. Listen carefully, and you will hear it. As soon as you do, raise your hand (or finger)."

Should the subject fail in the last test, he is told: "You are responding well to suggestions. The next time you will be able to hear the bell more distinctly."

After this, the subject is told, "I'm going to pick up a small bottle. Visualize me doing that. You are curious about what is in the bottle. You look at the label and notice a flower on the label. You realize that there is perfume in the bottle. Visualize a flower; as you do, you will smell the perfume. I am going to place the bottle under your nose, and you will smell perfume." The operator may then remove the cork from a small empty bottle for the sound effect. Then he places the bottle under the subject's nose, remarking, "As soon as you smell the perfume, indicate it to me by lifting your left hand (or finger)."

Fantasy and dream induction

These two techniques are extremely valuable in permitting the analyst who uses hypnosis to work dynamically with his subjects. Here is an example of the kind of instructions that are given: "As you sit there, I'm going to ask you to visualize yourself inside a theater. You are sitting in a seat in the second or third row, and observing the stage. You notice that the curtains are drawn together. Raise your hand (or finger) when you visualize this." When the patient raises his hand (or finger), suggestions continue: "You are curious about what is going on behind the curtain. Then you notice a man [or woman if the subject is a woman] standing on the stage at the far end of the curtain. He has an expression of extreme fear and horror on his face, as if he sees the most terrifying thing imaginable behind the curtain. You wonder what this may be, and you seem to absorb this man's fear. In a moment the curtain will suddenly open, and you will see what frightens the person. As soon as you do, tell me about it without waking up. As soon as you see action on the stage, tell me exactly what you see."

After the subject describes what he sees, he is told, "You continue to sit in the theater observing the stage. The curtain is again closed. You see the same man, but this time, instead of having a frightened expression on his face, he seems happy. It is as if he is filled with unbounded happiness and joy. As you watch him, you begin to share his happy feelings. You wonder what causes him to be so glad. In a moment the curtain will suddenly open, and you will see what makes him so happy. You will see the most delightful and joyful thing that can happen to a person. As soon as you see action on the stage, tell me exactly what you see."

Upon describing his fantasy, the subject is told, "What you have observed are fantasies. Fantasies are thought processes that occur in a state of reverie. They are related to dreams. As a matter of fact, dreams are nothing more than fantasies in a state of sleep. In the future, whenever I ask you to dream while you are relaxed, it will be possible for you to let your mind wander and to have a series of thought processes similar to those I have just descibed. Or you may have an actual dream. When I give you the suggestion to dream, just let yourself relax deeply enough to allow a series of images to come into your mind. If you find it difficult to dream, imagine yourself in a theater, sitting in the second or third row, looking at the stage. As you watch the drawn curtain, it will suddenly open, and you will see action. For example, as you sit there now, I want you to go into a deep state and to have a dream—anything that happens to come to your mind. As soon as you have had this dream, tell me about it without waking up."

The subject's fantasies about situations of fear and happiness may yield important clues to his conflicts. When this technique is perfected, it is usually possible to get the subject to dream about or to produce fantasies relating to specific problems, such as existing anxieties, resistance manifestations, and transference feelings toward the analyst.

Opening the eyes without awakening

The ultimate aim of training in depth is to get the subject to a point where he is able to open his eyes in a trance without awakening, to develop amnesia, and finally to respond to complicated posthypnotic suggestions. The subject can be taught to open his eyes without awakening by an exercise like this: "As you sit there, imagine that I am holding a bottle of water close to your eyes. You notice that it is colorless, but as you watch it, it slowly changes to a pink color, and then to a reddish color. As soon as you see the color change, as soon as you visualize the color changing to red, indicate this by raising your left hand (or finger)."

When the subject responds, he is told, "Even though you are asleep, deeply asleep, it will be possible for you to open your eyes slowly without awakening. At first things will be hazy; then they will become more clear. But you will still be asleep, deeply asleep, even though you have your eyes wide open. You will continue to stay asleep with your eyes wide open until I give you the suggestion to awaken. It will be possible for you to stand up and walk around the room, just as a person walks in his sleep. It will be possible for you to observe things that I point out to you. When you open your eyes, you will notice that I hold a bottle of clear fluid in front of your eyes. As you watch the bottle, it will slowly change to a pinkish color and then to a reddish color, just as it did when your eyes were shut. As soon as you see the color change, indicate this by raising your left hand (or finger). Now slowly open your eyes; very slowly open your eyes. Things will be blurred at first, but as you look at the bottle, they will clear up, and you will notice that the color will change to a pinkish, then to a reddish color. Slowly open your eyes; open them wider and wider." A bottle containing water may then be brought close to the subject's eyes, and he may be asked to gaze at the bottle until he notices that the color changes to pink or red.

As soon as the subject acknowledges the fact that he sees the color change, he may be given another hallucinatory suggestion. "Look at the table in front of you, and you will see that there is a candlestick there with a burning candle. Go over and blow it out." This direction is repeated several times.

Developing amnesia

If a subject has reached the somnambulistic state, he will probably awaken with spontaneous amnesia. In some cases subjects need special training to forget certain aspects of the trance or the entire experience. The first step consists of finding out how much has been forgotten. Should the subject recall everything, then a method to help him forget can be tried. Immediately before the end of the next hypnotic sessions, the operator will tell him to imagine that he is at home asleep. Then he will be told that he will have a short dream, after which his eyes will open, and he will believe he has just aroused himself from a sound slumber. He will remember the dream vividly, but immediately after recounting it, he will have a hazy recollection of the events in the trance. He may even forget some of them when questioned.

If the subject develops partial amnesia as a result of these suggestions, he is told during the next hypnosis: "Forgetting is a perfectly normal experience and a means of preventing an overloading of the mind. It is easy to forget by shifting attention from some things. For instance, last time you forgot certain experiences that happened. (*The specific experiences are mentioned.*) This is perfectly normal. Today you will probably forget many, most, or even all of the experiences you are having now. You will, before you awaken, have a dream. As soon as you dream, awaken with a start, as if you are at home in bed, and have just awakened from a sound sleep. You will remember the dream, but you will forget all or most of the other events that have happened."

There are some subjects who seem unable to develop the capacity for amnesia. For one reason or another they need to retain enough control of their faculties to enable them to remember what has occurred in the trance state. Suggestions to forget are met with an embarrassed or defiant remembering. Therefore, a proposal that the subject remember some minor aspect of the trance is sometimes included in the suggestions for amnesia.

Posthypnotic suggestion

If the patient responds positively to suggestions for posthypnotic dreaming, he is then given a suggestion that after he awakens he will, at a given signal, carry out instructions that were given in the trance. For instance, extreme sensitivity (hyperesthesia) in the right hand and numbness (anesthesia) in the left hand may be induced during hypnosis. The subject is told, "After you awaken and have been awake a while, I will tap three times on the desk. At the third tap you will notice that your right hand will tingle and be sensitive, while the left hand will be numb. This will last until I tap once more on the desk, when the hands will return to a normal sensation." The hyperesthesia and anesthesia are then removed.

Another posthypnotic suggestion that is often effective is requesting the subject to dream in hypnosis, to awaken upon completing the dream, but to forget the dream on awakening, as if he has just come out of a very deep sleep. He will be unable to remember the dream until the operator taps on the desk three times, whereupon the dream will suddenly pop into his mind and he will repeat it.

The subject accordingly is given the following suggestions: "I want you now to have a dream. As soon as you have the dream, your right hand will rise straight up in the air until it touches your face. As soon as it touches your face, your eyes will open, and you will awaken with a start. But you will have forgotten the dream completely. Every time you think of it, your mind will go blank. However, I will rap on my desk three times, and when you hear the third rap, the dream will suddenly pop into your mind, and you will tell me about it."

In giving posthypnotic suggestions, most operators repeat them several times and ask the subject whether he understands what he is to do upon awakening. His ability to recount what is expected of him usually insures success. When a specific action is suggested, the subject is often given a cue, such as tapping on a desk. After the tapping he is supposed to perform the posthypnotic act. When therapeutic posthypnotic suggestions are made, these are presented in a way that will not conflict too drastically with the patient's personalty and inclinations. Responsible operators never ask a subject to perform a ridiculous act, since this could well arouse resistance that would interfere with a proper relationship. Often, subjects who are somnambules are protected by their hypnotists, who give them posthypnotic suggestions to the effect that they will not be hypnotizable by anyone except the operator they have been working with.

Conditioning hypnosis to a given signal

In many cases a subject's ability to sink more and more easily into a deeper trance improves with each succeeding induction. In some cases this does not happen; subjects continue to display the same trance depth session after session. Should the trance evoke anxiety, the subsequent sessions may be much lighter or trance induction may be resisted altogether. In the second or third session some operators condition their subjects to enter hypnosis upon a given signal. This signal can vary. It can be a certain word or sentence, an auditory stimulus such as a bell or buzzing sound, a visual stimulus like a blinking electric light, or a touch on the shoulder. While in hypnosis the subject is given a suggestion something like this: "Now listen to me carefully. From now on it will not be necessary to go through the process of hypnotizing you each time you come here. When I give you a certain signal, such as tapping on the desk, you will immediately and easily enter in a state as deep as the one you are in now."

This suggestion is repeated, and then the subject is told: "I am now going to awaken you. As soon as I awaken you, I am going to give you the signal. The moment you get the signal, you will again fall into a sleep as deep as the one you are in now. Do you understand?" After this, the subject is brought out of hypnosis, and the signal is immediately given to show him that he will be responsive to it. As soon as he enters hypnosis again, the suggestions are repeated, and the patient is then asked to acknowledge the fact that he understands he is to go into a deep state when the signal is presented to him.

At the next session the subject is told that he will be given a signal, whereupon he will automatically start relaxing. The signal is then presented, and after the patient has entered hypnosis, the suggestion is reinforced.

Arousing the subject

To arouse a subject, a technique that aims at a slow awakening is generally used. It usually goes like this: "Relax completely. I am going to start bringing you out. I will count slowly from one to five, and as I do, you will gradually become more and more awake. At the count of five, your eyes can open, and you will be completely out of it. If you wish, you can take a couple of minutes to come out. One, you are becoming more and more awake now; two, slowly awaken; three, you begin to feel more awake now; four, you are becoming wider and wider awake; five, your eyes will open gradually when you are ready."

On rare occasions, some subjects experience somewhat disturbed psychosomatic effects upon being aroused. These can take the form of shivering, confusion, nausea, and headache. When these aftereffects are present, the subject is rehypnotized, and it is suggested that his symptoms will not be present when he awakens. These side reactions are most often present when the subject has been given a posthypnotic suggestion that he attempts to resist, either because it is opposed to his standards, or because he desires to maintain control of his actions and not yield to the commands of the operator. In such cases, rehypnosis and suggestions that symptoms will disappear are usually made to no avail. During rehypnosis the operator informs the subject that he will not have to follow the suggestions given to him. Sometimes, even this release will not neutralize the former suggestions, and psychosomatic symptoms will not disappear until the subject carries out the posthypnotic suggestion that has been made. At any rate, all unusual symptoms following hypnosis generally disappear shortly after the termination of the trance.

In isolated instances, the subject will refuse to awaken from hypnosis following suggestions that the trance be terminated. (This is extremely rare and has happened in only two cases during the many years I have practiced.) The reasons for this sometimes lies in an expressed or unexpressed posthypnotic suggestion that the subject refuses to fulfill. Escape from conflict is sought in sleep. Sometimes the subject feels such great pleasure in the trance that he wants the state to continue. Where the subject persists in "sleeping," he may be asked why he refuses to waken and what the operator may do to wake him up. The operator is firm, but never threatening. If exhortations fail to arouse the subject, there is no need for alarm, since the subject will always awaken spontaneously after a nap. This sleep will not last more than several hours.

The various reactions that subjects have to their trance experiences are summed up in the following frequently made observations. My comments are given.

I don't believe I was hypnotized because my mind was wandering. I could hear everything you said.

Hypnosis is no bludgeon that knocks a person out. It would be totally without value if the subject could not hear what was said.

One is supposed to be aware of everything and even hypersensitive to stimuli. One is in contact at all times. If one goes in deeper, one's mind may bounce around from one thought to another.

Shouldn't I be deeper?

Deep states of hypnosis, while useful for stage tricks and the like, are not necessary in most forms of therapeutic hypnosis. As a matter of fact, a light form of hypnosis may be advantageous. If a deeper form is necessary, you may be trained to enter it. It takes time for a person to learn how to enter into a deep trance.

I could have opened my eyes if I had wanted to.

Of course you could have, because you were not out of control. But the fact is that you didn't want to open them.

I am afraid hypnosis will not help me because I wasn't able to do everything you suggested.

In the next few sessions I am going to suggest that you observe a number of different kinds of phenomena. You will be able to observe some, but not all of them. It is not necessary for you to be able to observe everything that I bring to your attention. All hypnotized people are capable of doing certain things and not others in the trance. What you have experienced is perfectly normal.

I do not believe I was hypnotized because I was in full control at all times and could have resisted suggestions.

Hypnosis is a co-operative enterprise, and I don't want you to lose control of yourself. Indeed, my aim is to give you better control of yourself and your functions so that you will become stronger. If you have a desire to resist suggestions, there are reasons for this resistance, and I shall try to help you understand them. In the next few sessions you will develop greater confidence in your ability to enjoy the experience of hypnosis, and it will be of value to you in overcoming your problems.

When you tell me to do things, should I do them voluntarily?

It is not necessary for you to do things deliberately. If you make your mind passive, things will happen in the natural course of events. Just relax and enjoy the experience of watching how things come about as the result of suggestions. You don't have to try too hard.

Preferred Methods of Induction

Psychotherapists generally select induction techniques on the basis of personal taste after experimenting with a number of methods, none of which universally possesses any superior virtues over the others. Whirling disks, flashing lights, electronic instrumentation and other mechanical aids offer no advantages, except in rare instances, where because of the expectancy of certain patients a strong placebo effect is exerted. Ample illustrations of induction procedures can be found in the literature (see Bibliography). I personally prefer a simple relaxation technique and avoid the mention of the word "hypnosis." Other therapists favor eye fixation or hand levitation. I rarely test for depth, assuming that the patient will find his or her own level. An uncomplicated posthypnotic suggestion tells me if the patient is capable of achieving a deep enough trance for us to utilize the hypnoanalytic techniques of regression and revivification and the setting up of experimental conflicts. In most cases, irrespective of depth, it is possible to stimulate dreams and to study transference and resistance mobilized by hypnotic induction and trance utilization. Such reactions can yield useful clues about basic conflicts and character organization. Hypnosis lends itself to the making of a relaxing and ego building tape and to the training of the patient in self-hypnosis, which can be invaluable for "homework" and for continuing self-therapy after the formal treatment period has ended. All therapists will introduce into any methods they learn their own unique approaches to hypnotherapy.

5

The Happenings in Hypnosis

There is a wealth of evidence that the mind exercises an enormous influence over the physiological functions of the body. This fact was dramatically impressed on me early in my career as a psychiatrist. A patient was referred to me for the treatment of depression, which was only one of his complaints. Since childhood he had suffered from an allergy that affected his nasal and respiratory tract, a condition brought on during seasons when roses were in bloom. Intense itching of the nose, burning and watering of the eyes, sneezing, headaces, insomnia, and asthma made his life miserable. According to his internist, allergic tests definitely pinpointed rose pollen floating in the air as the source of his trouble. On one occasion he walked into my office and began his session. In the course of relating a current matter of concern, he started to sneeze, then wheeze. He insisted that there was rose pollen in he room. With this announcement, he turned his head to the back of the office and triumphantly pointed to a rose in a thin glass vase. I agreed that it was indeed a rose but pointed out *that it was made of plastic.* He would not believe me until he had touched it. The artificial rose had registered in his peripheral vision as he entered the room, but his attention was diverted at seeing me. The visual stimulus automatically set in action a physiological response based on years of conditioning.

In hypnosis, suggestion may release certain conditioned patterns in a similar way. Obviously, each subject's responses are unique and depend on previous experience. These reactions are not specific to the trance state but may be confused with it.

The question of what *is* specific has been central to arguments that have gone on for years among professionals. The fact that all the manifestations observed in hypnosis may also be encountered in other situations has tended to obscure the issue of specificity. Another complicating factor is that there is a wide range of responses that can merge, on the one hand, with normal behavioral manifestations and, on the other, with neurotic and even psychotic symptomatology. The nature of hypnosis varies with the level of anxiety, the habitual modes of reaction to external stress and inner conflict, the depth of trance, and the many fluctuating attitudes that the subject has toward hypnosis and the hypnotist.

There are few objective signs by which the hypnotic state can be differentiated from other states of consciousness. Laboratory studies reveal no reliable chemical criteria to distinguish hypnotic from "normal" physiological variables. Electrical brain (electroencephalographic) and muscle (myographic) tracings, and scrutiny of a wide range of physiological measurements yield ambiguous results. Even the subject's personal account of what he believes is happening to him may be fundamentally no different from what he describes in normal ego states. What is specifically characteristic of hypnosis is difficult to say, apart from the subject's avowal that there is something "different" about it. This cannot be considered too reliable a statement, since all psychological states, from excitement to relaxation, may be interpreted by him as distinctive. It should not cause surprise, therefore, if, in surveying the happenings of hypnosis, we find that they do not come from another planet.

Because some research psychologists have arrived at this discovery, they tend to downgrade hypnosis as an authentic experience and to insist that the word "hypnosis" itself is neither useful nor meaningful. On the other hand, there are psychologists who oppose this point of view. They have presented evidence from their own studies that hypnosis can bring about extraordinary occurrences not possible in the waking state.

All this is, of course, confusing to the average person, who will ask, "what difference does it make? If hypnosis works, why not use it irrespective of whether or not its manifestations are commonplace?" There is much to be said for this argument. We are still far away from the day when we can positively define the physiological, psychological, interpersonal, and spiritual elements that make up hypnosis, or consciousness for that matter. Let us nevertheless examine some of the classical manifestations of hypnosis. For convenience these may be divided into rapport, catalepsy, hypersuggestibility, physiological signs, effects on sensory and intellectual functioning, time sense, regression, posthypnotic suggestion, and general performance.

Rapport

Rapport is defined as a relationship between the hypnotist and subject, in which the subject is absorbed almost exclusively with what the hypnotist says and does. This does not mean that he cannot perceive other stimuli around him. The focus of his attention is more or less directed by the hypnotist, who may persuade him to concentrate on bodily sensations, experiences in his everyday life, memories going back into remote childhood, conflicts and anxieties raging within, fantasies, and sounds, smells, and sights, real or imaginary. The subject, however, can interrupt any of these activities if they stir up too much anxiety, or he can conjure up illusions dictated by his present needs and defenses.

A subject's performance will shift from day to day, according to his mood at the time and particularly the immediate quality of his relationship with the hypnotist. The depth of trance will fluctuate—sometimes it is light and sometimes deep—and the reported experiences will vary accordingly. Rapport, therefore, is an arbitrary and unpredictable quality that can be broken by the subject at any time, although it is a consistent element of hypnosis.

Catalepsy and Other Muscular Phenomena

An impressive phenomenon often demonstrated to an audience by a stage hypnotist is a hypnotized person in a muscular bind suspended by his heels and neck between two chairs. So rigidly does the subject hold himself that it is possible for someone to stand on his chest without causing him to buckle. Actually, this dramatic happening is not as spectacular as it appears, because many people, by forcing themselves voluntarily to keep their muscles taut and rigid, can do the same thing while fully awake. It is true, however, that because a subject is more highly motivated to follow suggestions in the trance state, he will more likely be able to retain fixed and uncomfortable postures of the body or limbs, sometimes for incredibly long periods of time. In such induced "catalepsy" he can maintain an unstrained positioning of any muscles singled out for suggestion.

Catalepsy, therefore, does not happen only in hypnosis but can also be brought about through suggestion in waking life. Indeed, a variety of muscle phenomena besides spasms may be produced.

Suggestions for muscle relaxation and paralysis usually cause the subject to feel a lazy disinclination for active movements or an inability to make up his mind about whether or not to move his limbs. There is no loss of motor power, merely a temporary suspension of tonicity and motion. Suggested paralysis may involve small groups of muscles, such as the eyelids, or large groups like the limbs or trunk. It may be of a flaccid or spastic nature. The paralysis is not controlled by the motor nerves and is based entirely on the subject's conception of how a paralyzed person behaves. Some subjects made no effort to struggle against suggestions of paralysis, while others vigorously attempt to move the extremity in spite of the hypnotist's command. The subject usually fails in such struggles, and as he contracts the muscles of the paralyzed part, one may observe antagonistic muscles opposing the action. If he is told he is totally paralyzed and cannot walk, he will earnestly make an effort to ambulate, but fail, often to his consternation and amazement. This development is not so frightening as it seems because, were the place to catch fire, the subject would spontaneously come out of the trance and become active. Even though a dangerous situation does not exist, some persons will attempt to overcome inhibition by a ruse that may or may not be successful. They usually sense their helplessness, and this realization may precipitate panic in fearful subjects.

More dramatic are induced convulsions. Here the subject (usually one who has a hysterical disposition) will put on a display of violent, sustained (tonic) and intermittent (clonic) contractions of certain muscles and roll his eyeballs upward, symptoms that closely resemble epileptic seizures. These "attacks" may occur spontaneously at the induction of hypnosis, or they may be brought on by pointed suggestions from the operator. There is a close imitation of convulsive attacks that the subject has observed in genuine epileptics or in "possessed" souls who are inspired to throw themselves about during religious revival meetings.

Hypersuggestibility

If we were to point to the most outstanding feature of hypnosis, we would select its enormous influence on a subject's suggestibility. Man seems to possess a built-in suggestibility mechanism that appears to be responsible for a good deal of his educational grounding and development. The child learns by imitation, following the precepts of his parents and teachers. His suggestibility level is high, and this is an enormous asset because it diminishes trial-and-error experimentation. His concepts of the world, his values and attitudes are molded to a great extent by his acceptance of the pronouncements of the important adults at home and school. The stamp of authority is later transferred to other individuals and even to communication media. What he sees on television, hears on radio, and reads in books and magazines possesses a special aura of credibility. To challenge the validity of all their pronouncements is to belittle the parental image itself. In cases where the child has been brought up to respect or fear authority, such heresy may create great anxiety. As the child grows into an adult, he tends to utilize his own critical judgment more and more and to reserve the right to independent thought and action. But still lurking within him is the highly suggestible child, who continues to follow magisterial commands.

Evidences of man's irrational suggestibility are to be found everywhere. The advertising business, for example, is in large measure directed at the suggestibility of prospective clients. A major premise in advertising is that if one feeds sufficient data to people through such media as television, radio, newspapers, and magazines, they will eventually become consumers irrespective of the virtue of the advertised products.

Politicians, also, often depend on the suggestibility of their constituents. William G. Sumner in his classic work *Folkways* illustrates this in the story of a man seeking nomination for office. He appeared before the party convention to make a speech and began by promising that he would state his position completely and frankly on a difficult question causing conflict within the party. "But first," he said with emphasis, "let me say that I am a Democrat." This released a great round of applause. Then he proceeded to boast of his services to the party. He stopped at this point without having said a single word about the great question. He easily won the nomination. The opinions of popular and much-admired personalities are often held in high regard, even though they are not at all qualified to decide on the issues in question. Political parties scurry to enlist the support of movie stars, popular athletes, beauty-contest winners, and other celebrities who are idolized and whose convictions are accepted by the suggestible public without challenge.

In hypnosis, as a consequence of submitting to the authoritative intoning of the hypnotist, the subject tends to revert to a childlike submissiveness and heightened suggestibility. A good deal of what happens in and after hypnosis is a result of this enhanced capacity to accept suggestions. There are, or course, some people who actively resist suggestions in both waking and hypnotic states because of their painful experiences with authority. But more people find themselves absorbing with relative ease in the trance suggestions that may enable them to secure effects they could not otherwise achieve. There seems to be an unqualified acceptance of the hypnotist's injunctions.

However, there are definite limits to suggestibility, and subjects will emphatically resist, and resist successfully, any suggestion that arouses too much anxiety. As long as suggestions do not involve a questionable issue, they will conform without hesitation. But when a basic conflict is touched on, resistance is the rule. For example, a woman with a mouse phobia may develop anesthesia on suggestion and will permit her arm to be burned by a cigarette without flinching. But when it is suggested that she no longer fears mice and is threatened with real exposure to a mouse, she will in all probability awaken.

The critical faculties are thus never truly suspended. Even when the subject is a responsive somnambule, who is able to execute foolish posthypnotic suggestions made by a stage hypnotist, his automatic compliance will cease if he recognizes the senselessness of his behavior. Of course, if he has a bit of the ham in him, he will enjoy performing for the amusement of the audience, and he will then have motivation to continue his antics. In therapeutic hypnosis the operator enlists the co-operation of the individual and does not suggest anything foolish or anything that may be against the best interests of the patient. Instead, he works toward handling the patient's anxiety and removing resistance to change.

Physiological Happenings

If a person were given a suggestion that his blood pressure suddenly rise and his heart rate increase, we would be surprised indeed if his pressure did bound up and his pulse raced beyond its normal limits. If, on the other hand, we were to ask the same person to imagine himself engaged in a life-and-death struggle with a burglar who is half strangling him, we would expect his excitement to register an accelerating effect on his circulatory system. In the latter instance his emotions would be inflamed and his body would release hormones and enzymes that would have a direct effect on his body organs.

It is not surprising, then, to learn that in hypnosis great physical upheaval can take place during a similar situation. This is especially true, since the imagination is more active in hypnosis than in waking life. If a patient were asked to imagine himself in a dangerous predicament, his agitation would express itself in the upheaval of his various organ systems and body functions. The resulting disturbances could be recorded and measured by the sensitive machines that are used to diagnose such manifestations.

In studying the results, our conclusions would probably be that emotions aroused during hypnosis directly affect the functions of body organs and processes. Because people vary in their physiological sensitivity (some are more impressionable than others), we would anticipate a great variety of response. Moreover, a suggestion can take on added meaning for an individual in terms of his own experience. Thus, if a subject has actually been assaulted and robbed in the past, he will probably react explosively to the suggestion of a robbery and personal attack. Finally, people vary in their physical vulnerability to emotional stimuli. Some respond with high blood pressure, others by blushing, still others with painful abdominal cramps. As a result, the same suggestion to different subjects may bring about totally different physical reactions.

Researchers who try to measure body changes under hypnosis find themselves under a great handicap because they are not able to determine how much of what they observe is caused by the special sensitivity of the individual, how much by the particular significance of the suggestion in terms of the subject's past conditioning, how much by what is going on in the immediate relationship between the subject and hypnotist, and how much by the trance experience itself. This probably accounts for the ambiguous results that are described in the research literature.

There are some professionals who are convinced that they can direct their suggestions to a specific organ through word pictures without any preliminary conditioning. I know of one operator who believes that he can influence one of his subjects' blood count by merely telling him that his white or red cells will increase or decrease. Most impartial observers would doubt that such a dramatic reponse is possible without emotional preparation. But the operator in question insists that he can bring this about, and he presents impressive evidence as proof. Other reports, equally difficult to believe, detail the direct effects of suggestion on specific targets of the body.

A considerable number of clinical "cures" of obstinate skin ailments have been recorded. After traditional medications failed to heal these disorders, a cure was said to have been effected when the operator merely told a subject that a selected lesion would disappear. For example, some physicians claim to have eliminated by simple hypnotic suggestions one of the most persistent and ugly skin maladies, fish skin disease (ichthyosis), a hereditary familial disease characterized by dryness, scaliness, and abnormal keratinization. What is interesting in these report is the indication that only the lesions singled out for cure are eliminated; the rest persist until they are directly treated. There are other focal cures described in the literature, for instance, moles, eczema, and neurodermatitis. Before one rejects these reports as of questionable authenticity, he should consider the effect of suggestion on warts. Tom Sawyer was well aware of this, and folk medicine aimed at wart elimination is largly dependent on the suggestive effects of the prescribed remedies. I myself have been able to eliminate warts in certain subjects under hypnosis by merely touching them and suggesting that they disappear. What the mechanism is behind this phenomenon is hard to say. Does the brain shoot impulses to the selected areas? Does the circulation in these areas become activated, delivering more healing blood to the chosen zone? We do not know. All we can say is that the mind has a stronger influence on areas of the body than many of us are ready to admit.

It is possible to bring about heart (cardiac) and blood vessel (vascular) responses by means of verbal cues after an initial learning process, in which key words and suggestions are associated with certain emotions. Responses ordinarily produced by emotional reactions can later be elicited in trained subjects by mere verbal suggestions. This fact holds true not only for cardiovascular responses, but for other physiological activities, which may, through the process of conditioning, be influenced by verbal command.

Emotional states can influence other somatic reactions during hypnosis. Excitement, for example, may produce an increase in the number of red blood corpuscles, probably through contraction of the spleen. Tear production may be caused by appropriate depressive moods. Cold sores have been produced in a subject by the hypnotist's recounting of unpleasant experiences while stroking the lower lip and suggesting itchiness, as in a cold sore. A swelling of the lip develops followed by a real cold sore. Contraction and dilation of the pupils can also be emotionally incited.

Some of the more spectacular physiological effects of hypnosis are difficult to believe. For example, there are a number of accounts of blister formation produced in the exact area of the skin touched by the operator. The authors of these reports are reputable practitioners, and their statements bear a good deal of weight. However, the possibility of fraud must always be kept in mind. Knowing that the hypnotist expects certain things of him, the subject may contrive to please with remarkable ingenuity. He may later develop amnesia about his connivance. For instance, I once suggested to a subject that he would develop hives over the forearms after hypnosis. I asked that he report to me as soon as hives appeared. Several days later, he demonstrated a markedly irritated skin, but there was no evidence of hives. He denied that he had in any way irritated the skin, insisting that when he awoke from sleep that morning he found the skin scratched and inflamed. Under hypnosis, however, he confided that after the trance he had taken a walk through the woods. Here he picked poison ivy and rubbed it vigorously on the inner surfaces of his arms. Later, he developed a complete loss of memory about this, probably to convince me that he had spontaneously complied with my request.

The old-time hypnotists reported such rare phenomena as bleeding from the mucous membranes, local redness of the skin, burns, and changes in milk secretion induced by suggestion. Such reports must be accepted with caution since unconscious deception might have been involved.

Studies about the influence of hypnosis on metabolic processes are almost as incredible. One observer noted that the calcium content in blood could be brought down by hypnotic command. Others reported that there was a marked increase in the blood sugar of subjects to whom it had been suggested that they were eating large amounts of honey. On the other hand, when suggestions were made that there was an absence of sugar and sweetness in food eaten, the blood-sugar rise is said to have been inhibited, even though sugar was ingested. A hypnotist suggested to his subjects that they were first drinking bouillon and then eating butter. He had the contents of the duodenum examined and after the first suggestions found these to be thin and yellow. After the second suggestion they were dark, viscous, and increased in quantity to the extent of what would have occurred had the suggested substances actually been incorporated.

In another experiment, it was suggested to a subject that he was eating a meal consisting, first, of protein, second, of fats, and third, of carbohydrates. When the contents of the stomach were examined, it was discovered that the corresponding enzymes for each type of food had been manufactured during each process, just as they are when real food is eaten. In a similar study with a group of subjects, some where told that they relished the food and the rest that the food was repulsive to them. Analysis of the stomach contents is said to have shown a greater acid content than normal in the first group, and greatly reduced acid in the second group. A researcher suggested to his subjects the ingestion of an imaginary meal and claimed to have produced gastric secretions, the amount and content of which corresponded with what one might expect had the foods actually been eaten. In another experiment, he suggested to his subject that he was taking a constipating dose of opium under the guise of castor oil. The results were cathartic. Another subject was told that he was drinking large quantities of water from what was actually an empty glass. The operator noted that the urinary output was markedly increased with a loss of body fluids. Russian authorities have reported that they were able to cause symptoms of acute alcoholic intoxication to disappear by hypnotic command. Both elevation of temperature and altered basal metabolism are claimed to have been brought about by hypnotic suggestion.

These effects are not as unusual as one would believe. If a person is given a barium meal and his stomach is watched under the fluoroscope, definite changes in gastric motility may be observed with various suggestions. When told he feels disgusted or that he has no appetite, gastric and intestinal sluggishness occur. When suggestions are made that he has eaten a delicious meal or that he feels relaxed and comfortable, normal peristalsis is restored, and tonicity reappears. During hunger contractions, suggestions of eating stop the contractions.

A hungry man, asked to think about a sizzling steak, will find his mouth watering and his stomach making importunate demands for food. Under hypnosis, suggestion works the same way, but because the imagination is more vivid, and since the situations brought to mind seem more real, the psychological and physiological reponses are even more intense. Were we to suggest to a person in a deep trance that a stack of blotters was a tender piece of meat, an examination of the stomach might easily reveal digestive juices preparing the way for protein foods.

It is also possible that where certain maladies such as skin ailments and gastric ulcers have a possible emotional origin, suggestions that these conditions reappear may serve to bring on a recurrence. We may emphasize that not all of these effects can be obtained in every subject. A special disposition seems to be essential.

To summarize what we know or believe to be valid about the physiological effects of hypnosis:

1. *Circulatory system*

The heart, blood vessels, and content of the blood are indirectly influenced by emotions suggested or spontaneously evoked in the trance. Reduced bleeding from wounds is also probably an indirect phenomenon associated with the existent reduction in tension and heart rate. Changes in the blood vessels that cause an increased supply of blood to areas of poor circulation, as in vasospastic conditions, have been reported, but there are no controlled experiments to substantiate this. Irregularities in the heart recordings registered by an electrocardiograph may be provoked by emotive suggestions that bring about anger or fear.

2. *Respiratory system*

The respiratory rate is lowered by suggestions to breathe slowly and by tension reduction. It is heightened by suggestions of pain, fear, and anger, or by induced fantasies of muscular activity. It is claimed that cases of asthma may be helped through hypnotic suggestion. However, the reassuring effect of the interpersonal relationship in hypnosis cannot be ruled out as the principal healing agency.

3. *Gastrointestinal system*

This entire system, from mouth (*e.g.*, increased salivation) to stomach (*e.g.*, vomiting) to intestine (*e.g.*, alterations of motility) to rectum (*e.g.*, diarrhea) can be influenced through induced fantasies, dreams, and emotive suggestions. Both gastric secretion (free and total acid, total volume and pepsin activity) and motility of the gastrointestinal tract may be increased or inhibited in this way. Hypnosis has been employed with success in duodenal ulcer, in the nausea, vomiting and weakness ("dumping" syndrome) following gastric resections, and in vomiting during pregnancy.

4. *Genitourinary system*

The effect of hypnosis on kidney function is not established. Through alleviation of tension and diversion of thinking, urinary frequency and spasm that prevent free urination may be controlled. Sexual problems, such as impotence, premature ejaculation, and frigidity may be approached through the adjunctive use of hypnosis during psychotherapy. They are not particularly influenced by the hypnotic state itself.

5. *Metabolism*

Relaxation, whether it occurs in the waking state or in hypnosis, has a lowering effect on the basal metabolic rate. When emotions are aroused during hypnosis, the rate will increase because of the accompanying release of energy. There are reports that the body temperature may be raised by inducing feelings of warmth. Such suggestions may enable a subject to endure cold better than in the waking state since he will pay less attention to his discomfort.

6. *Brain-wave studies (electroencephalography)*

The brain emits characteristic waves during waking and sleep, and these can be recorded by an electroencephalographic machine. We would expect a special pattern of brain waves to come through during hypnosis. Most investigators have found nothing distinctive in the brain recordings of subjects under hypnosis. It may be that our instruments are not refined enough to disclose minor changes.* It may also be that the choice of subjects has an effect on our results. The subjects who are usually chosen for experiments are highly susceptible to hypnosis. They may show brain rhythms that respond differently than subjects with low susceptibility. At any rate, for all practical purposes, we are not able to record anything that identifies hypnosis electrically. Of course, if a subject passes from hypnosis into a temporary sleep, we then observe brainwaves characteristic of sleep, but this should not confuse us into identifying hypnosis with sleep. So many contradictory reports have been issued on brain-wave studies in hypnosis that we must wait for future findings to settle the dispute of whether or not the hypnotic state per se has an influence on cerebral electrical activity.

Effect on Sensations of Touch and Pain

There is evidence that a subject's sensory reactions are the products of suggestions, or result from a conviction of how he is supposed to behave. Paresthesias in various areas are relatively easy to produce. Among these are numbness, tingling, itching, prickling, burning, sensations of coldness, and increased sensitivity to stimuli of pain, pressure, temperature, and touch. On suggestion, a subject may be made to distinguish variations in texture and temperature that could not be differentiated in the waking state. This does not mean that hypnosis gives a person facilities he does not latently possess; it merely supplies greater motivation to bring out his hidden capacities.

Hypnotic anesthesias, like hysterical disorders of sensation, conform to popular notions of function rather than to anatomic areas. In suitable subjects, suggestion will produce a loss of the sense of touch (anesthesia), pain (analgesia), and temperature (thermoanesthesia). Often this loss is relative, and the subject

*Some researchers claim that with special instruments and methods distinctive brain waves can be elicited in hypnosis. This work is still in the process of being evaluated.

will attest to a diminished rather than to a total absence of sensation. In trained subjects, however, sensory loss can be complete: dental work, obstetrical procedures, minor and, in somnambulistic subjects, even major surgery may be possible. Whether anesthesia is real or whether the subject is playing a role and merely acting as if he did not feel pain is a question about which different opinions have been expressed. In a later chapter this question will be explored more thoroughly.

Effect on Vision, Hearing, Taste, and Smell

Through suggestion, and perhaps because of a loosening of controls in the trance state, hypnosis can produce distortions of the special senses in the form of flashes of light and color (photomata), hearing, such as buzzing or roaring in the ears, altered taste sensation (parageusia), and smell (parosmia).

In profound somnambulistic states the eyes may be opened without awakening. Visual hallucinations may often be induced in these states, which evoke the same kind of behavior that might be expected were the perception produced by a real stimulus. The subject will flee in terror from imaginary lions or, upon suggestion, he will pick up and pet tenderly a hallucinated kitten. If it is suggested that he go into a restaurant to appease his hunger he will go through the motions of entering it, seating himself, scanning the menu, inquiring about the various dishes, imbibing the ordered courses from cocktail to dessert, even wiping his mouth with a napkin and leaving an imaginary tip for the waiter. Stage hypnotists depend upon such hallucinations for their effects, and they will select from the audience somnambules who are most likely to comply.

Crystal gazing or mirror gazing are forms of visual hallucination. Upon suggestion the subject will gaze intently into the crystal or mirror and see scenes that are the product of his own imagination. This tactic is sometimes used in the exploratory phases of hypnoanalysis. Taste, smell, and hearing hallucinations, both pleasant and unpleasant, may also be induced. Thus the subject will listen intently to an orchestra or a speech, reacting with appropriate facial expressions and other gestures. "Shell hearing," in which comunications from a seashell or a teacup held over the ear are received on suggestion, is a type of auditory hallucination.

In hypnosis a degree of keenness in vision, hearing, taste, and smell—which is not fully realized in the waking state—may occur. The subject may perceive stimuli that would escape ordinary observation. A favorite trick of stage hypnotists is to show the subject a blank card, then ask him to select it from a shuffled pack of apparently similar blank cards. Telepathic abilities and powers of second sight are held responsible for a successful performance. What actually happens is that the subject observes creases or imperfections on the card, which will enable him to distinguish it from others later on. These flaws are so slight that they are not noticeable unless the attention is specifically focused on the most minute details. Increased sensitivity to noises, tastes, and odors are also evident in these situations.

Negative hallucinations, that is, a blotting out of areas in the visual or auditory range, often observed in hysteria, are possible only in the deepest somnambulism and require a careful formulation of commands. In the visual area the hypnotist can bring about through suggestion an elimination of specific objects in the environment, blindness of half the visual field (hemianopsia), the development of various blind spots (scotomata), color blindness (achromatopsia), concentric narrowing of vision, and total blindness (amaurosis). Suggested deafness may involve one or both ears and may be partial or total, with loss of varying portions of the tonal range. The complete absence of taste (ageusia) and of smell (anosmia), or the obliteration of specific taste sensations or odors may also be brought about.

The nature of these sensory changes has been debated. Some observers believe that they are merely the result of a changed attitude and that all elicited phenomena can be explained on the basis of playing a role. Other researchers, however, believe that an organic change is involved. One group of experimenters held open with adhesive the lids of their subject so that it was impossible to close the eyes. They then measured the brain potentials with an electroencephalographic apparatus. At alternate fifteen-second intervals they suggested to the subject that first he was totally blind and then that his vision was normal. In every case where it was suggested that the subject could not see, brain waves characteristic of a totally blind person, or of a person whose eyes are shut, appeared. These ceased upon suggestion that the subject could see. Other researchers have not been able to duplicate this result, which raises the question of its validity.

Contradictory opinions have also been expressed about pupillary reactions to hallucinations of light. In hypnotic blindness there is usually a normal pupillary response to light stimuli, and even hallucinations of light produce no contraction of the pupil. However, in very deeply hypnotized subjects who have been conditioned properly, pupillary contractions have been obtained. Suggestions of hallucinatory color visions were given to a group of subjects, who responded by seeing afterimages of complementary colors, even in cases where preliminary word tests showed no correct associations of the various colors. Hypnotically induced deafness, which observers claim was not distinguishable from neurologic deafness by any of the ordinary tests, has been produced.

It is a scientific principle that in order to verify the result of an experiment, the test should be repeated. When the results are not the same, questions are raised about the accuracy of the experiment. Some competent experimenters insist that hypnotically produced color blindness and deafness result from a mental set in the subject rather than a true inhibition of sensation. The subject acts as if he has a visual or hearing loss. Tests do not detect a real organic loss. By the same token, visual and hearing acuity are increased only if motivation to respond more intensely to stimuli can be created. There is no question of deception or simulation; the subject is truly convinced of the truth of his responses. Questions of how genuine the reactions are and how closely allied to organic deviations cannot yet be fully answered at this stage of our scientific knowledge. For example, in true blindness there is no pupillar reflex in response to light. In hypnotically produced blindness the individual, when walking, will avoid dangerous obstacles, and his pupils will respond to light stimulation. Hypnotic deafness seems merely to deaden an awareness of stimuli.

Intellectual Functions

The thinking process is not suspended during hypnosis. In fact, it can be quite active, with the subject entertaining spontaneous ideas sometimes wholly divorced from the situation at hand. The induction of hypnosis may release thoughts, memories, and feelings that are held in abeyance by purposeful repression during the waking state. However, problems that cause too much anxiety will in all likelihood continue to be concealed, or be so highly disguised (symbolized) that they will escape precise identification. The creative imagination is sometimes stimulated during hypnosis, and artists in particular are often pleased by this, since new concepts and fresh ideas come to the surface. Quite a few writers have come to me for therapy and the treatment of specific symptoms that seemed to have nothing to do with their work. Hypnosis gave them an added dividend by freeing their creative imaginations to work more fully and effectively for them.

Certain studies indicate that the learning process is improved through hypnosis and that established habits can be broken more easily. Russian researchers have demonstrated that conditioned reflexes are easier to set up and that they last longer than in the waking state. The faculty of memory also functions better in hypnosis. This "hyperamnesia" can be demonstrated by hypnotizing a person and testing his memory of recent events. He will often be aware of situations that had not seemed to register on his conscious mind because his attention apparently was directed elsewhere. I believe that most people observe more about their environment than they can consciously recall. For example, I have asked several patients to describe my waiting room before hypnosis. I discovered that their memories were patchy, even though they had just left the room. Yet interrogation under hypnosis produced an astonishing recall of detail, even to the most minute description of the pictures on the wall and the dates of magazines on the table, which they had glanced at casually. These observations had been beyond the range of their recollection a few minutes previously.

There is good reason why we screen our perceptions, selecting some to remember and storing the bulk in a reserve storehouse. In waking life and even in sleep, our sensory organs are constantly being bombarded by stimuli from the outside world. These are sifted out by a process of conscious or unconscious selection. A person reacts to stimuli as a result of set conditionings or because he is motivated to do so through needs that operate on various levels of awareness. It is simply psychologically economical to pay more attention to matters of greatest concern at the moment.

Remembering incidents that occurred during childhood and even infancy may sometimes be achieved by inducing hypnotic regression. This is because hypnosis can remove some inhibitions and repressions that block early memories. The recall of forgotten events depends to a large extent on the amount of the nascent anxiety associated with a specific memory. It depends also upon the degree to which the process of forgetting is a purposeful defensive mechanism shielding the individual from conflict.

On the other hand, the learning process can also be impaired or blocked by certain suggestions. In deep hypnosis, induced amnesia may produce a forgetting of entire segments of experience, which is what happens without hypnosis in hysterical amnesia. False memories may also be invoked with acceptance of these falsifications as factual. The latter phenomenon is often used in experimental conflicts and in provoking dreams and fantasies that will give clues to unconscious conflictual situations.

When the hypnotist employs probing techniques, such as automatic writing, hypnotic drawing, and regression with subjects who are able to enter somnambulistic trance states, he sometimes encounters the kind of bizarre images and associations largely associated with dreams. This is probably because it is the same subconscious areas of the mind from which dreams emerge that are being explored. At first glance, the weird outcroppings of the unconscious appear senseless, and one might suspect that the levels of mind reached through hypnosis are disorganized and absurd. This is by no means the case, for unconscious thinking has a definite purpose and function.

Subjects in deep hypnosis can often reproduce the distorted ideas and symptoms that are affiliated with neuroses and psychoses, which proves that elements of mental illness and the defenses that neurotic and psychotic people employ are potentially present in all of us. If, for example, an obsession or delusion is introduced into the mind of a normal subject, he will defend it vigorously with fabrications and rationalizations. Even absurd or foolish ideas may seem sound to the subject if it suggested to him that he will remember them as true facts after he awakens from the trance.

On one occasion, in a demonstration of this phenomenon before a group of medical students, I suggested to a volunteer subject that he had attended the Kentucky Derby several days before and that he would remember this upon awakening. In talking about his experiences, the subject skillfully wove in the fact that he had recently won a sizable sum of money in the Kentucky Derby, but that he had lost it at the track. It was pointed out to him that he could not possibly have gone to the Kentucky Derby since the race was scheduled to take place several months in advance of the day he claimed to have attended it. He quickly manufactured the story that because of unusual conditions a number of races were being run that year. Several of his colleagues testified that he had been in New York City on the day he said he was away. They reminded him that they had been in several classes with him. The subject then asserted that he actually had been in New York in the morning, but that in the afternoon he had boarded an airplane to attend the race, flying back again when it was over. No amount of argument or logic could dissuade him from this idea. Later on, he had amnesia for this incident and was amused when informed of his behavior.

Situations created during hypnosis can seem as real to the subject as if they actually happened. During a play-therapy session with a patient who had been regressed to a ten-year level, he got into an imaginary fight with another boy over the disputed occupancy of a swing. The fight became so extreme and the rage of the patient so intense that the dispute had to be stopped.

Time Sense

The sense of time is actually subjective. We have all felt that a few minutes in the dental chair during a tooth drilling seemed interminable. On the other hand, how rapidly time passes during pleasant experiences. Suggestion can affect the time sense by shortening or lengthening the awareness of an interval. It can also enable some people to estimate a time span with little error.

There is conflicting evidence about whether or not the average person has a greater ability to gauge the passage of time in hypnosis than he has in the waking state. If a subject under hypnosis is asked to perform a task after a certain number of minutes has passed, he will often do so with considerable precision. Similarly, upon appropriate suggestion, a subject may punctually carry out a posthypnotic act or series of acts after a prescribed interval.

Perhaps the most intensive work in this field was done many years ago by old-time hypnotists, whose subjects displayed an uncanny time sense. Their work, however, has never been duplicated. In controlled experiments, some modern researchers have reported that the ability to judge time is not greater during hypnosis than in the ordinary waking state, provided the individual concentrates on the task.

Although it is dangerous to generalize, it seems safe to say that the varying results obtained in time experiments probably depend upon differences in the aptitudes of the subjects under test. It is possible to train a hypnotic subject to judge time with extraordinary accuracy. On the other hand, there are persons who are capable of estimating time with a remarkable degree of exactitude in the waking state. Appropriate suggestions prompt the subject to concentrate more intensively on the passage of time during hypnosis. Were he to devote himself to the problem as keenly in the waking state, he might be able to obtain the same good results that he does in the trance.

Taking advantage of the fact that the concept of time can be altered by suggestions, some therapists distort the time sense in hypnosis. They either prolong or condense it in order to explore the past. In this way their patients can be helped to use the insights they gain for self-improvement. Milton Erickson, for example, a remarkably inventive hypnotherapist, describes a technique he employs with some hypnotized subjects, in which they are asked to discuss their wishes, hopes, and possiblities for the future. A suggestion is made that they will report on the progress they have made in therapy, describing what they think they have accomplished in the way of normal adjustments. After this they are reoriented to the current time and given posthypnotic suggestions to insure complete amnesia. While they are in the trance the hypnotist suggests that various developments and events in their lives will determine the time and nature of the next appointment. In susceptible subjects these suggestions are apparently acted on as rapidly as internal resistances are resolved. In projecting a more integrated and more balanced conception of the self, the subject may start a re-educative process and reinforce new, more-productive patterns in living. The pseudo-orientation in time may permit the patient to adjust more easily to the anxiety that results from accepting normality as a reality in the here and now. The hope for a more fulfilling life and the possiblity of success in the future help reduce resistance to change and lead to increased efforts to become more like the healthy self visualized in hypnosis. Obviously, the method is applicable only to a small number of patients who not only are somnambules but who are able to project a reasonable conception of normality into the future without too great anxiety. In addition, they must be able to accept suggestions that influence them toward more normal actions, and to consolidate their new behavior patterns by ensuring that they carry them out in favorable environmental circumstances. Through hypnotic time compression the patient is directed to abbreviate an experience so that is seems to pass very quickly. This technique is sometimes used in a pain syndrome so that the time of suffering appears greatly diminished. In time expansion, sensations of pleasure are stretched out so that moments seem like hours. Occasionally this is used in depressed persons to enhance acceptance of enjoyment and to dull the sodden mood.

Regression

One of the most vivid and dramatic happenings in hypnosis is the ability of deeply hypnotized subjects to turn back the clock and to play back, as one would a recording, the events and fantasies of early childhood. If one asks a subject in this state to return to the time when he first entered school, he is often able to recall the names of his school friends and his teachers in kindergarten and the first grade. He can also recount in vivid detail experiences that were exhilarating, upsetting, or otherwise important to him. Such memories could not be summoned in the waking state.

Some reports of phenomena elicited through regression sound incredible. In one study an epileptic was regressed to an age before his first attack. At that point the electroencephalograph recorded his brain waves as normal. There was reversion to the abnormal brain waves when it was suggested that he reach and go beyond the age of the onset of epilepsy. Other reports deal with the re-establishment of an infantile foot-nerve reflex (Babinski reflex) when subjects were regressed to the first year of life. In this case the subjects could not possibly have known what reflexes they had when they were infants. The drawings made by a regressed subject and his responses to psychological tests also approximate those of a child. For example, the drawings on this page were done under hypnosis. When the subject was in a waking state, he was asked to imagine himself at the corresponding age levels, but he could not duplicate the drawings.

Adult Hypnosis

Regression to Age 6

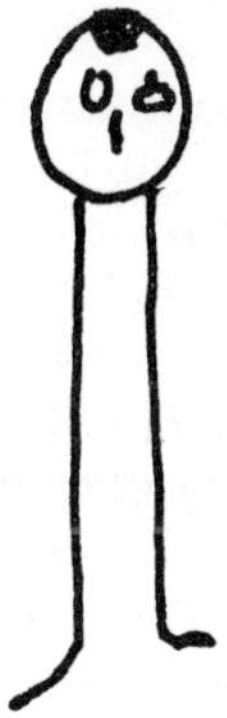

Regression to Age 3

However, there is considerable disagreement about whether hypnotic regression is valid, in the sense that it is a recapitulation of a previous state of development, or whether the subject merely re-enacts and dramatizes an earlier development stage according to his idea of what a person at the suggested age level is supposed to do. Hypnotic subjects without question are capable of simulating behavior at suggested regressed ages much better than conscious subjects. They're also able to remember things at regressed age levels that they cannot recall at adult levels.

On the basis of intelligence tests, some hypnotists claim to have regressed patients to infancy, and a few believe that it is possible to secure regression to a state before birth, that is, to the experiences of the fetus in the womb. They report that the results of intelligence tests at regressed ages correspond precisely with performances at actual chronological levels. Attempts have been made by a similar method to show that the transformation in the subject during regression is an actual reliving of an earlier developmental period. Each of the subjects who regressed to an earlier age was able to pass only those tests that did not go beyond the corresponding age as established by the Binet-Simon method of intelligence measurement. Furthermore, the behavior of the subject during regression was similar in all details to what one might find in children at those ages. For instance, at four- and six-year levels, the subjects were very fidgety, easily distracted and fatigued. When given complicated tests, they faltered and refused to go on. At the regressed age of ten, their behavior changed completely, and they worked quietly and attentively. Handwriting also corresponded to various age levels. In the waking state the subject easily passed all tests, including those at the adult level.

The conclusions were that these results definitely disproved any kind of simulation or role-playing. The phenomenon of regression is explained by some on the basis that conditioned reactions, once developed, do not disappear completely but leave patterns of behavior that are never thoroughly erased in the nervous system. This makes possible an actual reproducing of previous development stages later on. Word stimuli in hypnosis activate earlier conditioned reflexes. Thus suggestion brings forth a playback of the recordings in the brain, that were formed in earlier periods of the individual's life.

On the other hand, there are researchers who have criticized these findings on the basis that there has not been enough conclusive experimentation to warrant such sweeping generalizations. For example, one well-known researcher regressed fourteen trance subjects to their third birthdays and found that intelligence tests revealed an average mental age of six. Although their speech and grammar, as well as their mannerisms, were very childish, the subjects did not enter into activities typical of a three-year-old child. Seven unhypnotizable control subjects who were asked to simulate a three-year-old child approached more closely a three-year level of performance than did the hypnotized subjects. The researcher concluded that hypnosis is playing a role and that regression in hypnosis means the subject acts a part. Carefully planned studies have shown that Rorschach and drawing tests administered in the regressed state yield results not really characteristic of childhood and that the personality organization is for the most part typically adult.

In response to the reports of altered brain wave findings in regression, the skeptics insist that electroencephalographic studies of average subjects during hypnotic regression show no evidences of brain-wave alterations from the normal mature waves to the normal immature waves of childhood. As for the Babinski reflex, presumably produced in regression to infancy, they state that this infantile reflex may be obtained normally during sleep. Therefore, it can also occur in hypnosis when the trance is so deep that it borders on sleep. It has nothing to do, they say, with the suggestions to regress. In their opinion, there is no basis, therefore, for the assumption of physiological alterations during regression.

Robert Rubenstein and Richard Newman of Yale Medical School have introduced another dimension that they believe detracts from the validity of regressed phenomena. Instead of regressing their subjects, they advanced them in age. A vivid living-out of "future" experiences was obtained in all of their five subjects—experiences that sounded possible and well within the realm of probability. Since these experiences could be the product only of the imagination, having no basis in reality, the researchers suggest that many descriptions of hypnotic regression also consist of fabrications and simulated behavior. However, they qualify their opinion by stating that a past true traumatic situation that has been repressed could be recovered with hypnotic regression and would not be imagined.

In contrast, an interesting case reported in 1970 by Erika Fromm provides evidence in favor of the theory of true regression. A twenty-six-year-old, third-generation Japanese American, born in California five days before Pearl Harbor, assumed that he knew no Japanese whatsoever. Regressed to levels below the age of four, he spoke Japanese spontaneously, but could not do so when he was regressed to five or above. I have had two similar experiences with people who had been brought to this country as young children. They were unaware that they knew their native tongue until regressed to an age prior to their entry into the United States. In both cases, when in the waking state, they were not able to speak the second language upon being asked to imagine themselves as young children in their native land.

We may hypothesize that regression is likely to reproduce early behavior in a way that precludes all possiblity of simulation. My own studies have convinced me of this fact, although the regression is never stationary. It is constantly being altered by the intrusion of mental functioning at other age levels. These shifts are probably the result of certain psychological needs or defenses that are being stirred up by the experience. Regression, then, is never complete or total, since there is always an encroachment on one age level by more mature levels. Sometimes the patient reacts as if he were reliving a scene exactly as it happened, without any reference to later events in his life. Sometimes he responds as if he were judging an earlier actual event from his present point of view. Dramatic overacting and vivid embellishments of fantasy are often intermingled with real-life experiences. These constructions should not be considered as ingenious maneuvers that must be scrupulously discarded. Rather, they are motivated by neurotic defenses and needs, and they may be profitably explored by an analytically trained hypnotherapist in the course of psychotherapy.

In certain cases, hypnotic regression can be used to trace the development of a current symptom to the environmental source that precipitated it, or to go back to the roots of fundamental conflicts within a subject. It is like playing a tape recording that was made years ago.

The difference of opinion about the nature of regression is probably the result of the two types of phenomena that can be observed during this process. In the first type there is an actual return to an earlier stage of development, in which events subsequent to that period are totally forgotten. For example, if a subject is regressed to a five-year level, he will remember experiences at that level and will completely forget all the events following that period. He will even fail to recognize the hypnotist and may lose rapport with him. Drawings made at a regressed age level are so genuinely childish that simulation seems improbable. Even an accomplished artist will draw grotesque figures typical of the suggested age level. Motor-behavior patterns also correspond to the regressed age level, and a re-enactment (revivification) of past experiences may occur. On the other hand, suggested regression in some subjects brings about not an acutal experiencing of an earlier childhood state but a simulated model of what this state must have been. The fact that both these forms of behavior occur may explain why opinions differ over the actual nature and meaning of hypnotic regression. When it can be obtained, the first type of regression approaches a definite and genuine re-experiencing of a developmentally earlier period.

The earliest age to which a subject can be successfully regressed is difficult to state with certainty. On one occasion I attempted to regress a somnambulistic subject to the first year of life. He was unable to speak and exhibited definite sucking and grasping movements. The subject was instructed to remember his experiences when brought back to an adult level. He revealed the following details: "I was very small. I didn't understand anything. Everything was new. I didn't know what things meant. I was trying to get hold of things, reaching for things. I didn't know what I was doing. I didn't know the meaning of things. Somebody was leaning over me, my mother. She picked me up and held me tight. She was fixing things around me. She was fixing my body, the clothes where I was lying. I had all kinds of sensations. I didn't know what anything meant. I saw different kinds of things. I saw mother, I didn't know the names of anything. I took hold of things that came toward me, the covers. They dropped to the floor. I didn't know what made them drop. I didn't know what became of them when they dropped. I didn't know why mother was there. I took hold of her, I played with everything. I was reaching out, grabbing things, clothes, feet, everything."

As fascinating as this material is, one cannot be certain whether the subject actually returned to an infantile state or whether he was trying to please me by complying with my suggestion. Responses in hypnotic regression must be carefully checked, since there is an intensification of the imaginative life and sometimes a need on the part of the subject to live up to the expectations of the operator. There are also tendencies toward dramatization. Thus the subject may "remember" his own birth, intrauterine life, and even conception. Constant shifts in levels of regression occur, and role playing is often superimposed upon any existing true regression.

Posthypnotic Suggestions

A subject in a somnambulistic trance may be given a suggestion to carry out a series of acts at a certain point or upon a given signal after awakening. The response is usually automatic, and even though it serves no purpose, it may be defended and rationalized by the subject without awareness that the impulse had been implanted in him by the hypnotist. In some cases, posthypnotic suggestions will be carried out even if the trance has been relatively light and in spite of the fact that the subject remembers the suggestions. Such subjects are probably extremely suggestible and would be easily influenced in the waking state also. In most cases, however, posthypnotic suggestions are effective only after the subject has developed a deep trance, which has been followed by amnesia.

To illustrate how sincerely the subject believes in the authenticity of his posthypnotic experience, I give here an example of a posthypnotic negative hallucination induced in a man in the presence of one of my colleagues. Dr. S., who was skeptical about hypnosis, came to my office unexpectedly at a time when a volunteer subject, known to both of us, was in a hypnotic trance. I suggested to the subject that when he woke up he would neither see nor hear Dr. S. Upon awakening, the subject started to talk to me about the pennant possibilities of the Dodgers. In the middle of our conversation he casually asked if I had seen Dr. S. recently. I in turn asked him the same question. All this time Dr. S. was leaning against a window. I told the subject that I was expecting Dr. S. and asked him to look out the window to see whether he was in sight. The subject looked directly at Dr. S. and said, "No, he isn't." When I asked him what he saw, he remarked that he noticed the usual trees, grass, and buldings. At this point, Dr. S. addressed the subject. The latter interrupted him in the middle of a sentence with a remark directed at myself. Dr. S. continued talking, but the subject paid absolutely no attention to him; it was as if he were not in the room. At this point, I held up an inkwell and asked him if he saw it. Perplexed, he said that he did and wondered why I had asked him such a silly question. I then handed the inkwell to Dr. S. and asked the subject again if he could see the inkwell. He looked intently at it and exclaimed, "My God, you'll think I am crazy, but the inkwell is floating around in space." He appeared to be genuinely alarmed. I took the inkwell from Dr. S., and the subject said, "You have the inkwell now." Even though I insisted that Dr. S. was in the room and pointed him out, the subject maintained that I was joking. He remarked that fortunately he had not yet lost his mind. He was certain that there was no other person in the room until I rehypnotized him and removed the suggestion. Was the patient play-acting the absence of Dr. S.? The possibility exists, although my guess is that an actual alteration of his perceptions had occurred.

The compulsive nature of the posthypnotic act is one of its most characteristic features. This is not to say that the suggestion cannot be resisted. Usually, however, resistance takes a tremendous effort. The famous psychiatrist Eugen Bleuler underwent hypnosis to the test this point, and gave this description of his experience in attempting to resist a posthypnotic suggestion: "I was able to resist the carrying out of a posthypnotic suggestion. However, this cost me considerable trouble, and if I forgot for an instant during talking my resolve not to take any notice of the plate, which I was supposed to place somewhere else, I suddenly found myself fixing this object with my eyes. The thought of what I had been ordered to do worried me until I went to sleep, and when I was in bed I nearly got up again to carry it out, merely to ease my mind. However, I soon fell asleep and the action of the suggestion was then lost."

Commands that are reasonable and in keeping with a persons's personality are usually carried out. Unreasonable or ridiculous suggestions, and those antithetical to an individual's personality may not be carried out, even though the subject is a somnambule. I once gave a patient a posthypnotic suggestion to reach for a cigarette and light it as soon as I returned to my chair. He did not follow the command. When I inquired whether he remembered my giving him any posthypnotic suggestion, he declared that he did not. At the next hypnotic session he confided that his doctor had advised him against cigarettes because of a heart condition. He insisted that his refusal to comply with my suggestion was based upon a feeling that it might do him harm. When the posthypnotic command is resisted without conscious awareness of the command, the subject may complain of certain psychosomatic symptoms like headache and dizziness.

In certain cases, suggestions that are incompatible with the subject's customary behavior or outlook may be carried out with great resistance. Often, a tremendous struggle against compliance takes place, with resulting anxiety or emotional disturbance that can assume frightening proportions. This struggle has been ascribed to a conflict between commands given the subject by the hypnotist and the unconscious commands of his own conscience, which would be violated by the posthypnotic act. Sometimes the compulsive quality of posthypnotic suggestions may be so intense that anxiety will force the person into compliance.

The manner in which a posthypnotic suggestion is given also influences whether or not it will be followed. If the subject detects in the hypnotist's expression the implication that obedience is not mandatory, he will better be able to resist the command. If, however, he believes that he is expected to obey, he will feel more obliged to carry out the suggestion.

Frequently, the enactment of a posthypnotic suggestion is defended by numerous rationalizations. The subject may refuse to believe that the act had been suggested by the hypnotist, and he may justify it as his own impulse. A physician friend of mine, skilled in hypnosis, often used his wife, who was a good subject, to demonstrate the induction of trance. On one occasion his wife decided to defy him. Upon awakening from the trance she suddenly felt great thirst. She assumed from the compulsive nature of her desire to drink that her husband had given her this suggestion, which was, of course, correct. In spite of her resolve she felt herself being lifted out of her chair and pulled toward the kitchen. However, she clutched the chair and was for a while able to resist the compulsion. But she soon experienced such an extreme dryness of the throat that she felt it was foolish to torture herself. She then went to the kitchen, quenched her thirst, and explained that the only reason she had done this was because she really was thirsty and had intended to get a drink anyway.

An experimental neurosis that I unwittingly produced in a medical student illustrates the compulsive character of posthypnotic suggestion. In order to illustrate the induction of hypnosis, a student volunteer was hypnotized in front of the class. A suggestion was given to him that upon awakening he would return to his seat and listen attentively to the lecture. As soon as I went to the blackboard and wrote the word "psychiatry," he would write his name, but would misspell it. Before awakening, he was instructed to sleep for three minutes, after which I would arouse him by rapping three times on the table top. After three minutes, the rappings failed to arouse the subject, who was still in a deep trance. Five more minutes passed without my being able to awaken him; his only response was violent shaking and tremors. Finally, I told him that the posthypnotic suggestion might have aroused some resistance in him and that he did not have to comply if he did not wish to.

He then aroused himself and opened his eyes, but his shaking became even more violent. He took his seat, but his tremors became so strong that he could hardly sit. I rehypnotized him and attempted to remove the tremors by direct suggestion. Although his tremors were diminished somewhat in intensity, they were still present, and he was obviously uncomfortable. He complained of nausea and feelings of tenseness and anxiety. He remembered the posthypnotic suggestion I had given him, and he recalled also the instruction that he did not have to carry it out.

I then went to the blackboard and wrote the word "psychiatry." As soon as he saw the word, he reached for his pencil, but he paused in mid-air and forcefully brought his hand back. His tremors and anxiety became much more intense. I then advised him that it would probably be best for him to write his name in spite of his resistance. He grasped the pencil, but his fingers would not move. When he started to write, his hand shook violently, and he was unable to form letters. He tried to steady his right hand with his left, but his pencil moved so slowly that it took him almost five minutes to write his first name. His hand stopped, and he seemed to exert a superhuman effort in forcing himself to write. Upon reaching the last two letters, his hand refused to go further. Finally, after a pause of several minutes, he finished his name. To his amazement he had misspelled it! His anxiety and tremors vanished immediately, and he became extremely cheerful. He was able to write his name then without any difficulty.

He offered the information that he resented deeply any misspelling of his name. People frequently misspelled it, and he often wondered why they could not accurately write such a simple name. In commenting on the experiment, he said that he did not want to write his name incorrectly, and yet he found himself forced to do so for reasons he could not understand.

It seemed obvious that his sleeping beyond the signal to awaken was a mechanism to avert conflict. The release from the obligation to write his name inaccurately was sufficient to arouse him, but he felt compelled, nevertheless, to react to the command. The phenomenon acted as an excellent demonstration to the class of the dynamics of neurosis.

A letter written to me by this subject is interesting in its description of his subjective reactions:

> When the experiment started, I found it very easy to concentrate. When you told me I was asleep, I truthfully didn't believe it because I could still hear you talking and was still conscious of the fact that I was being hypnotized. I believe I remember everything you told me to do, since I do not feel that I lost consciousness during the hypnosis. I simply felt more or less drowsy. The best comparison that I can make is this: I felt that I just ingested some alcoholic beverage (which I very rarely do because I never got into the habit) and was just about to doze off. When you told me that my right arm felt very light, it really did feel that way, and the same held true when you told me that my left arm felt heavy. And yet throughout all of this, I kept being amazed at it all, because I didn't see how it could be possible. When you gave me the command to write my name incorrectly, I was not conscious of the fact that such a task would be distasteful, nor that it would create an experimental neurosis. When you asked me to dream, I did not dream but felt very relaxed and saw a soothing red or pink color in front of my eyes. When you tried to waken me, I felt very much as I do when I wake up in the morning, i.e., I hated to awaken, I know I trembled while still under hypnosis, and even after I came out (I'm not sure that I did come out when you told me to), I could not stop trembling no matter how much self-control I tried to exert.
>
> When I sat down in the chair, I wanted to write my name on the paper largely because of curiosity, especially since you began to analyze the situation at the time, referring to experimental neurosis created, etc. When I tried to write, I could hardly hold the pencil, since I was shaking so violently. As you well know, it turned out to be a child's scrawl. I had difficulty in getting out every single letter. I just could not get it out. All through this performance, I kept murmuring to myself that the whole thing was ridiculous, especially the tremors and trembling which affected my entire body. Finally, in exasperation, I murmured, "What the hell," and ended my name wrong against my will. When I did this, the trembling immediately ceased, and I felt kind of relieved. Someone then asked me to misspell my name again, and I could do it with no trouble.
>
> After this I felt tired because of the strain of concentration and trembling. But sure enough, on my way home from school on the

train, I felt very gay and lively, in spite of the fact that I was up late the night before and would ordinarily be tired. I was with some friends. I kept joking with them, inviting them to come out with me that night to "tear the town apart" and felt very contented as one does in the early stages of alcoholic intoxication. When I got out of the subway, for some strange reason I ran all the way home and did not feel at all tired when I got there (and I'm hardly in good athletic form at this time). That evening I felt very well, not at all tired as I usually am (from a full day at school), and studied very efficiently. When I turned in, I was not tired, and I think that I could have worked efficiently the entire evening. (We'll have to try this again before finals.)

The nature of posthypnotic behavior has been intensively analyzed by a number of observers, who contend that posthypnotic suggestions are not carried out in a normal condition, but in a state that resembles hypnosis. During the performance of a posthypnotic act, a spontaneous self-limited posthypnotic trance develops, according to this hypothesis, a point of view that incidentally is not accepted by other researchers. One observation is that some subjects act dazed during the execution of a posthypnotic act, as if they were automatically carrying it out. This is especially true when the subject is forced to interrupt one action to perform another that differs markedly from what the individual was previously doing. Amnesia for the posthypnotic act occurs particularly when the action is unusual or ridiculous, or conflicts with the customary behavior of the subject. Forgetting may serve the purpose of avoiding embarrassment or anxiety.

In other cases, when the act is in harmony with the personality of the subject and with his surroundings, he may appear fully conscious during its execution. He will then remember his behavior, often rationalizing it as a product of his own will. This occurs most often when the suggestions are so phrased that he can perform the act according to his own timing. Unconsciously, he will wait for an opportune moment to perform the act as inconspicuously as possible and in such a way that it does not conflict either with his standards or with what other people are doing at the time. This is not to say that the subject may not be in a special form of trance while he carries out the posthypnotic act. However, it is usually impossible to differentiate this behavior from the ordinary waking state.

An interesting question arises in regard to the actual extent and duration of posthypnotic suggestions. Do the suggestions themselves fade eventually or can they be made to persist indefinitely? Many observers have corroborated the fact that when a posthypnotic suggestion is to be executed at a much later date, the passing of time does not obliterate the intensity of the compulsion. For example, I once told a subject that exactly two years and two days from the date of trance he would read one of Tenneyson's poems. He complied with this suggestion on that date, having a week before developed a yearning to read poetry. While perusing the bookshelves of a library, he picked out one of Tennyson's volumes and looked through it. The poems interested him so much that he borrowed the book. He then placed in on his own desk until the prescribed day, when he suddenly found an opportunity to read the poem. He was positive that his interest in Tennyson was caused by a personal whim.

The well-known psychologist G. H. Estabrooks mentions the case of a person in whom a posthypnotic suggestion was strong after twenty years, and he believes that with occasional reinforcement the posthypnotic suggestion can last indefinitely. Without reinforcement, a posthypnotic suggestion often persists for many days. In one subject, a student, I induced a craving for vinegar during hypnosis. This led to such an intense desire for vinegar that for several days he doused all his food with it, to the disgust of his roommates.

Another psychologist, W. R. Wells, urged three of his subjects in a hypnotic trance to memorize a series of nonsense syllables. Posthypnotic amnesia was suggested for one year, and an appointed hour was set for remembering the syllables. This suggestion was carried out precisely by each subject. Further experiments by Wells proved that hypnotically induced suggestions were not necessarily obliterated by time, a fact that can have great therapeutic significance.

We come now to the subject of the posthypnotic forgetting of trance events (amnesia) that occurs in the small number of subjects who are capable of entering somnambulistic states. The subject may remember all details of the trance state upon awakening and then gradually forget some or all of his experiences. He may remember nothing, and then later recover some or all of the events. Although some authorities deny that these "lost" memories can ever be recalled through association of ideas, experience does not corroborate this.

Posthypnotic amnesia is probably due to a direct or implied suggestion to forget what has occurred. Because many subjects automatically equate hypnosis with sleep, they assume that events during the trance must not be remembered. Complete posthypnotic amnesia occurs only after the deepest hypnotic states. In certain instances the subject's character structure demands that he maintain control and even though he succumbs to a deep trance, he will recall all his experiences or a sufficent number of them to satisfy his personality needs. Trance events shielded from consciousness by purposeful forgetting are usually remembered in subsequent trances, unless there are specific directions to the contrary. If, on the other hand, a person is directed during hypnosis to remember events that have occurred, he will in all likelihood have no amnesia. In somnambulistic subjects, posthypnotic amnesia may be induced for events in one's past life. The amnesia may even involve the individual's name, age, and address, much as in hysterical amnesia.

The phenomenon of posthypnotic amnesia raises an important question in therapy. To what extent does amnesia nullify curative, persuasive, and re-educative suggestions given during hypnosis, and will it cause the repression of forgotten memories recalled in the trance? There is considerable evidence that even a so-called complete posthypnotic amnesia is not perfect. Subjects will often remember hypnotic incidents, but will consider them a product of their own fantasies. Sometimes they confuse events that took place during hypnosis with actual happenings. I have repeatedly observed that subjects, through free association or slips of speech, will bring up material of the trance state without being fully aware of the origin. Some subjects, upon leaving the hypnotist's office, will gradually recall all or most of the forgotten trance events. Suggestions given to the patient during hypnosis, even though not remembered, can be effective, perhaps operating from the more subconscious layers of the mind. This has important therapeutic implications.

Can Hypnosis Improve Performance?

In both the professional and popular literature on hypnosis one reads that it can enhance strength, endurance, co-ordination, memory, and learning. Generally this is true, but such increments are not a product of the hypnotic state itself. Rather, they are produced by incentives released within the individual during the trance experience.

Every person has latent talents and capacities. Ordinarily these are dormant, but they may come to the surface under special circumstances. Consider the feats of great courage and endurance that many people perform in emergencies or during natural disasters. In wartime soldiers may drive themselves for days, going without sleep for long periods, and enduring hardships they would find impossible if danger did not threaten. The urge to win in competitive sports and contests can spur a contestant toward record achievements. Successful athletic coaches know the value of the preliminary "pep talk" that hopefully will spur each member to "give his all" for the team. Impelled by their desire to excel and reach new heights of achievement under the press of special needs, actors and musicians may give stellar performances. Students who have had only a casual interest in their education will, when the stakes are especially high, immerse themselves so deeply in their books that their marks begin soaring. We are all familiar with such examples.

It should not be surprising, therefore, that an individual under hypnosis, motivated by the operator's suggestions to transcend his usual capacities, shows an improvement in performance. Take the case of a frail woman who cannot lift more than a fifty-pound weight before trance induction. Under the excitement of a hypnotic suggestion that a seventy-five pound weight pinning her child to the ground must be removed, she can mobilize enough energy to raise the weight zestfully. Even if the simple suggestion is given to her that she simply feels stronger and more energetic, she might be able to perform the same lifting feat, provided her desire to please the operator or to feel stronger is sufficently great. But if the same woman were in the actual position where she had to summon enough strength to release her child from a dangerous weight, she would be able to perform this act just as well as, or better than, in the hypnotic state.

Personal need and motivation, then, are the keys to the transcendence of normal capabilities. However, the capacity for heightened abilities must be latent within the subject. If such aptitudes do not exist, they cannot be created by hypnosis. Any improvement in performance—intellectual, emotional, and behavioral—is probably the result of changed attitudes in the subject rather than the creation of new powers that did not exist before. Enhanced performance may be reinforced and continued in the waking state through posthypnotic suggestions. In this way, therapeutic effects can be sustained.

6

How People Become Emotionally Ill and Get Well Again

To be a fully adjusted person is to greet the dawn of each new day with hope, to relate to one's fellow men with genial good will, to approach the tasks that face one with confident joy, and to embrace all the pleasures of living. If we gauge adjustment by this yardstick, we must regretfully admit that there are few, if any, human beings who qualify. One reason for this is that we live in a world torn by problems. Natural disasters, wars, race prejudice, pollution, crime, unemployment—the list is endless. But equally important is the inner turmoil of emotional disturbance, which casts a shadow on the most benevolent environment. Conflict and anxiety can deaden the joy of living and blunt the exciting sounds and smells and tastes and sights of life, transforming feelings of well-being into suffering.

There is no such thing as a completely adjusted person. There are possibilities for mental illness in everyone, and it is often difficult to distinguish clearly the psychological areas that can cause trouble from zones of mental health. "Normality" is a misleading conglomerate, for it lumps together all human strengths and frailties. John gets headaches for which no organic cause can be found. Mary experiences periodic depressions from which she eventually emerges happy as a lark. Phyllis cannot stand mice and "goes berserk" when she sees one. Her husband Joe, who chides her for this foolishness, is himself inclined to drink too much. Alice is sexually frigid. Charles is an avaricious grouch. George is a bore. Edith is too masculine. Frank is too passive. And so on. One can catalogue friends and acquaintances into long lists of symptoms and syndromes. Were we to examine closely the habits of any person, we would find few who could escape some categories of neurosis. But we would not classify all those who display certain symptoms of disturbance as abnormal, since some maladjustment seems to be the price of human existence.

It is easy to exaggerate the implications of the discovery that emotional illness is ubiquitous. Certainly there is no reason to fear that most people on earth will be candidates for mental institutions. But the fact remains that a great many of us struggle along with neurotic handicaps that we may not even recognize. And the society we live in does not do much to discourage them.

This was brought into sharp focus in the "Midtown Study" conducted in Manhattan some years ago by a group of social scientists. These specialists examined a cross-section of New York's population, interviewing so-called average "normal" citizens and instituting diagnostic tests for psychological problems. They discovered that the great majority of persons, indeed over 80 per cent, were suffering from definable neurotic difficulties that could qualify for psychiatric help. Yet they were functioning at work and in their social relationships, perhaps not as well as they might, but still with sufficient effectiveness to hold jobs and to adjust to marriage and other close interpersonal relationships. In other words, their undiscovered emotional illnesses did not cause them to drop out from the mainstream of life. Needless to say, they were not operating with full efficiency, and some of them were sitting on an emotional time bomb. It could explode at any moment, detonated by a crisis in their environment with which they could not cope, and result in emotional breakdown.

The factor that decides whether the individual will adjust to average stress or will break down in his personality structure is the flexibility of his defenses. Personality is shaped by one's early upbringing. In childhood, habit patterns are recorded in that most wonderful of all computers, the human brain. This complex bundle of nerve fibers is housed in a vast observation tower (the sensory apparatus that scans the environment) that monitors every operation of the body, including physiological and biochemical activities, emotional transactions, relationships with people, functions of judgment and reasoning, and co-ordinations in behavior. Like any other computer, it has to be programmed; data is fed into the brain from the moment of birth and perhaps even during intrauterine life. Perhaps the most crucial programming occurs in the first years of existence, in relationships with parents and other important authorities. The child's personality mechanism, indeed his very survival, is dependent on how adequately his needs are gratified and how constructive the disciplines and reinforcements are that he receives from the people around him and from his milieu.

The kind of information that is fed into his brain computer will have an immense bearing on what will later come out of that computer. If the individual is programmed with the wrong kinds of data, he will probably have faulty reactions to life. When the original programming is salutary, his responses should result in productive and satisfying relationships to life and people. Under these circumstances, even though problems arise in his environment and inner conflicts develop, he will still be able to make a satisfactory adjustment. When the programming has been inadequate or unhealthy, the resulting disturbed emotional patterns and weak capacity for adaptation may prevent the person from managing even normal problems.

Let us look at some aspects of the evolving personality and the patterns that issue from it. A child at birth comes into the world helpless and dependent. He needs a great deal of affection, care, and stimulation. He also needs to receive the proper discipline to protect him from his primitive impulses like unreasonable rage and incessant pleasure urges. In an atmosphere of loving care and discipline, in which he is given an opportunity to grow, develop, explore, and express himself, his independence gradually increases and his dependence decreases, so that in adulthood there will be a healthy balance between the two. In the average adult they are soundly balanced, a certain amount of dependence being quite normal, but not so much that it emotionally cripples the person. Normally, a person's dependence level may go up temporarily when he falls sick or feels insecure. Under these conditions his independence will temporarily recede. But this shift is only within a narrow range. However, in the case of bad or deprived experiences in childhood, the dependence level is usually high, and the capacity for independence is weak. This seems to be a common denominator in neurosis.

What happens when a person in adult life is excessively dependent and has a low level of independence? Most people with strong feelings of dependence attempt to find persons who are stronger than they are and who can do for them what they feel they cannot do for themselves. It is as if they are searching for idealized parents—not the kind of parents they had, but much better ones. But a dependent person soon becomes disillusioned in his relationships. First, he feels disappointed in the people he chose as idealized parental figures; they never come up to his expectations, and he feels cheated. For instance, if a man marries a woman who he expects will be a kind, giving, protective mother figure, he will become infuriated when she fails him on any count. Second, he finds that when he does become involved with a person onto whom he projects parental qualities, he soon begins to feel helpless and vulnerable. There is a sense of being trapped and a desire to escape from the relationship. Third, the awareness of being dependent makes him feel as passive as a child. He may associate this with being nonmasculine, with turning homosexual and relating passively to other men. This role in our culture is more acceptable to women, but they too fear excessive passivity, and in their relation to mother figures, they may feel as if they are breast-seeking and homosexual. It is as if a dependency motor were operating incessantly in these people, compelling them to seek a parental image that will inevitably disappoint them.

The dependent person also has a second motor going, a resentment motor that operates constantly, whether he is trapped in dependency or whether he cannot find an idealized parental figure, or because he feels or acts passive and helpless. This resentment generates tremendous guilt feelings, since all religious and ethical teachings state that one is not supposed to resent or hate one's fellow men. But hate feelings do escape sometimes in spite of this. And if hate feelings are strong, the person may become frightened and think he is losing control. The very idea of hating may be so upsetting to him that he pushes this impulse out of his mind, with resulting tension, depression, physical symptoms of various kinds, and self-hate. The hate impulse, having been blocked, is turned back on the self. This creates "masochism," the wearing of a psychological hair shirt, with self-punishment resulting from feedback of resentment.

A third motor runs alongside the other two. High dependence means low independence. A male with meager feelings of independence usually suffers a good deal because he does not feel adequate or competent within himself. He feels nonmasculine, passive, helpless, dependent. Because it is so hard to live with such feelings, he may try to compensate by being overly aggressive, competitive, and masculine. He may even act in a destructive manner to make up for his inadequate feelings of masculinity. He may indulge in fantasies of becoming a strong, handsome, overly active sexual male. When he sees such a figure, he may try to identify with him. This can create conflicting desires in him: attraction to and repugnance of homosexuality. If he does not really want to be homosexual, he can become quite terrified of his own impulses. Interestingly, a low independence level in women is compensated for by competing with men, wanting to be like a man, acting like a man, and resentment at being a woman. Homosexual impulses and fears in women may also sometimes emerge as a result of a repudiation of femininity.

Low feelings of independence often result in a devalued self-image, and this starts a fourth motor going. The person begins to despise himself, because he assumes he is weak, ugly, and contemptible. He will search for supporting evidence of this conviction, becoming critical of his stature, or complexion, or physiognomy. If he happens to have a slight handicap, such as a physical deformity or a small penis, he will use this as a focus to justify his feelings of having been irretrievably damaged. This self-devaluation gives rise to a host of compensatory drives like perfectionism, overambition, and power hunger. As long as he can do things perfectly and operate without flaw, he will respect himself. If he is bright enough, and his environment is favorable, he may boost himself into a successful position of power. Often, he will gather around himself a group of sycophants, who will worship him as the idealized authority, and whom in turn the person may resent and envy while accepting their plaudits. He will feel exploited by those who elevate him to the position of a high priest. "Why," he may ask himself, "can't *I* find somebody strong *I* can depend on?" What he actually seeks is a dependent relationship, but this role entails such conflict for him that he becomes fiercely competitive with any authority on whom he might want to be dependent.

To complicate matters, some of the drives to overcome the devalued self-image become sexualized. For instance, when a dependent person relates to someone in the way a child or infant relates to a parent, a powerful suffusion of good feeling may be experienced, which can bubble over into sexual feeling. There is a great deal of sexuality in a vague form in all infants, which adumbrates adult sexuality. And when a person reverts emotionally to the dependency of infancy, he may reexperience diffuse sexual feelings toward the new parental figure. If a man is dependent in his relationship with a woman, he may harbor a kind of incestuous attitude toward her. The sexuality will not be that of an adult to an adult, but of an infant to a mother, and these feelings for her may be accompanied by tremendous guilt, fear, and perhaps an inability to function sexually. If the parental figure happens to be a man instead of a woman, the person may still relate to him as to a mother, and emerging sexual feelings will stimulate fears of homosexuality. A parallel situation can develop in women who find a parental substitute. In this case, a woman may experience again the emotions of her childhood, when she sought to be loved and protected by her mother. Through body closeness she may have a desire to fondle and be fondled, and this will stir up sexual feelings and homosexual fears. In sexualizing drives for independence and aggressiveness, a man may identify with and seek out powerful masculine figures to fraternize with. This may stir up homosexual impulses. When aggressive sadistic and masochistic impulses exist, these may be fused with sexual impulses for a number of complicated reasons, punishment becoming a condition for sexual release. Thus the dependence motor, and the self-devalution motor, are accompanied by complicated compensations and sexualizations.

In the midst of all this trouble, how do some people find peace? Often by means of a fifth motor—detachment. Detachment is a defense that can be used as a way of escaping life's messy problems. One withdraws from relationships, becomes isolated, runs away from things. A person will try to heal himself by not becoming involved with other people. But this usually does not work, because after a while a person becomes terrified by his isolation and inability to feel. People cannot function without other people. They may succeed for a short time, but then they realize that they are drifting away from happiness and depriving themselves of one of life's prime satisfactions. Compulsively, then, the detached person may try to re-enter the warm atmosphere of close human relationships by becoming gregarious. In desperation, he may force himself into a dependency situation with a parental figure as a way out of his dilemma. And the whole neurotic cycle will start all over again.

As a consequence, the victim keeps getting caught in a web from which there is no escape. As long as he has enough fuel available to feed his various motors and keep them running, he can go on for an indefinite period. But if opportunities to satisfy his different drives do not present themselves, and if he cannot readily switch from one to another, he may become excessively tense and upset. If too much tension builds up, if he encounters serious problems in his life situation, or if his self-esteem is crushed for any reason, he may develop a catastrophic feeling of helplessness and expectations of being hurt.

When tension becomes unbearable, and there seems to be no hope, anxiety may overwhelm a person. This is perhaps the most frightening and catastrophic of all human experiences. A person will build up strong defenses to cope with his anxiety, some of which may succeed and some may not. For instance, excessive drinking may be one way of managing anxiety. Fears, compulsions, physical symptoms are other means. These defenses often do not work. Some, like phobias, may complicate a person's life and make it more difficult than before. Even though various ways are sought to deal with anxiety, these prove to be self-defeating.

For a while, the victim of neurotic symptoms may manage to get along, particularly when he can control his environment. But when pressures are too strong, or when he is unable to fulfill his various needs, he may break down. It is at this point that he may seek professional help.

This is not to say that psychotherapy is the only answer for neurosis. There are many factors in one's everyday environment that may serve as a healing force. There are also healthy elements in all personalities that can prompt a person to seek alternatives to professional help in order to restore psychological equilibrium. A person may spontaneously figure out which situation in his life is upsetting him the most; he may then deal with it directly or remove himself from it. Thus a man who is victimized by an unusually demanding and hostile employer may either assert himself and insist on his rights, or, making no impression, change his job. A single adult living with his parents may conclude that it is better for everyone concerned if he takes an apartment of his own. Some people find hobbies, vacations, and other recreational pursuits of value in diverting their minds from pressing conflicts. Others discover that religion or a special philosophy helps immeasurably. A constructive relationship with a clergyman, physician, or mature friend may supply both the solace and direction that can restore emotional balance.

Such stopgaps are normal and may be all that is required. When the individual's personality structure is fairly intact, that is, when his difficulties do not involve too great a dependency or masochism or devalued self-esteem, he may restore himself after a while to his customary ways of feeling and behaving. If he cannot do this by himself, or if the resources he tries do not provide relief, professional help may be the best answer.

The problems that confront him then are finding the best therapist and the best kind of therapy for his particular problems. Not surprisingly, in a field as new as psychotherapy there are disagreements over what constitutes the most adequate treatment measures. Therapists are trained along different lines, and their points of view may seem radically different. Moreover, they usually endorse their own methods with dedicated zeal. Some therapists also tend to be critical of or underestimate the contributions of other schools.

In the main, two philosophies of therapy are currently in vogue. The first contends, "Treat the symptom, and the person as a whole will benefit." The second states, "Treat the person as a whole and the symptom, which is only a by-product of conflict, will abate or vanish." The first, which advocates symptom removal as the primary goal of treatment, is founded on the premise that faulty responses to anxiety are learned, an unfortunate "programming-in" of flawed and deleterious information . This, in turn, leads to a destructive pattern of behavior, whereby the patient responds to all experience with habitually neurotic reactions. The second philosophy, which maintains that insight is the prime force in treatment, looks upon symptoms as manifestations of unconscious conflicts. These conflicts give rise to defense mechanisms. According to this philosophy, the emotions experienced during crucial relationships in the individual's early life are preserved through transference of these feelings toward other people or situations. When the patient continues to express self-destructive attitudes and feelings, he is actually reacting according to an emotional pattern established in his formative years.

Adherents of these two theories follow different procedures in therapy, in accordance with their interpretation of the basic cause or source of neurosis. Each therapist proclaims the virtuosity of his method, which, from his own accounts, sounds effective and impressive. Thus a symptom-oriented therapist dedicated to drug treatments may treat the anxiety response with tranquilizers. A behavior therapist will attempt to break up the connections between stimulus and response through various techniques designed to create new, healthier habits. A classical analyst will direct his "insightful" efforts toward "expanding the strength of the ego," resolving resistances to unconscious conflict, and working through the "infantile neurosis" via the "transference neurosis." A non-Freudian analyst, acknowledging the unconscious origin and defensive role of symptoms, may work toward his patient's understanding and mastery of them with a number of psychoanalytically oriented techniques. The methods leading to elimination of symptoms are more or less short-term, while those geared toward insight are long-term. Both symptom-oriented and insight-oriented therapists may decide to employ hypnosis as an adjunct.

When we view the results of the symptom-oriented versus the insight-oriented therapies, we must admit that the former *seem* more successful insofar as the rapid disappearance of symptoms is concerned. A leaky roof can be repaired expeditiously with tar paper and asphalt shingles. This will help not only to keep the rain out, but also ultimately dry out and eliminate some of the water damage to the entire house. We have a different set of conditions if we undertake to tear down the structure and then rebuild it. We will not only have a watertight roof, but we will have a better house, that is—and this is most important—if the fundamental foundation of the house is strong, if the carpenter is good, and adequate financing is available. Too often we find attempts at reconstruction of both houses and personalities on foundations that are too weak to support new edifices or that are fabricated by builders who are inept. Personality reconstruction is long-term, tedious, expensive, and risky. Not all efforts are successful; when they are, the results can be most rewarding and beneficial. The tolerances, however, in terms of therapist competence and patient accessibility are unpredictable. If the object is merely to keep the rain out of the house, short-term repair focused on the roof alone will be better, without the bother of more hazardous, albeit ultimately more substantial reconstruction. **In both short-term and long-term therapy, hypnosis, if used properly, may catalyze the therapeutic process.**

It is unfair to compare the symptom-directed and insight-oriented therapies. Each has different dimensions and disparate therapeutic goals. When the patient has a resilient personality and his symptoms have not become too chronic, short-term therapy may be all that is required. When problems date back to childhood, obviously more time will be needed to resolve the source of the difficulty and to help reconstruct the personality to a point where it is stronger and can cope more adequately with living problems.

When a patient with whom we aspire to do depth therapy enters into treatment, he is often bewildered, confused, and upset by what is happening to him. His symptoms seem more or less dissociated from the mainstream of his life. Consequently, he is confounded by attempts to investigate in detail aspects of his experience that he considers irrelevant to his disability. Not realizingthat his symptoms stem from bad patterns of long standing, which are presently being reflected in his disturbed relationships with people, he expects rapid results. In this respect, he is rather like the obese patient who wants the physician to remove in two weeks the excess weight that has taken ten years to accumulate, while at the same time refusing to exercise or diet. The patient tries to retain his dependency and his fixed ways of dealing with people and situations, although these provoke and exacerbate his symptoms. At the same time, he demands that the ingrained habits of his problematical behavior be quickly extirpated.

With this in mind, the patient wants to relate to the therapist in the same way patients traditionally seek aid from a physician. He usually demands some kind of immediate and dramatic assistance, or, in his helplessness, the working of a miracle by means of a mysterious nostrum or formula. He thinks of the therapist as a powerful authority who will palliate his suffering and expeditiously lead him to health and personal success. The sicker the patient the more likely he is to consider therapy a conjuring trick.

It may require a great deal of perseverance on the part of the therapist to show the patient that his symptoms do not occur at random but are intensified by certain life situations that involve his attitudes toward people and his estimate of himself. Before progress can be made, however, it is necessary for the patient to realize that his symptoms are not independent manifestations but are, rather, the outer warnings of inner difficulties of which he is only partially aware. Once the patient accepts the principle of a connection between his symptoms and specific problems within himself, he will be more capable of abandoning hope for immediate magical repair through some spectacular performance on the part of the therapist. Motivated by the discomfort of his symptoms and the desire for a more fulfilling life, he may acquiesce to a deeper inquiry into himself.

Soon, the patient will understand that his symptoms vary according to the happenings of his daily life and the difficulties encountered in interpersonal relations. Awareness of these facts will tend to divert inordinate attention from his immediate complaints. As soon as this occurs, an inquiry into basic motivations becomes a possibility.

To bring the patient to such an understanding, however, can prove to be a difficult task. The patient often has so habituated himself to his various traits and attitudes that he can scarcely accept the fact that they are not usual or in any way out of the ordinary. The possibility that his behavior is abnormal may be not only unacceptable, but unbelievable. Nearly all neurotic people assume that their own particular pattern of living is average, if not universal. If they do recognize themselves as deviating from the norm in some ways, then they consider their case as special and attribute it to the uniqueness of their own makeup and to particular external conditions that offer them no other course than the one they are pursuing.

This attitude is responsible for obstinate resistance to change. The patient cannot easily be made to see that his attitudes and fears are projected outwardly without any actual basis. But in the course of therapy he may learn to see that what he has assumed to be normal may actually be unusual. Clues to his fundamental difficulties will be pieced together for him by the therapist. The unique relationship that has developed between the patient and the therapist will help him to accept interpretations of his behavior and his unconscious life, revealed in symbolic ways—through verbalizations, dreams, and fantasies.

The identification of significant behavior patterns is often startling to the patient, and he may counter with resistance, since basic adaptional patterns are being challenged. Although these are unsatisfying and produce anxiety, they are nonetheless the only way of life the patient knows. Moreover, the patient derives many hidden spurious benefits from his neurosis, which he does not want to forfeit. Debilitating as they are, many neurotic symptoms serve a protective purpose in the psyche. To give them up threatens exposure to inconveniences and discomforts far greater than anything the patient already suffers. He will, therefore, in an exasperating way, tend to obstruct his own progress.

Thus it seems that the patient does not entirely want to get well. What he wants is a magic recipe from the therapist whereby he may retain his neurosis, yet be free of any suffering. He wants to be dependent, yet secure and strong within himself. Or he wishes to detach himself, to keep his freedom, yet at the same time to form successful and gratifying relationships with people. He will resent the attempt to change his life in a significant way, and, in order to hinder the therapist, he will continue in his attempts to impede the treatment process.

It is in the resolution of resistence that hypnosis may serve its most useful purpose. The patient may finally come to realize that while he is a prisoner of his past, it is he who functions as his principal jailer. Such "insight" may give him the incentive to experiment with new and more constructive patterns of behavior. He may become motivated for reconstructive therapy aimed at a true alteration of his personality structure.

This reconstructive goal may be divided roughly into two phases. The first involves an uncovering process, during which the patient becomes aware of impulses, fears, attitudes, and memories that have interfered with wholesome relationships with the world and people. The second is reeducative and consists of an elaboration of new and adaptive interpersonal patterns. Social reintegration does not occur automatically. It is a slow reconditioning process, necessitating the establishing of fresh habit and reaction patterns to displace the old destructive ones. Both phases of the reconstructive process may initiate resistance, and a therapist may decide to utilize hypnosis as an aid to its resolution.

With growing emancipation from his past, the patient becomes more self-confident, assertive, and expressive. He accepts it as his right to make salutary choices and decisions, and to establish new values. As his feelings about himself improve, his conscience becomes less punitive. The patient learns the joy of living and the satisfaction of being a creative human being. Finally, he no longer requires help from the therapist, and the world itself offers possibilities for fulfillment, which, prior to therapy, he felt to be utterly beyond his reach.

7

How Does Hypnosis Work

It is generally believed that enhanced suggestibility is the key to how hypnosis works. If this were true, then the more suggestible the subject, the easier it would be to predict a successful outcome for hypnotherapy. According to the standard literature on suggestibility, which describes research and empirical findings, a composite type of a highly suggestible individual would be a young undernourished, feeble-minded, emotionally disturbed girl. She would be fatigued, in illhealth, and educated in conformity, docility, and deference. Years ago I attempted to treat such a patient, and she turned out to be the worst hypnotic subject I ever had. She resisted every suggestion that I tried to give her. Finally, I told her parents, who had brought her to me, that there was no sense in her coming back until she herself decided that she wanted some help.

Suggestions are never accepted by subjects at their face value, no matter how suggestible the person may be. They are always integrated, augmented, or neutralized in accordance with their potential significance, their influence on existing psychological defenses, and the specific meaning to the subject of his relationship with the hypnotist at the time.

The actual words used to phrase the suggestion and the manner in which it is presented by the hypnotist have some influence on the effect it will have. But the special needs of the subject are most important. They will be responsible for the way in which he will interpret the suggestion. This interpretation will correspond to his current psychological condition.

This is not to depreciate the role of suggestibility in the trance. It does play a signal part in the hypnotic *Gestalt,* but it is only one aspect of a complex pattern of factors. Different individuals will respond in various ways to the experience of hypnosis, using one or several of these factors that seem most attuned to their needs. Their suggestibility will seem greatest in those areas that are most meaningful to them, whether it has to do with tension, the lessening of anxiety, or the relationship with the hypnotist.

Reduction Of Tension

A highly tense and distraught individual may find a means of reducing his tension in hypnosis. We know that tension, irrespective of its source, promotes disturbing physiological reactions. It can aggravate any existing organic illness and delay the healing process in damaged tissue. As a result of overwrought glandular and nerve reactions, tension can also stir up pathological body effects (psychosomatic symptoms). On a psychological level it can produce a catastrophic sense of helplessness, which promotes anxiety and releases a host of neurotic defensive reactions, such as phobias and compulsions. The ability to cope with and adjust to life's responsibilties is impaired.

Any measure that lessens tension can help restore lost equilibrium and give a person the strength to deal more constructively with his problems. When tension is reduced, it is gratifying to see how the latent strengths of the person come to the fore. He is much more capable of dealing with troubles that confront him on the outside and with inner conflicts. Sometimes, when the goal in treatment is merely to restore the person to the levels at which he was operating before he became ill, no further psychotherapeutic measures may be necessary. Understandably, no changes will have been produced in the psychological structure; it has merely been given a chance to rest and will respond the same way as before to overwhelming stress. If, however, the stress situations that were responsible for throwing the person psychologically off balance are eliminated, or if he is shown how to manage them more appropriately, he may not break down again. This is obviously what we try to do in psychotherapy.

Because hypnosis has proven so successful with tension reduction in many cases, some hypnotists emphasize this aspect of hypnosis to the exclusion of almost all others. Indeed, they may credit the total influence of hypnosis to the lowering of tension exclusively. I know of one therapist who has given up delving into the nature and sources of his patients' difficulties, or even allowing them to be discussed. Disregarding the patients' complaints and symptoms, he teaches them how to relax by inducing a trance with a minimum of words and suggestions. All his patients, he claims, experience an abatement of symptoms and some even achieve a complete cure. While I am convinced that relaxation, with or without hypnosis, may prove helpful for the average person, I doubt that we can explain how hypnosis works solely by this one factor. There are many other vital elements that enter into a hypnotic relationship, and I believe they have an even more important impact on the subject than the mere reduction of his tension level. Moreover, unless some change is brought about in the existing psychological disposition which will assist it in dealing with greater stress than it habitually can mediate, the individual will not be helped to achieve his potential for better adaptation. This requires other techniques besides comforting him through a lowering of tension.

The Placebo Factor

The faith that a person has in the measures prescribed for him is an important factor in his progress. This "placebo" reinforces the techniques used in his treatment. The reproduction on page 130 of a poster circulated in England during the eighteenth century is an example of how a placebo can relieve even a severe toothache in persons willing to put their trust in it.

Placebo action has long been recognized by the medical profes-

A Surprising Cure for the Tooth-Ache.

I am come to you to get Relief for a most violent Tooth-Ache.

My Letter, that smells so very pleasant, when delivered, is your Relief.

WHICH

Has never been known to fail.

TO the Nobility, Gentry, and Others. If the Pain be ever so violent, and if the Teeth are rotted away below the Gums, nay even to the Stumps, the Patients are sure to get rid of the Pain, caused by the Tooth-Ache, and that in less than two Hours, after I have delivered to them a small Letter (sealed up).

This Letter smells very pleasant when delivered, which the afflicted are to put into their Pocket, and as the Tooth-Ache leaves them, this agreeable Smell leaves the Letter. But if not the Tooth-Ache, this reviving Smell will not leave the Letter.

Any one that is not satisfied in their own Opinion of the above Cure, and think it impossible, I beg leave to mention those Families I have cured, and I believe that will give them the greatest Satisfaction. I have cured several Thousands of the Tooth-Ache, for above these Twenty-three Years. But I shall only trouble you at present to read these few Names, and where they live, which are as follow:

Mrs. King and her Daughter, No. 19, Old Bailey.

Mr. and Mrs. More, No, 42, St. James's-street.

Mrs. Griffiths and Mrs. Richards, Tufton-street, Westminster.

Mrs. Crowder, No. 9, Queen's-Head-Court, Pater-noster-row.

Mrs. Jordan, No. 100, St. Martin's-Lane.

Mrs. Salt, No. 21, Panton-street.

The two Head Cooks of St. George's Hospital.

If not cured, nothing is expected; but I am sure, with God's Blessing, to cure every one that comes to me with the Tooth-Ache; and before they go from me, they are desired to return the small Letter to me again, and on telling me they have no Tooth-Ache, I then leave it to their own Generosity to satisfy me for their Cure.

My Patients often get rid of their Tooth-Ache in less than One Hour after coming to me, but I am desirous that every one who comes to me to be cured, will stay at least Two Hours with me. This great Secret is not known to any one but myself.

Removed from No. 9, YEOMAN'S-ROW, BROMPTON, to No. 100, ST. MARTIN'S-LANE, opposite MAY'S-BUILDINGS, near CHAIRING-CROSS. Where I attend at my Apartments every Day, from Eight o'Clock in the Morning till Eight in the Evening, except Sundays.

☞ For the Good of Mankind, it would be a Charity to let this Bill be put up in some Part of your House, that this Cure may be made as public as possible to those who have the Tooth-Ache.

N. B. The poorest Sort of People cured gratis, from Eight till Ten every Morning.

[1757.]

sion as a potent healing force. Indeed, the prescription of inactive substances was a standard part of medical practice for many years, typified by the tradition of giving pink sugar pills or injecting sterile water for suggestive effects. These measures can be quite powerful in their results, even where prejudicial statements or innuendos about a presumed drug action induce a psychological reaction diametrically opposed to the true effects. Exploratory research on new medications in the form of double-blind studies, employing first a drug and then a harmless pill that looks and tastes exactly like the drug, is a routine part of tests, since it is recognized that mental influence can affect the impartial appraisal of a substance. If the placebo pill causes a desired effect as great as the drug pill, the drug is considered valueless. It happens very often that this is the case.

What holds true for drugs probably also holds true for adjuncts in psychotherapy, including hypnosis. A person often projects into these treatments expectations of cure, and he may react quite remarkably to techniques and agencies, attributing powers to them that they may not actually possess. During the heyday of orgone therapy, many intelligent people benefited by interludes in an orgone box. An acquaintance of mine claimed that he had got more out of three months of stepping inside a box than he did from three years of intensive psychotherapy with a well-known and skilled psychiatrist. In fact, he was so impressed by the results that he bought a "his" and "her" box for himself and his wife. He also built a small orgone box for his cat. These boxes, he insisted, reduced his psychiatric, medical, and veterinary bills to negligible amounts. It requires no great exercise of logic to charge these effects to pure suggestion.

Psychiatric therapies that are believed by patients to possess mystical qualities are most likely to secure results. Thus hypnosis, with its aura of esoteric characteristics, is apt to instill in the patient a feeling of magical persuasion. Although this is a superficial notion, it may provide the essential push toward health that the patient needs. By the same token, a negative placebo effect may occur. If the patient has a lack of faith in hypnosis or fears being hurt by it, his imagination may be a powerful deterrent to any change. The chances are that his attitude will inhibit the effectiveness of treatment.

During the past few years, I have had an opportunity to test this hypothesis tentatively. Because of the intensive publicity given to hypnosis as a treatment method, I have been consulted by a considerable number of persons whose sole motivation for therapy was to control obnoxious habits and symptoms. Chief among these have been obese persons who have wanted to reduce but were unable to stop overeating, chain smokers whose physical well-being was being threatened by their excessive intake of nicotine and coal tar, and impotent men whose sexual problems threatened their marriages, as well as their self-esteem. They all asked the same question: "Can hypnosis cure me?" In roughly one-third of the cases I replied, "It is impossible to say. Generally, problems such as yours require deeper psychotherapy over a long-term period, since the basis of the trouble is in personality difficulties and insecurities that originated in childhood. However, there is a fifty-fifty chance that you might feel better with hypnosis if you turn out to be a good subject." In one-third of the cases I answered enthusiastically, "Yes, hypnosis can definitely help symptoms such as yours. If you keep at it, it is bound to work. You can't help yourself from responding." In the other one-third my pessimistic response was: "Probably not. Hypnosis is no cure-all. It can help some problems, but not all. In your case, the difficulty seems to be too deep-rooted, and the habit too firmly entrenched to respond to anything but long-term psychotherapy. However, if you want to try hypnosis first, we can." Symptomatic responses to hypnosis have been directly in proportion to my positiveness and enthusiasm. Apparently, the hope that I inspired and the patient's conviction that the method could work acted as an influential motive in marshaling curative forces.

The powerful factor of confidence in the method of treatment as an incentive to cure is well documented. Among native groups who practice magic and witchcraft, even the effective administration of scientific medicine can produce meager results in cases where an afflicted member of the group is convinced that his suffering is the consequence of a curse or other evil magic from an offended spirit. In a surprising number of instances, the adroit use of a fetish or the exorcism of the force believed responsible for the bewitchment will bring about the improvement of even longstanding illnesses. These effects are undoubtedly of a placebo nature.

We need not go to primitive tribes to detect evidences of susceptibility in psychological cures. In our own culture, patients hospitalized with bleeding peptic ulcers were given hypodermic injections of distilled water accompained by the statement that this was a remedy for bleeding ulcers. Seventy per cent improved remarkably over a long-term period. In a number of studies of psychiatric outpatients for whom the sole therapy was the administration of inert placebo substances, 55 per cent showed marked progress.

In an article published some time ago in the *Journal of the American Medical Association*, an experiment is described in which eighty patients over sixty years of age were suffering from a combination of symptoms including depression, restless agitation, and paranoidal thinking. Half of the patients were given powerful tranquilizing and sedative drugs; the other half were given placebos. A third group of patients was given no medication whatsoever. The latter group showed an increase in anxiety, while the group receiving medication demonstrated a lessening of anxiety. However, the best results were obtained in the placebo group, who, in addition to experiencing a lowering of anxiety, also exhibited better spirits and greater spontaneity. Perhaps the most interesting experiment on placebo action was also reported in a later issue of the *Journal of the American Medical Association*. One hundred and twenty hospitalized psychiatric patients were given sugar pills by nurses and psychiatrists, who were told they were new and effective tranquilizers and energizers. From 50 per cent to 80 per cent of the patients benefited from these new "drugs," an astonishing finding to the experimenters. The experiment was considered especially significant because medical personnel, as well as patients, believed the drugs to be genuine. The experimenters believed that this intangible but positive aspect of the test was important.

Placebo effects are usually, but not always, temporary. In many instances the temporary improvement is an incentive for a patient's more permanent adjustment. The way in which the placebo influence exerts a more than temporary effect varies with the nature of the underlying problems. In some instances, the idea of being protected brings about a feeling of security that results in greater self-assuredness and an increased capacity for handling challenging relationships with people. The placebo may thus act as a basis for reorganization of attitudes, which may become firmly established in a favorable milieu.

Placebos, therefore, often produce, momentarily at least, the exact effect suggested by the operator who administers them. Some time ago the findings of a research project completed at the University of Michigan were reported. The researchers concluded that "about one-third of the effectiveness of many modern drugs depends upon the personality of the physician. If a patient desperately wants relief and trusts his physician, he sometimes gets as much relief from a sugar tablet as from a drug." This kind of influence operates in all therapeutic situations, and its importance should not be minimized. On the other hand, one should keep in mind the fact that even an unskilled person can operate as a "healer" through the placebo influence. Let us say that the power of placebo will make him effective in one-third of the cases that he handles. Naturally, he will advertise his one-third "successes" and not mention his two-thirds failures. The crucial distinction between a quack who relies on the placebo influence and the trained person who relies on the placebo influence *and* his training and experience falls in the area of the "two-thirds," where skill, not suggestion, is the vital factor.

The placebo effect operates in hypnosis as strongly as in other phases of medicine, and probably more intensely. This is because the suggestibility index is heightened in hypnosis. The commands and dictates of the hypnotist, unless they are too distasteful to the subject, are generally accepted and acted upon less critically than in waking life. What really counts in therapeutic hypnosis are the influences beyond the placebo effect, and these can be implemented only by a trained professional person. Although he makes use of the powers of suggestion, he does so with a structured design and therapeutic plan in mind.

The Relationship Factor

Every remedial situation is characterized by a special kind of relationship that develops between the client and the person who helps him. In this relationship the client invests his guide with benevolent protective powers and relates to him with expectant trust. Implicit, if not explicit, is the understanding that the counselor has the knowledge, skill, and desire to help the client overcome the problem for which he has sought professional assistance. The more bewildered and helpless the person in trouble, the greater the reliance he places on professional practitioners.

A moving testimony to this relationship appeared in an article called "Treatment for Modern Medicine—Some Sympathy Added to Science," published some years ago by *Life* magazine:

> Of all human acts, few can match the quiet splendor of the moment when the pale and tremulous fingers of a sick person are grasped in the firm reassuring hands of a compassionate physician. This simple act mutely promising that all the powers of modern science and human thought will be unsparingly invoked to restore health is among the finest deeds of humankind. It is more than ritual. When pain and fear make a sick person feel that all is lost, the laying on of healing hands brings solace and hope. Its strength can even turn the tide of illness and amplify the curative effect of the strongest wonder drug. It remains today as it always has been—man's oldest medical miracle.

The bedside manner of the physician is based on this "miracle."

It is this influence also that seems to operate during the phenomenon of hypnosis. We might say that all physicians practice a kind of "waking hypnosis," exercising their healing capacities in part through their relationship with their patients. This element of the healing process can help speed the patient toward health. It is certainly true in the case of a sick patient afflicted with a physical ailment who relies on his physician for relief from pain and suffering. It is also a most important factor in a psychotherapeutic situation, particularly at the beginning of the treatment.

Most patients experience an immediate relief upon receiving hypnosis, or indeed any form of psychotherapy. Generally this relief stems from the relationship itself. No matter how nondirective the therapist may be or how much he discourages any dependency on the part of the patient, the latter will almost inevitably project his need for solace and comfort onto the therapist and the therapeutic situation.

This contingency is, of course, an aspect of every verbal pro-able time may be needed for the relationship to jell, rapport begins almost from the start in hypnosis. The patient will quickly respond with hope, trust, and a lessening of inner tension. In such receptive soil the roots of therapy are quickly embedded, and prone to be greatly advantageous in short-term therapy. The influence of rapport is particularly helpful in distrustful, despairing, or detached patients who often hold themselves aloof, refusing to enter into a constructive relationship except perhaps after many months of testing of the therapist. This is an extravagance one cannot provide in short-term treatment.

The importance of the relationship factor is too frequently minimized, and credit for cure is often incorrectly attributed to the particular techniques and methods used by the therapist. Yet it should be stressed that in some cases improvement is sustained for an indefinite period only because of the relationship and not because of the type or depth or real worth of the psychotherapy being practiced. It must be remembered, however, that the benefits gained from the relationship are only the forerunners of therapy, not the end-all. Unless there is a correction of stress sources, and/or a restructuring of personality, the improvement may cease upon termination of treatment.

The Factor of Verbal Unburdening

The sheer act of talking can provide a person with considerable emotional relief. This release from mental stress can happen with many kinds of listeners—a sympathetic friend or a respected authority such as a physician, teacher, lawyer, or minister. Talking is the basis for most psychotherapy in the waking state. It is an even more effective release in the trance. Indeed, hypnosis can liberate a flood of buried emotions and bring them to the surface with dramatic force. The ability of people to tolerate decisive feelings during hypnosis appears to be greater than in waking life, and more flexible expressions of emotion may continue after hypnosis is over.

Verbal unburdening not only furnishes a motor outlet for the release of tension but softens inhibitions and liberates conscious and unconscious conflicts that have been held in check. It exposes suppressed attitudes and ideas that the person has been concealing from himself and encourages him to subject them to critical reasoning. It brings to the surface frightening impulses that have been rejected, and their attendant feelings of shame. It opens up avenues for the discharge of emotion, freeing the individual from the burden of a dynamic charge that is a constant threat to his stability. In this way, it takes the strain off physiological channels that have been used to unload accumulated neurotic energy.

In the unburdening process, there is often a relief from guilt feelings resulting from past experiences. Guilt is appeased as fantasies and forbidden impulses are examined. Discussing these with an understanding authority gives a person assurance that he is not a helpless victim of uncontrollable drives and that he has not been irreparably damaged by his past. Reviewing incidents in which one has been hurt, humiliated, or exploited also tends to put them into proper perspective. Sharing one's fears of disease and mutilation deprives them of their frightening quality. The conscious restraints that rob a person of his spontaneity are relinquished. In short, putting diffuse and terrifying feelings into words and having one's pronouncements accepted by the hypnotist without condemnation or rejection enable a person to gain greater control over his emotions.

8

How Hypnosis Influences Psychotherapy

In psychotherapy, where the goal is to restore the individual to a satisfactory level of functioning rather than to effect a structural change in the personality organization, hypnosis often serves as an effective treatment for a limited objective. It is particularly suited for the patient who is paralyzed by resistance, which develops in many forms during psychotherapy. Resistance can be observed in overt or covert defensive maneuvers that the patient develops to preserve his neurotic behavior patterns. Usually, the patient is unaware of such maneuvers. For example, a subtle form of resistance is the patient's denial that there are things going on within him of which he is unaware. He often is certain that he knows all about his attitudes, prejudices, and conflicts, and he will stoutly deny the implication that he is under the influence of forces over which he has no control or does not recognize. If the patient is a fairly good hypnotic subject, he can be given a posthypnotic suggestion to show him that he has acted on impulses not determined by his conscious self. This may enable him to accept the fact that other drives may also be operating within him. Resistance can also develop toward the special techniques that are employed in psychotherapy or psychoanalysis. Hynosis can help resolve such resistance and enable the person to respond to treatment.

Hypnosis may be advantageously employed in the course of psychotherapy under the following conditions:

1. When the patient lacks motivation for treatment.

Hypnotic techniques may be helpful in convincing an unmotivated patient that he can derive something meaningful from treatment. A patient can feel resentment toward people who insist that he get psychological help; he can be afraid of revealing secret or disgusting aspects of his life; he can feel distrust for the therapist or refuse to recognize an emotional basis for his complaints. These and other obstructions that contribute to the lack of incentive for therapy can usually be handled by a skilled therapist in the initial interviews without recourse to hypnosis. But occasionally even skillful approaches do not resolve the patient's resistance in accepting help. At thus point, if the patient permits induction, hypnosis may provide him with a positive experience that significantly alters his attitudes.

For example, a patient who had great resistance to psychotherapy was referred to me by an internist. He suffered from urinary frequency, which had defied all medical intervention and had become so serious that it threatened his livelihood. He resented being sent to a psychiatrist and announced that he could see no sense in starting what might prove to be a long and costly process when he was not fully convinced that he needed it. I accepted the patient's negative feelings, but I speculated that his tension might be responsible for at least some of his symptoms. I offered to show him how to relax so that he might derive something beneficial out of the present session. He agreed, and I then induced a light trance in the course of which he achieved a general state of relaxation. After the trance was terminated, the patient spontaneously announced that he had never felt more relaxed in his life and asked if he could have several more sessions of hypnosis. In the course of hypnorelaxation, I casually suggested to him that there might be emotional reasons why his bladder had become tense and upset, and I inquired whether he would be interested in finding out whether this was so. When he agreed, I gave him a posthypnotic suggestion to remember any dreams he might have within the next few days.

He responded with a series of dreams in which he saw himself as a mutilated and frightened person escaping from situations of danger and being blocked in his efforts to achieve freedom. His associations were about the democratic rights of oppressed people throughout the world and the futility of expressing these rights in the face of cruel and uncompromising dictatorships that seemed to be the order of the day. When asked how this affected him personally, living as he did in a democratic regime, he sarcastically repiled that one could be a prisoner even in a democracy. Since his father had died, he had been obliged to take over the responsibility of looking after his mother. Not only did she insist that he stay in her home but she demanded an account of all of his movements. He realized that she was a sick, frightened woman and that consequently it was his duty to devote himself to her comfort for her few remaining years. These revelations were the turning point at which we were able to convert our sessions into explorations of his wishes and conflicts. As he recognized his repressed hostility and his tremendous need for personal freedom, he realized that he himself was largely responsible for the condition that was virtually mutilating him. It was then possible for him to help his mother find new friends and to move into a retirement village. When he resolved the problem of his deep resentments, his bladder symtoms disappeared completely. More significant was a growth in assertiveness and self-esteem that promoted a much more constructive adaptation to life.

2. *When the patient refuses to begin therapy unless he is assured of immediate relief of his symptoms.*

Symptoms may be so upsetting to the patient that pe refuses to engage in therapy unless there is first a reduction or removal of his symptoms. When symptoms are so severe that they create physical emergencies, as in cases of persistent vomiting, hiccuping, or paralysis, the therapist may be able to restore function through suggestions in hypnosis. After this, he may proceed with other psychotherapeutic techniques. In less severe cases, insistence on symptomatic relief may be a tactic for demanding that the therapist prove himself a sympathetic person concerned with the suffering of the patient. Hypnosis with suggestions aimed at relaxation, tension control, and symptom reduction can create an atmosphere conducive to a therapeutic working relationship. Hypnosis can also expedite the learning of new habit patterns through desensitization and reconditioning (behavior therapy).

A patient who came to me with an obessional neurosis complained of belching and hiccuping after meals. This caused her great embarrassment and frequently forced her to skip meals. She was so preoccupied with whether or not her symptoms would overwhelm her that she could scarcely enjoy food when she did dine. Weakness forced her to seek medical help, in the course of which she was referred to me. At the initial interview, she testily protested being sent for psychiatric treatments, particularly in view of a past unsuccessful psychotherapeutic experience. What she wanted, she insisted, was sufficient relief from physical distress to enable her to function at work and in her relationship with her family. In light of her disappointment with her former therapist, I suggested hypnosis as a possible way of helping her to achieve some lessening of her trouble. She agreed to give it a trial. The next five sessions were spent in teaching her how to relax and how to control her symptoms. Her response was dramatic, and her attitude toward me changed from suspicion and hostility to friendly co-operativeness. She readily entered into a therapeutic relationship, and once therapy had started, there was no need for further hypnosis.

3. *When the patient has such deep problems in relationships with people that he cannot relate to his therapist.*

A good working relationship between patient and therapist is mandatory for any kind of psychotherapy. This is particularly essential in therapy that tries to bring about an extensive modification of the personality that is prone to anxiety. This type of personality often feels great stress when the therapist probes for conflicts and challenges habitual defenses. With some sick patients the proper working relationship may never develop or may take many months to appear because of such factors as fear of closeness or intense hostility toward authority. Relaxation during hypnosis can resolve fears, reduce hostility, and cut down the time period required for the development of rapport. As a result, the patient often feels an extraordinary warmth and closeness toward the therapist even after only one or two hypnotic sessions. A therapeutic relationship may crystallize under these circumstances, and it will then be possible to proceed with psychotherapy without hypnosis.

One of the most difficult patients I ever treated was a paranoidal man who upbraided me severely during our first session for my delay in arranging a consultation with him. He was upset, he said, because he was involved in litigious proceedings against his business partners, who had presumably deceived him about their business prospects when they first induced him to buy a share of the company. Another legal case was pending against a neighbor who had built a garage that the patient considered an eyesore. But what he most desired from the consultation with me was to determine the feasibility of hypnotizing his wife in order to obtain from her the truth of her exact whereabouts during an evening when he was out of town on business. He had carefully examined her tube of contraceptive jelly before his departure and again upon his return. At first he could see no difference, but he compulsively returned to it, ruminating about whether he had not made a mistake in his original conclusion about his wife's innocence. For weeks he had been subjecting her to cross-examination, carefully tabulating contradictory remarks until he had convinced himself that she was concealing the truth about a rendezvous with her lover. The poor woman, protesting her innocence from the start, had become so confused by his confrontations that she desperately tried to make up stories to cover tiny discrepancies in her minute-by-minute account of activities on the fatal evening. With a sharp eye for her inconsistencies, the patient had seized on her flounderings to trap her into an admission of lying, which then convinced him all the more of her infidelity. A firm believer in the powers of hypnosis, he challenged her to submit to a hypnotic reliving of the evening in question.

Upon finishing this account, the patient inquired about my methods of trance induction. I volunteered to demostrate the hand-levitation technique to him, and he cautiously agreed to be a subject. Before too long he entered into a deep trance, during which I suggested that he would soon begin to feel more relaxed, secure, and self-confident. If he visualized a happy scene or had a dream about the most wonderful thing that could happen to a person, he would probably feel free from tension and enjoy a general state of pleasure that would make him happier than he had ever been in his life. After an interval of ten minutes he was brought out of the trance. Upon opening his eyes, he revealed with humor having had a dream of lying on a hammock while lovely slave girls circled around him with baskets of fruit. I suggested that he return in two days and bring his wife if she wished to accompany him.

During the second session, his wife tearfully proclaimed her innocence, whereupon the patient petulantly asked her to leave my office if she was going to "act like a baby." When she promised to control herself, he requested that she wait for him in the reception room. He then told me he had felt so well since his first visit that he had decided that several more sessions of hypnosis would be valuable for his insomnia. His wife's problem could wait, he claimed, until he had "healed his own nerves." After this initiation into therapy, he underwent ninety sessions of psychotherapy with and without hypnosis, during which he worked out several important aspects of his personality problem. He ended therapy when he had achieved a marked reduction of his symptoms, an easing of his tensions with his partners, and the reestablishing of a satisfactory relationship with his wife.

Another patient spent the first three months of his treatment with me in fruitless associational explorations. He protested that "nothing was happening" in regard to his symptoms or "anything else." He did not have either a warm or hostile attitude toward me. Indeed, he avowed, I was "neither his friend nor his enemy." He resented any continued questioning concerning his feelings about me, insisting that I was being paid to do a job and that it was necessary not to get too personally involved. There was a constant negative reaction to my interpretations. After I induced him to try hypnosis, he was able to achieve a medium trance. From the very first hypnotic session, his enthusiasm and energy increased. From then on, he stopped breaking appointments. His activity and productivity improved remarkably, and we were able to achieve a good therapeutic result. Without hypnosis, I am convinced his detachment could not have been penetrated.

4. When the patient is unable to verbalize freely.

When communication is blocked, there can be no therapy. Sometimes, the usual unblocking techniques may fail to restore verbal communication. In such an event, hypnosis can often be effective, although the way in which it is used will depend on the causes of the difficulty. The mere induction of a trance may uncork explosive emotions against which the patient has defended himself by refusing to talk in the waking state. Cathartic release in the trance may restore normal verbal expression. If the patient's silence is due to some resistance, it may be possible to explore and resolve it by encouraging the patient to talk during hypnosis. In speech paralysis (aphonia) resulting from hysteria these techniques may not suffice, and direct suggestion may be needed to lessen or eliminate the symptom. Speech disorders may occasionally be helped by lessening tension during the trance, and there may then be a carry-over into the waking state. When speech difficulty is caused by needs that forbid the expression of painful sounds or ideas, an explosive outburst during hypnosis may not only release the capacity to talk freely but will also open up areas of conflict that can be beneficially explored.

A young woman, a severe stammerer, came to me for therapy because of incapacitating phobias. Once she had established rapport with me, she expressed herself satisfactorily, but as we began to examine her fantasies and dreams, she experienced so pronounced a relapse in her speech disturbances that she was almost inarticulate. She complained that while she could talk better than ever before with her friends, she could scarcely communicate with me. Since progress had come to a halt, I suggested hypnosis as a way of helping her to relax. She reacted to this suggestion with anxiety, but nevertheless agreed to try. During the process of deepening the trance, she suddenly broke down and cried fitfully. Encouraged to discuss what she felt, she clenched her fits and shrieked, "No, no!" After exploding into a coughing spell, during which she could hardly catch her breath, she gasped over and over that she was choking. At my suggestion that she "bring it up," she broke into a torrent of foul language, pronouncing the word "shit" repeatedly, and spitting with angry excitement. A few minutes of this frenzied behavior were followed by complaints of exhaustion. Thereupon she resorted to normal speech, which continued for the remainder of the session, even after she had been aroused. This performance was repeated in subsequent sessions, although the patient responded with diminished fury. The therapeutic process gained great momentum, and the young woman was able to curb her stammer. The experience opened the door to a discussion of her great concern over bowel activities. This stemmed from extremely rigid toilet training as a child by an obsessive, overdisciplinary mother, who made her feel guilty and frightened about toilet activities. Feces were equated with poison and destruction. Our therapeutic sessions were largely concerned with clarifying her misconceptions. As she developed a more wholesome attitude toward her bowel functions, her general feelings about herself improved, and her speech difficulty disappeared.

5. When, during psychoanalytic therapy, the patient is unable to engage in unrestricted verbal expression (free association).

A patient may maintain rigid control over his speech when he fears that psychological areas of conflict may be exposed. He is thus unable to permit his ideas to float freely and unrestrainedly in the process of exploring unguarded aspects of his psyche. In some cases free association is the preferred means of helping a patient; but when he is unable to engage in it because of resistance, hypnosis may be the best solution. Not only may it bring the patient into contact with repressed emotions and thoughts, but it also helps him to analyze his blocks.

This was true in the case of a former patient of mine. He had retreated from free association to a highly structured and rigidly directed form of verbal expression. Attempts to analyze his loss of spontaneity produced little response. After a week of floundering, with no improvement and mere repetition of insignificant items, I induced hypnosis and encouraged the patient to talk about what really was bothering him. He revealed that he had felt guilty in the past few weeks for having masturbated in my office bathroom after one of our sessions. He had not wanted to tell me about this incident because he knew it was not an adult act. He then associated this action with having been caught as a child masturbating in his aunt's bathroom. Not only had he been reprimanded and warned by his aunt, but his parents had promptly been told. The physician who referred the patient to me also frowned on his masturbatory practices, classifying masturbation as "idiot's delight, which is never indulged in by a mature person." Reassured by my handling of these revelations, the patient was able to continue with his free associations in the waking state.

6. *When the patient is unable to remember his dreams while in psychoanalytic therapy.*

Because it is a way of understanding the unconscious, dream interpretation is an important part of analytic therapy. The mind asleep seems to be able to conceptualize its inner problems in dream structure better than when it is awake. If a trained professional translates these dreams, he may be able to bring a person to an awareness of some of the unconscious conflicts with which he is struggling.

In instances where there is a dearth of dream material the patient can be trained to dream in the trance or through posthypnotic suggestions during normal sleep. General topics or specific topics may be suggested as the dream content. Once this process is started, it may be possible for the patient to continue dreaming without hypnosis. Hypnosis can also be used to restore forgotten elements of dreams, to clarify distortions elaborated to disguise their meaning ("secondary elaborations"), and to help the patient explore by means of dreams his attitudes toward people and elements in his everyday life. In patients who are unable to remember their dreams, hypnosis may be remarkably effective. In dreams that have been forgotten, hypnosis may activate the same dreams spontaneously.

In hypnosis dreams may be spontaneous, reflecting unconscious attitudes, memories, emotions, and conflicts. They can also reveal to the patient the meaning that the immediate hypnotic experience has for him, as well as distortions in his relationship with the therapist, caused by confusing him with early authority figures.

The improvement shown by one of my patients illustrates how valuable hypnotic dream induction can be. The patient came to me for psychotherapy when he could find no relief for severe rectal itching. He had tried various kinds of medicinal and injection treatment. Although we soon established a good working relationship, he was unable to remember his dreams. In the trance I suggested he would have a dream that would explain his rectal itching. He responded with an anxiety dream of a man with a huge penis approaching him from the rear. He was told to forget the dream or recall any part of it that he wished to remember after he had awakened. Upon opening his eyes, he complained of tension, but he did not remember his dream. He admitted some relief in his rectal itching. That same night he had a dream of riding a roller coaster with a male friend. Clearly, his dream suggested that he had unconscious fears of homosexuality. In later dreams he was able to countenance homosexual impulses and to discuss them during the session. Hypnosis was responsible for opening up a repressed and repudiated area of guilt and conflict.

7. *When the patient seems blocked in transferring to the therapist his distorted attitudes toward early figures of authority.*

Childhood experiences, particularly relationships with parents and siblings, have a formative influence and prejudice the attitudes, values, feelings, and behavior of the individual as an adult. The imprints can be indelible and affect the way a person responds not only to other people but the way he feels about himself. Because the most important formative experiences occur in very early childhood, they may be forgotten, or remain hazy, or be dissociated from the fears and anxieties with which they were originally linked. Yet they continue to influence faulty ways of thinking and acting in later life.

The hypnotic situation can be of great help in discovering conditioned responses when it takes on the character of a drama, in which a subject reveals underlying attitudes toward and problems with authority dating back to his earliest relationship with his parents. The therapist can use these "transference phenomena" to teach his patient how his early patterns, needs, and defenses repeat themselves in settings where they make little sense. The patient may then realize that the way he is reacting to hypnosis and to the hypnotist is unrealistic and that he responds in destructive and unnecessary ways in many other situations. The lesson he learns can serve as the basis of new, more wholesome attitudes to present-day authority, attitudes that, though new to him, will in all likelihood make his life more comfortable and productive.

A patient who came to me for therapy entered easily into the hypnotic state but became more and more recalcitrant to suggestions. He had always been submissive to his father (and later to other male authorities). As a result, he felt great inner rage, turmoil, and depression, although he was outwardly calm. It was apparent that his entering hypnosis was a means of pleasing me. This was his customary role with male authority, patterned after the way he reacted to his father. "For years I hated my father," he said. "He couldn't stand being contradicted. I remember needing to lose at cards deliberately so that father would not get upset over my winning. I am never able to be successful; it makes me too anxious." When I interpreted to him the way he was reacting to me, he at first denied it. But then he seemed to see the light, with the result that he challenged me by first resisting hypnosis, and finally by manifesting a total inability to enter the hypnotic state. I accepted his refusal to comply, even encouraged it. At this phase the patient experienced dreams of triumph. "It's healthier to dream of feeling love rather than hate. For the first time I realize I love my father. I cried in my sleep. I felt my father really loved me, but we had this wall between us. I awoke feeling I really loved him." This change in feeling resulted in an abatement of symptoms and a capacity to relate more co-operatively to men. From then on, the patient was able to enter hypnosis easily and without resentment, as a means of pleasing himself, not me.

Another patient, experiencing frigidity, was referred to me by her psychoanalyst for some hypnotic work. After the third induction, she told me that she felt the need to keep her legs crossed the entire trance state. So tightly did she squeeze her thighs together that they ached when she emerged from the trance. Before the next induction, I instructed her to keep her legs separated. As I proceeded with suggestions, she became flushed, opened her eyes, and exclaimed that she knew what was upsetting her. I reminded her of her grandfather, she said, who, when she was a small child, had tossed her into bed and held her close to his body on several occasions. She had felt his erect penis against her body, and this had both excited and frightened her. It became apparent that the hypnotic experience represented for her an episode during which she hoped for and feared a repetition of this sexual seduction. Her leg-crossing was the defense against these fantasies. Continued trance inductions with the patient diminished her fears, and she then was able to have better sexual relations with her husband.

Another patient, who suffered from periodic attacks of nausea, vomiting, and gastrointestinal crises, was referred to me for hypnosis after two years of traditional psychonalysis had failed to relieve her symtoms. Because she tended to shield herself from awareness of her problems with strong repressions, I felt that transference, which had not developed significantly during her previous therapy, might be important in helping her to gain insight into her problems. After she had been trained to enter a medium trance, I suggested that she would dream of her feelings about me. She failed to dream but instead had a hallucination consisting of a peculiar taste in her mouth, which she described as "bittersweet." This taste persisted for several hours after her session. That evening she had a nightmarish dream in which a woman, whose handbag bore the initials "B.S.," took a small boy into the bathroom to help him to urinate and wash up. She was unable to interpret the dream. A trance was induced in which she recalled forgotten elements of the dream, namely that the sexes of the two participants had changed as they had entered the bathroom; the adult had been a man, the child a girl. The next few sessions were spent discussing a "reaction" to me that the patient had developed and that made her want to stop treatment. She was positive that I resented her, and she recounted several minor incidents indicating to her that I did not have her best interests at heart. She was positive that I preferred a young man whose sessions preceded hers, because I once kept him late, thus overlapping her time.

In the trance that followed, she broke into hysterical crying, identifying me as her father, whose nickname was Bing. (The initials B.S. in the dream stood frador Bing and his last name Steward, as well as being linked to the "bittersweet" taste she had in her hallucination.) He had been both father and mother to her (changed from male to female in the dream), had preferred her brother to her (her reaction to the male patient whose hour preceded hers), and always reminded her that he regretted that she had not been born a boy (her being brought into the bathroom as a boy in the dream possibly indicated that she had finally succeeded in achieving a masculine status.) Thereafter, she experienced strong sexual feelings toward me and demanded that I express a preference for her among all my other patients. From then on, it was possible to analyze the origins of these feelings in her relations with her father and to see that some of her symptoms were associated with fantasies of wanting to be a boy through acquiring a penis. Hypnosis succeeded rapidly in allowing us to understand what was behind her difficulty.

8. When the patient has forgotten certain traumatic memories, whose recall may help the therapeutic process.

In certain emotional states, memories may be submerged. Because they constantly threaten to come to the surface, anxiety and defensive symptoms, which bolster repression, affect the personality. The trance can be instrumental in recalling the repressed experience, and the examination of the associated emotions helps to eliminate debilitating symptoms.

One of my patient suffered from periodic attacks of shortness of breath, an affliction that resembled asthma. He was given a suggestion in hypnosis that he would return (regress) to his first attack. In a scene in which he saw himself as a child of three standing in a snowsuit on a back porch, he described how he slipped and fell into a high snowdrift, gasping for breath as the snow filled his nose and throat. With panic, choking as he talked, he told of being rescued by his mother and father. This story was verified by his parents as a true experience. They were amazed that the patient remembered the exact details of the accident, and said that "asthmatic" attacks had begun soon after this incident. It was then established in therapy that interpersonal situations in which the patient felt trapped caused him to respond with the symptom of choking for breath. This pattern had originally been established when he actually had been physically trapped. With this recognition, the symptom lent itself to constructive working through.

9. When the patient seems to "dry up" in his conversations, being unable to produce any more significant material.

Periods of resistance may develop during the course of therapy characterized by an almost complete cessation of activity. The patient will spend many sessions in fruitless attempts at conversation; he seems to be up against a barrier that he cannot break through. Attitudes of disappointment and hopelessness contribute to his inertia until he resigns himself to making no further efforts. He may even decide to abandon therapy. When such circumstances threaten, hypnosis may be tried to stimulate productivity. A variety of techniques may be used, including letting one's thoughts bounce around without restraint ("free association") in the trance, dream and fantasy stimulation, mirror gazing, automatic writing, play therapy, dramatic acting, regression and reliving (revivification), and the production of experimental conflicts. The specific method employed is usually determined by the therapist's experience and preference as well as by the patient's aptitudes in working with one or another technique.

Another patient who had been working satisfactorily with me began to develop silences that greatly puzzled her since she had up to this time been quite garrulous in her ramblings. "When I try to think, my mind goes blank," she said. "Nothing comes to me." After several frustrating sessions, hypnosis was induced, and she was encouraged to talk about her mental meanderings. She began to moan and cry. "Grief, grief. It's all death—as if it's all over. It's my father; he died of cancer, and I took care of him. He keeps coming back. It chokes me up. It's as if it's all happening again." The patient then revealed, expressing great feelings of guilt, that while she had nursed her father during his illness, she had experienced tender and then voluptuous feelings for him. During his illness she was able to have him all to herself for the first time. Her mother was only too willing to let her take care of him. Sexual excitement was strong during this period, and she harbored guilt feelings during and after her father's death, scarcely daring to think about it. "I'm frightened. I know I felt guilty about my desire to be close to my father. After he died, I felt cold and detached. Maybe that is why I can't feel anything for men now. I realize I do this with all men, that is, I want to baby them. I had been taking care of one man I know who got sick with the flu. I sponge-bathed him and got so sexually excited I could hardly stand it. The thought occurs to me that I would like to take care of you too. I'm so ashamed to talk about this."

After the patient understood the reason for her guilt feelings and why they were causing resistance to progress in therapy, she was able to interpret the transference to me of her feelings for her father. From then on, she progressed satisfactorily in free association.

10. When the patient is unable to deal with forces that block the transformation of insight into action.

The mere development of insight is not enough to insure the correction of neurotic attitudes and patterns; it must be employed toward constructive action. Unfortunately, there are often anxieties and resistances that obstruct this process and bring therapy to an incomplete end. Hypnosis is sometimes useful in converting insightful perception into action, and it can achieve this goal in a number of ways. First, one can attempt by various techniques to explore resistance to change; the patient can make associations in his fantasies, dreams, or by the dramatic acting-out of certain healthy courses of action. Second, posthypnotic suggestions can be made to the effect that the patient will want more and more to expose himself to the actions that are necessary and that are being resisted. Third, role playing can be used, the patient projecting himself into various situations in the present or future, and acting out his insights or fears with the therapist. Fourth, in somnambulistic subjects experimental conflicts can be set up to test the patient's readiness to execute necessary and desirable acts and to investigate his reactions to their completion.

One of my patients, a man with a passive personality, had gained insight into the roots of his problem during therapy; he also realized the destructive consquences of his failure to be self-assertive. He wanted to change but was paralyzed at the thought of how to begin. The best he could do was to fantasize about walking into his employer's office and boldly asking for a promotion. In his fantasy he was rewarded with a higher position and a handsome raise in salary. But he could not muster the courage to face his employer in real life and expressed fears of being turned down. In hypnotic role playing, he took the part both of himself and his employer and vehemently discussed the pros and cons of his position. However, he still could not get himself to act. Since he was able to develop posthypnotic amnesia, I decided to try to set up an experimental conflict. I suggested that he imagine himself asking for a promotion. Then I told him to forget the suggestion, but, upon emerging from the trance, to feel as if he had actually made the request. The first two attempts were followed by tension, headaches, and discouragement. This indicated that the patient was not yet prepared to take the necessary step forward. We nonetheless continued discussion and role playing, and a third experimental situation resulted in a feeling of elation and accomplishment. The next day the patient spontaneously approached his employer and was rewarded with success. From then on, the patient began to act with more assurance, and his progress in therapy helped him to become more positive in everyday life.

11. When the patient has problems in terminating therapy.

Difficulties in ending therapy are sometimes experienced by patients who, having been freed of neurotic symptoms, are afraid of losing what they have gained and suffering a relapse. Patients with weak personality structures may resist ending treatment with astounding stubbornness. Contrary to what might be expected, the adroit application of hypnosis can help some of these patients toward self-reliance by relieving their tension at points where they ought to act independently. The patient can also be taught self-hypnosis for purpose of relaxation, and shown how to investigate spontaneously—through dreams, fantasies, and associations—the problems that arise daily from demands to adjust to specific situations. In this way, responsibility is transferred to the patient, and he may become more and more capable of self-determination. Intervals between visits with the therapist are gradually prolonged. In the beginning, the patient may resort to daily sessions of self-hypnosis because of anxiety. But as he develops more confidence in his ability to survive alone, he usually forgets regular self-hypnosis and finally resorts to it only when his tensions cause him to seek relief. Eventually, as his independence becomes stronger, he finds himself capable of functioning without props. In very sick patients, however, regular relaxation exercises are an important part of adjustment and may be prolonged indefinitely with beneficial effect.

The situations described above are no more than brief outlines of how hypnosis can be effective in psychotherapy, and only suggest the various ways in which the trance can be used as an adjunctive procedure. Since all psychotherapy is a blend of the therapist's individual personality and his techniques, no two therapists will operate identically. Each hypnotherapist has his own unique approach in working with his patients, and it depends on his particular philosophy about how people become neurotically ill and how they get well again. If a doctor believes that unconscious memories and conflicts are the basis for all nervous ailments, he will try to dig into the psyche of his patient to discharge the emotional conflictual poison that has accumulated there. Once it is released, the psyche will presumably heal. Freud and Breuer originally used hypnosis in this way and scored considerable success with some patients. They recorded their findings in *Studien über Hysterie,* a revolutionary book that was a precursor of psychoanalytic theories and methods. Although hypnosis is instrumental in releasing repressed memories, we now know that the majority of patients are not helped by this process alone. Interesting and dramatic as the results are, additional techniques are necessary if we are to achieve lasting benefit.

There are other therapists whose theories about how people become emotionally ill involve the concepts of faulty learning and conditioning. They use hynosis to reinforce their stratagem of teaching their patients new patterns of habit formation, thinking, and action. Although these "behavioral" methods are responsible for considerable progress in the treatment of some ailments, they are not successful in dealing with all problems. Different tactics are needed.

As in any field of medicine there is a variety of remedies and techniques. The most successful therapist knows when and how to apply the best method for specific problems and situations. He is "eclectic" in the sense that he does not hesitate to use proven procedures that have been shown to work over a span of time. One of the most important points to be made about hypnosis is that it can be helpful as a catalyst irrespective of the method of psychotherapy. Some therapists are not able to use hypnosis with any measure of success, either for personality reasons or because of unresolvable prejudices. This does not invalidate hypnosis as a procedure. Hypnosis, like any other area of specialization, requires particular abilities and skills. Not every therapist is able to amalgamate hypnosis with his personality and technical training.

It should be stressed again that hypnosis must be used intelligently within the context of a comprehensive treatment plan and with due regard for its particular assets and limitations. Applied indiscriminately, hypnosis not only fails to serve a therapeutic purpose, but its ineffectiveness tends to discredit it as a scientific procedure and to impede its acceptance. Used at strategic points in psychotherapy, hypnosis can facilitate progress. In this way it adds an important dimension to the technical skills of the psychotherapist.

9

Pain Control in Hypnosis

In her book *The Nine Lives of Billy Rose,* Polly Rose Gottlieb tells the story of how this creative showman suffered intractable and paralyzing pain after extensive vascular surgery for a circulatory disease. "He was weak and frail; a hawk imprisoned in a sparrow's crippled body," was the phrase used by the columnist Jimmy Cannon in an article about Mr. Rose. Neither opiates nor sleeping pills eased his pain or relieved his insomnia. He was confined to bed, hardly able to walk. When, in desperation, hypnosis was suggested to him, Billy replied: "You must be out of your cotton-pickin' mind to think I'd even entertain the thought of such nonsense." What convinced him to try it, however, was the revelation that Cary Grant had had a small growth removed under the influence of hypnosis. As it turned out, hypnosis did eliminate Mr. Rose's pain immediately and enabled him to get out of bed and walk. I can vouch for the truth of the story, since I was the hypnotist who was called in. I cite the story merely to illustrate how remarkably effective hypnosis sometimes can be in pain reduction.

Pain is a sensation that can be altered under a variety of conditions. It can be temporarily excluded from awareness when the attention is diverted from it. The physical agony that results from extensive injury to the body organs may go unnoticed in moments of great excitement, only to occur later, when the emergency situation is over. Soldiers in battle often become conscious of amputated extremities before they experience pain. Civilian antagonists in combact can inflict serious wounds on each other and not realize they have been hurt until the fight is over. There are many accounts of athletes sustaining sprains and even broken bones while continuing to play in the heat of competition.

On the other hand, pain can be intensified in various ways: by concentrating on the affected area; by overreacting to the painful sensation and giving it an exaggerated significance; by becoming increasingly tense, thereby causing the organism to be more vulnerable to nuances of discomfort.

Hypnosis can help to diminish an obsession with pain, shift the attention away from the stricken area, and reduce tension. This will help to raise the pain threshold so that the individual will be much less aware of his suffering.

Effect of Hypnosis on Pain Perceptions

If a person puts his hand into a pail of ice water, he will experience sensations of cold and numbness, followed by pain, which can soon become intolerable. Apart from the subjective feeling of pain, certain physiological effects will be registered in other parts of the body. For instance, pulse rate and blood pressure will rise. There will be psychological effects too—discomfort, irritation, tension, and anxiety. The intensity of these feelings will vary with the sensitivity of the person and his attitude towards pain. Sooner or later, he will remove his hand from the pail to escape these unpleasant effects.

If the same person were to be hypnotized and told, prior to immersing his hand in water, that he would become insensitive to cold, he would, if he were an average subject, be able to endure the experience with relative equanimity. Should hypnosis have been delayed until the painful impact of the cold water was felt, the chances are that he would undergo at least some reduction or absence of pain. There would be a lessening of the physiological response to the painful stimulus. This would show in the pulse rate and blood pressure, which would be lower than ordinarily occurs without hypnosis. Certainly they would be lower than if the person were trying voluntarily to suppress his reaction to pain by imagining that it did not exist. From this we would be inclined to conclude that pain reduction under hypnosis (hypnotic analgesia) is a real, not simulated, phenomenon.

It is understandable, in view of the practical uses that may be made of hypnotic analgesia, that researchers have tried to pinpoint the exact reason for this dramatic happening. Some observers believe that hypnosis sets up an actual blockage to stimuli between the area subjected to pain and the neural mechanisms that are activated by pain. One hypothesis is that the connections between nerves (synapses) in the spinal cord which are related to the painful area become temporarily suppressed in hypnosis. Another is that a morphine-like brain neurotransmitter, endorphin, is released. How this can happen through sheer suggestion is not explained. Most observers shy away from an organic in favor of a psychological interpretation. They believe that the secret of pain reduction lies in the lowering of tension and anxiety.

When a person is subjected to pain, the perception of it immediately stimulates some anxiety. This is nature's way of alerting the person to the presence of a dangerous or potentially dangerous situation. He is then in a better position to remove himself, if possible, from the threatening source of pain or to eliminate it directly. But even though tension and anxiety serve as warning mechanisms, they also tend to amplify the pain sensation. For this reason, various methods are usually sought to eliminate them. Tension and anxiety can be reduced and the mind diverted from an awareness of suffering. Pain then begins to diminish and even to disappear. This is apparently how hypnosis works to produce diminution of pain or an actual blockage of the pain sensation.

A number of studies have been done that validate the theory that the degree of physical suffering can be greatly influenced by social and psychological factors. Pain can be either heightened or lessened in situations that concentrate attention on the sensation or distract it. Pain can be reduced by entreaty, by appeals to bravery, and by reassurance. Dr. H. K. Beecher, an authority on pain, has shown that fully one-third of patients suffering pain after surgical operations are as easily relieved by a placebo (*e.g.*, a sugar pill) as they are by morphine. The placebo seems to lower the tension level. In an editorial in the *Journal of the American Medical Association*, Beecher wrote:

> Any small boy in a fist fight feels no pain at the time of injury. This comes later, when his bloody nose begins to drip or his mother arrives to console him. The severely wounded soldier, not in shock but clear mentally, has surprisingly little need for a narcotic. In the early hours after wounding, only a minority request it, whereas the civilian recovering from surgery with a much smaller wound receives two to three times as much narcotic as the soldier with his more extensive wound.

Specific experiments have shown that the primary effect of morphine on pain is the reduction of tension and that a mild tranquilizer or sedative will do almost as much good as a powerful narcotic. Perhaps the greatest tranquilizer is a good interpersonal relationship with one's doctor. The legendary "bedside manner" of the compassionate physician is based on this principle.

By acting on the tension and anxiety level, hypnosis can have a substantial and even astonishing impact on pain, particularly when the subject is convienced that it can help him. Pain affects the heart rate, breathing rate, skin resistance, blood pressure, and amplitude of respiration. People in a trance have been studied with instruments that record these variables. Although the subjects show all the physiological manifestations of pain, they are calm, and their minds are diverted from uneasy or distressing thoughts.

Hypnosis as an Anesthetic in Surgery

The anesthetic properties of hypnosis have been recognized for centuries, and advantage has been taken of the trance for a variety of surgical purposes. Although chemical anesthetics are more efficient and reliable, there are certain advantages in hypnotic anesthesia. All chemicals introduce foreign substances into the body, and large amounts pose risks. In serious heart, lung, and kidney ailments even "safe" anesthetics may prove toxic. Most important, painkilling drugs used to control postoperative pain or the suffering from organic illness may become habituating. Narcotic addictions often result from the well-intended prescriptions for continued use of a drug like Demerol.

Hypnosis may suffice by itself as an anesthetic in minor surgery, dentistry, and obstetrics. For a very small percentage of subjects capable of achieving somnambulistic trances the anesthesia may be sufficiently deep to permit major surgery, such as breast removal (mastectomy) or Caesarian operation. Such deep anesthesia, however, is most unusual and cannot be depended on in the average subject. The chief value of hypnosis is as an adjunct to chemical anesthesia, since a trance greatly lowers the quantity of anesthetic required for effectiveness. This reduces the toxic effect of the chemical on body tissues, which is especially welcome in the case of debilitated patients, those requiring heart and chest surgery, and in persons who must undergo long operations.

During the early 1900's the famous surgeon George Crile discovered that apprehension and tension were key elements in increasing the mortality rate of patients undergoing surgery for toxic goiter. Through his observations of many patients, he came to a significant conclusion. The mortality rate went down dramatically when he was able to earn their confidence by convincing them that they were in good hands and by teaching them to relax in advance of the operation. He also trained his staff never to carry on conversations about a patient's condition or the impending operation in the presence of the patient, thereby insuring a higher survival rate.

Tension is undoubtedly a factor in the outcome of all operations. Sensitive people are particularly susceptible to it, and all good clinicians take tension into account in dealing with patients. Realizing the importance of an optimistic outlook, they make a point of reassuring them in order to reduce the level of emotional unrest. Doctors who know how to use hypnosis may reinforce the impact of their efforts. This is particularly important when the patient fears that he will not recover from an operation.

An increasing number of anesthesiologists have been learning to use hypnosis as part of their technique in preparing a patient for surgery. Dr. Milton J. Marmer, a well-known specialist in anesthesia, has said that the average patient fears anesthesia more than surgery itself. He has written extensively on the advantages of hypnosis as an adjunct to chemical anesthesia. One of its greatest assets, he has stated, is the posthypnotic lessening of pain, nausea, hiccuping, and vomiting. And, because hypnotized patients are more aware of undue pressures in unanesthetized areas, such complications as neuralgias and neuritis after surgery may be minimized, when the patient is alerted to report pressures.

Hypnosis is possible as the sole anesthetic in minor operations such as incision and drainage, reduction of simple fractures, and uterine curettage. It has been used for the cleaning of dirty wounds, suturing of incisions, cauterization of tissues, and diagnostic procedures in examining the stomach (gastroscopy), the lower bowel (sigmoidoscopy), the rectum (proctoscopy), and the bladder (cystoscopy).

Writing in a medical journal, Dr. Herbert A. Ecker, a noted plastic surgeon, pointed out the advantages of hypnosis in his area of specialization. Patients requiring extensive repair of facial lacerations or the wiring of bones in the jaw, he said, do not have problems in breathing, due to a blockage of the upper respiratory tract, when hypnosis is used. In most cases a general anesthetic would be hazardous. "A surgeon will find hypnosis useful in other procedures," Dr. Ecker added, "such as removing sutures in nervous adults and children, especially in patients with cleft palates. We have had two recent cases in which patients with abdomen-hand flaps kept their hands against their abdomens for four or five weeks under the suggestion that their hands were stuck to their abdomens and could not be moved, no matter how hard they tried. Only two strips of tape were used to help them, serving quite a contrast to the plaster cast often employed."

Hypnosis in Childbirth

A woman is waiting comfortably in the anteroom of the maternity suite in a local hospital. To look at her one would not suspect that she is in labor. Her uterine contractions started at home two hours ago, and soon after this she entered the hospital and received the usual preparation and enema. From the "prep" room she went to a chair in the anteroom, accompanied by her husband. As she experiences each contraction, one can see her shut her eyes and breathe deeply. She has been trained to put herself into a hypnotic trance and to remain in the trance during the entire contraction. Thereafter, she opens her eyes, obviously refreshed, and participates in the activities taking place in the room. She may drink some fruit juice, smoke a cigarette, or eat. If a television or radio program is on, she may watch or listen to it between contractions. She speaks cheerfully to her husband as well as the nurse, a resident, or her attending doctor, if any of them enter the room. After an hour or so, she informs her husband that she feels like pushing or bearing down. The obstetric nurse and attending doctor are notified, and she is brought to the delivery room, where she continues to relax between contractions. During contractions she is enjoined by the obstetrician to work hard and to experience a tremendous sense of well-being. In another fifteen or twenty minutes she has easily delivered her baby. She is then told that she can see her baby and hear its first cry. Thereafter she is instructed to return to a relaxed state. The placenta is delivered, and if repair work is necessary, it is usually done without the aid of a chemical anesthetic. If the new mother is a good subject, she may remain in the hypnotic state with her eyes open, holding and admiring her baby. Before she comes out of hypnosis, a posthypnotic suggestion is given to her that she will be able to void spontaneously, move her bowels without enemas, enjoy her food, and experience little or no discomfort.

This excellent description of the use of hypnosis in childbirth was given in 1960 by Dr. William E. F. Werner, a gynecologist and obstetrician, and published in the *New York State Journal of Medicine.* In his article Dr. Werner points out the advantages to the infant when painkilling drugs and chemical anesthesia are not used or used sparingly. The possibility of reduced oxygen in the brain (cerebral anoxia) during labor and delivery is minimized. Since the breathing of the mother is easier, this can be of benefit to the circulation of the child too. He states that in over one hundred and seventy-five deliveries performed with hypnosis there has been no necessity to resuscitate a single infant.

Moreover, the death rate of the newborn is materially decreased. Ninety per cent of the babies were studied during the first three months of their lives. There was not a single case of colic. "We feel that a relaxed mother tends to deliver a relaxed baby."

There are also many advantages for the mother. In the training period the prospective mother is instructed about the nature of labor and delivery. This education, contends Dr. Werner, greatly reduces or eliminates her tension. And tension fosters pain. Several times in hypnosis she is given detailed information about the nature of labor and delivery so that she can anticipate what will happen and be able to co-operate more easily. The three stages of labor are described, and she is assured of a comfortable and wonderful experience. She is trained to develop anesthesia, which she will use during her contractions. In at least 90 per cent of patients trained in this way there is a complete or partial reduction of chemical analgesic or anesthetic agents. After the delivery there is no evidence of obstetric shock or extreme exhaustion. Because the patient has been taught to relax and to produce anesthesia of the perineum, there is less need for operations and repairs (episiotomies). Nausea and vomitimg are very rare. There is no difficulty in voiding, and over 90 per cent of patients have good bowel movements without enemas within forty-eight hours. Appetites are good, food is enjoyed, and subsequent recovery is accelerated. Patients are soon up and about and can attend to their personal needs. Morale is greatly enhanced. "Let me state," says Dr. Werner, "that since the science of obstetrics came into being we have been looking for a method to deliver mothers of healthy infants in a comfortable state. . . . I feel that with delivery under hypnosis we can attain these goals . . . ."

Most obstetricians who have employed hypnosis in childbirth endorse the method heartily. It is particularly valuable in a difficult labor that may go on for many hours and even days. In prolonged labor chemical analgesics and anesthetics have a toxic potential for both mother and child. When administered during the second stage of labor, they may also depress uterine contractions as well as impair the respirations of the infant. In an article in the *Journal of The American Medical Association*, Drs. Frank Moya and L. Stanley James reported that controlled clinical studies during the first hour of life have shown "a significantly greater ability of the hypnosis group of babies to recover from the asphyxia of birth, as compared to the non-hypnosis infants including a non-medicated regional anesthesia group." The group of mothers who used hypnosis were calm, relatively comfortable, and co-operative. They demonstrated an unusual degree of rapport with and confidence in their doctor, in contrast with the other mothers, who were experiencing moderate to severe pain. While Moya and James endorse hypnosis as a valuable aid in obstetrics, they stress the need for competent administration and careful observation because of the time factor in training preparturient patients.

Hypnosis and Dentistry

The walls of my dentist's waiting room are adorned with pithy, piquant slogans: "Don't just do something—stand there"; "A bachelor is like a good detergent; he works fast and leaves no ring." These and other mottos are, I am sure, intended to create a mood that distracts the patient from thoughts of the dental drill. Scattered among these maxims are reproductions of authentic old dental advertisements, which promise painless dentistry through the use of ridiculous devices, and amulets that are obviously of placebo value. Yet they indicate how important the dentists of old considered distraction by pain-reducing devices to be—no matter how inauthentic they were.

While hypnosis has nothing in common with these old measures, its aims are nonetheless the same. Its effectiveness in dentistry is due in part to the placebo influence, in part to distraction, and in large measure to its ability to dissipate tension and fear. A great deal of the discomfort people experience in dentistry is caused by the anticipation of pain. Most people have had one or more unpleasant encounters with a dental drill, so that the mere sound of it and the pressure of the instrument set off tensions that exaggerate reactions to even minor dental work. When fear is especially great the injection of an anesthetic itself may precipitate panic.

Because of their desire to escape pain, most people who are

frightened by dentistry are motivated to accept hypnosis as an aid. Its effect, even when the trance is a light one, can be most gratifying. The chief benefit is the reduction of apprehension, which in turn raises the pain threshold. To some extent suggestions of anesthesia may be helpful, but this is secondary to tension alleviation. Hypnotic suggestions will also help control excessive salivation and bleeding, probably through tension reduction.

Novocaine or Xylocaine are so easy to use and so effective that it would scarcely seem profitable to invest time-consuming hypnosis in the average patient. However, there are certain conditions and situations that are greatly helped by hypnosis. Recognizing this, some dentists take the added time to work with it. In cases where extensive restorations are essential, considerable gum work is needed, fear of dentistry is especially pronounced, or where gagging is uncontrollable, hypnosis may offer the patient substantial relief. Not only is less chemical anesthetic required, but there is added benefit from the patient's greater co-operation during the appointment hour and lessened discomfort later on. Through posthypnotic suggestion, some dentists have prolonged the anesthetic effect for several days after the dental visit, enabling their patients to function with greater comfort.

Hypnosis also helps patients to become accustomed to and tolerate dentures. There are many people who psychologically resist dentures and make themselves and their dentists miserable with incessant complaints. Positive suggestions that encourage the patient to stop thinking about his teeth may make an enormous difference.

Hypnosis in dentistry may readily be employed with children, most of whom are excellent subjects. It may be the only means of keeping a child in a dental chair. Asking him to imagine himself watching his favorite TV program during induction may divert him from what the dentist is doing.

Thumb-sucking is a practice among young children that can have serious consequences for the proper alignment of teeth. The question of the value of hypnosis in stopping this habit is often asked. Generally it is not wise psychologically to interfere with thumb-sucking in a very young child. But because of the risk to teeth formation, hypnotic treatment may be of help in certain cases. Some dentists believe that proper suggestions to children under hypnosis will make them want to stop the practice. The approach must be permissive, since a disturbed child may respond catastrophically to authoritative suggestions. When a child continues to suck his thumb beyond the age of four, hypnosis may help with this problem, but suggestions must be couched in a nonauthoritative and nonthreatening way.

In teeth-grinding (bruxism) the careful use of hypnosis may prevent the condition from developing to the point of extensive tooth damage. Techniques vary, but a common one is to condition the patient to awaken when he starts gnashing his teeth. If there are other signs of emotional distrubance, referral to a psychotherapist should be considered.

In summary, then, there are some persons whose anxieties are so strong that they can scarcely co-operate with their dentist for necessary work. When the dentist is skillful in hypnosis, he can overcome this handicap. However, not all dentists use hypnosis. Some are afraid of it or are prejudiced against it. For the dentist who is willing to give his patient added time, and who knows how to use it, hypnosis can be a valuable aid in his work.

Hypnosis for the General Relief of Pain

A person's attitude toward pain, conscious or unconscious, will largely determine how he reacts when he experiences it. Pain can be a complex phenomenon in its causes and origins. Whereas the source of organic pain is for the most part obvious, psychosomatic pain—or what is sometimes called a pain syndrome—is more difficult to treat. In both cases, hypnosis can help to reduce tension and distract the attention from suffering. In addition, the solace afforded by the relationship between hypnotist and patient is another significant factor in the hypnotic process. A person in pain reaches for a soothing authority who will bring comfort and freedom from stress. This effect is assured by the doctor's sympathetic manner.

There are various psychological reasons why an individual develops a pain syndrome. It may be a way of punishing himself for thoughts, feelings, and experiences that he considers wrong or sinful. It may be a means through which he fulfills his need for martyrdom, or a technique of demonstrating to the world how badly he has been treated. Pain with no organic cause is common in certain hysterical states (conversion hysteria). It is important, then, to try to understand the reasons for resorting to pain as a symptom, in addition to attempting to alleviate pain through hypnosis. Accordingly, the victim of pyschological pain can be helped to develop motivation in dealing with the source of his difficulty.

In organic pain, hypnosis may occasionally prove to be of great help to the patient. It has been employed in both acute and chronic conditions. For example, in severe burns the loss of fluids, the toxemia, and the pain cause a loss of appetite, tension, and the shattering of morale. Hypnosis has been used on badly burned victims to anesthetize the affected areas, which not only makes the patient more comfortable, but also facilitates the changing of dressings, the cleaning of wounds, and skin grafting. In some cases hypnosis has helped the patient to begin drinking more fluids and eating properly. A depressed, nauseated, listless patient who has resisted drinking and eating may suddenly show an interest in living. With posthypnotic suggestions, there is a reduction of postdressing pain, and the patient is able to get out of bed and move about, thereby avoiding becoming bedridden.

In intractable neurologic conditions and advanced cancer, hypnosis may be able to control pain, reduce suffering, and help the patient face the present and future with greater courage. When possible, a very deep trance state can bring about an almost total relief of pain. But even light or medium trances can help patients to eat, sleep, and feel better. In cases where drugs are administered to kill pain, some patients have been able to give them up entirely; others have reduced the dosage. There have been instances in which hypnosis has removed the necessity of scheduled operations to cut nerve tracts for relief of intractable pain. Because it has no side effects, hypnosis can be a valuable adjunct to radiation, drugs, and surgery.

Some hypnotists use simple tricks to help a subject master pain. For example, an operator may suggest to a patient that he will picture himself in a corner of the room watching his body yield up its pain. A subject may be regressed to a time in life before he suffered pain and given a posthypnotic suggestion that the absence of pain will continue for a designated period. A child may be told that he will see himself eating ice-cream, which will ease his pain. When some honorable motive may be ascribed to the pain, as in battle wounds, a dramatic easing of suffering may be brought about. The subject can be told, for instance, that his tolerance of pain proves the worthwhileness of the sacrifice made for one's fellow men. Dr. Milton Erickson has accomplished some astonishing effects with pain reduction by the use of time distortion in hypnosis. He has asked patients to condense their mild suffering over an entire day into several minutes of agonizing pain and to replace day pain by night pain, during which sleep is maintained. In some cases, there is only a direct suggestion for the diminution or absence of pain.

There are therapists who rely on the patient's unconscious, enlisting it in cases of chronic pain to help in the search for a meaning of the experience and even to prescribe ways of overcoming the pain. This is done by using finger signals. The patient is asked to lift the index finger of a hand when the answer is "yes," the middle finger when the answer is "no," and the thumb when he does not know or does not wish to reply. How reliable this method may be is hard to say, but some therapists find it of great value. Other therapists employ some ingenious tricks, such as asking the patient to imagine himself holding an ice cube against the painful part to make it numb. I have often helped patients control their pain by simply telling them in hypnosis: "Your pain will get less annoying, and you will be able to pay less and less attention to it, until you are able to go about your business as if the pain didn't exist. In fact, the pain will be replaced by a dull feeling, and you will feel little discomfort." Such suggestions are greatly reinforced by teaching the patient self-hypnosis. Teaching the patient to produce a glove anesthesia and then to transfer the numbness by touching the anesthetic hand to his ailing part is sometimes an effective technique.

10

Relieving Symptoms Through Hypnosis

The year was 1897 and the place was St. Petersburg. The occasion was the première of the twenty-four-year-old composer's (Rachmaninoff) First Symphony. It was a complete fiasco, and Rachmaninoff himself described how he sat in rapt horror through part of the performance and then fled from the concert hall before it had ended. At a post-concert party which had been arranged in his honor for that evening he was further shaken and ill at ease, but the crowning blow came the next morning when the reviews appeared. In *The News* César Cui wrote: "If there was a conservatory in hell Rachmaninoff would get the first prize for his symphony, so devilish are the discords he places before us." This combination of events was too traumatic for a personality as sensitive as Rachmaninoff's. He was seized with a fit of depression and apathy from which he could not rouse himself. For two long, black years it lasted. Finally, friends persuaded him to see one of the pioneers in the field of auto-suggestion, a Dr. Dahl.

Rachmaninoff, in his memoirs (*Rachmaninoff's Recollections,* told to Oskar von Riesemann), tells the story: "My relations had told Dr. Dahl that he must at all costs cure me of my apathetic condition and achieve such results that I would again begin to compose. Dahl asked what manner of composition they desired and had received the answer, 'A concerto for pianoforte,' for this I had promised to the people in London and had given it up in despair. Consequently I heard the same

> hypnotic formula repeated day after day while I lay half asleep in my armchair in Dr. Dahl's study, 'You will begin to write your concerto. . . . You will work with great facility. . . . The concerto will be of excellent quality. . . .' It was always the same, without interruption. Although it may sound incredible, this cure really helped me. Already at the beginning of the summer I was composed once more. The material accumulated and new musical ideas began to stir within me—many more than I needed for my concerto. By autumn I had completed two movements (the Andante and the Finale). . . . These I played that same season at a charity concert conducted by Siloti . . . with gratifying success. . . . By the spring I had finished the first movement (Moderato). . . . I felt that Dr. Dahl's treatment had strengthened my nervous system to a miraculous degree. Out of gratitude I dedicated my Second Concerto to him."*

It should not be assumed from Rachmaninoff's experience with hypnosis that total symptom removal always takes place. Nevertheless, in some circumstances dramatic results may be achieved through the sheer force of suggestions. One such case involved a child of three who was sent to me because he was virtually starving to death. He refused to eat solid food and gagged when forced to do so. Finally, his diet became completely liquid, which he would often regurgitate, to the distress of his mother. I consented to use hypnosis, and after the consultation, during which I induced a trance, I never saw the patient again. Because I was so deeply involved with other matters at the time, I never followed up the case, assuming that the parents had decided against treatment. Five years later, the pediatrician who had referred the patient telephoned me and said, "Since you did such a wonderful job with that child who gagged, maybe you can help another one of my patients." I vaguely remembered the old referral. Having the name and address of the patient's mother, I wrote to her inquiring about what had happened. Her written reply was accompanied by a photograph of a plump little boy of eight. In the letter she said that when her son came out of my office into the waiting room, he had asked his mother for some cooked potatoes, the first time he had requested such food. And he had

*Martin Bookspan, in notes from the record album Vox Box, containing Rachmaninoff's Piano Concerto No.2 in C Minor, Opus 18.

been eating very well ever since. "And, doctor," she continued, "you do not know this, but while you were in your office with my son, I walked over to your door and put my ear to it to listen to what was going on. I heard you say, 'You will want to eat; you will have a strong desire to eat because you want to, not because anybody else wants you to.' And, doctor, *I* gained twenty-four pounds."

The moral of the story is not only that suggestions can be effective even through a closed door, but also that a thorough, deep exploration of inner problems is not always essential for symptom relief. This point of view is not completely accepted in some psychological circles. There are those who still believe in the old idea that all symptoms are like a safety valve for steam. Block the release and steam will build up and break out in new and perhaps more disabling symptoms. By and large, the time-honored dictum that symptoms removed by hypnosis must return in the same or substitute form, or that the psychic equilibrium will be upset, precipitating a psychosis, is purely fictional. Relief can be permanent, and advantage may be taken of the symptom-free interlude to encourage a better life adjustment.

Therapists frequently treat people whose lives are made miserable by distressing symptoms, such as functional paralysis, facial tics, obesity, impotence, and other afflictions. They become so unhappy and so upset by their failure to fulfill themselves that they are handicapped in their ability to function. To tell such people that they will have to delay dealing with their immediate complaints until the cause of their problems is understood is both illogical and unfair. Trying to bring about as much relief as possible in a short period of time shows the therapist's regard and concern for the patient and can help the therapeutic working relationship immeasurably. If the symptom is relieved, and the person is able to function again, then often his self-respect is restored, and he can go about improving his interpersonal relationships in the interest of a better total adjustment. Indeed, the resolving of one aspect of a person's problem may start a chain reaction that reverberates through the entire personality structure and influences other dimensions. I have witnessed some surprising examples of how a few hypnotic sessions can alter even the most serious pathological patterns. The fact that this happens is testimony to an inherent adjustability in human beings, which hypnosis can sometimes take advantage of to uncover dormant strengths as well as healing forces. One patient of mine provided a striking example of this phenomenon. He came from a distant state and had dedicated a good part of his life to charitable work. At the age of forty, six years before his first interview with me, he had become obsessed with homosexual yearnings. His desires were so strong that they drove him to prowling the streets, looking for physically attractive men. To his horror he found himself entering toilets to observe the genitals of strangers. Self-castigation, prayer, and the imposition on himself of harsh disciplines failed to prevent what he described as forays into "sin," or to quiet his conscience. A respected member of his community, he knew he was jeopardizing his reputation and security with conduct that could bring only disgrace to himself, his wife, and two children. His homosexual desires had started after a gradual loss of sexual interest in his wife. Except for sporadic mutual masturbation with a male companion during early adolescence, his sexual proclivities had been exclusively toward women. His choice of a wife was a good one, and his early sexual adjustment with her, he claimed, was excellent. He was unable to understand the unusual inclinations that had overwhelmed him and threatened his reputation, security, and sense of intergrity. Looking for answers, he had explored medical journals, and in one of them had come across an article by me on hypnosis. It intrigued him so that he had saved as much money as his small salary would allow, an amount sufficient for a three-day trip to New York. He was sure that one consultation with me, in which I induced hypnosis, would save him from ruin and put him firmly back on the heterosexual path. I scarcely shared his confidence in my talents or his exuberant assurance that his problem could so easily be put to right. Nevertheless, in view of his great sacifice, I could not bring myself to deflate his optimism.

I scarcely had time to do more than listen to a sketchy account of his story and induce hypnosis, during which I told him that my impression was that he was not as sick as he imagined and that in view of his past good adjustment with his wife he had sufficient strength to stop himself from homosexual explorations. There must be reasons why his interest in his wife had waned. Perhaps he had become angry at her for certain reasons and had bottled up his resentment. Since he had given up so much to come to visit me, he inwardly wanted heterosexuality, and he would soon find his desire for his wife returning. He would begin to have dreams in which he would recognize why he had turned away from his wife and dreams of feeling close to her physically. He would be able to practice self-hypnosis and give himself suggestions for self-observation. This would help him to work on the sources of his trouble and restore his faith in himself as a man. Before the session ended, I instructed him briefly in self-hypnosis.

Regular weekly letters for a few months gave me details of his practice and recounted dreams that indicated fear of and hostility toward female figures. But his feelings about women in later dreams gradually became more benign. After a while, sexual fantasies of a heterosexual nature returned. Although he found it difficult at first, it became progressively easier to restrain himself from homosexual excursions. In a few months sexual relations with his wife were re-established, with steadily increasing satisfaction. Over an eight-year period he wrote follow-up letters and visited me once. His overall adjustment would have been considered strikingly successful had prolonged therapy been the prescribed approach. I am not certain what happened to alter the patient's complex intrapsychic mechanisms, whether changes were sponsored by faith in hypnosis, by the healing influences of self-observation, or both. Whatever the *modus operandi,* the interlude with hypnosis played a signal part in his improvement, and may do so even in some patients considered hopeless.

I have had a great deal of experience with chronic obessive-compulsives who were tearing themselves apart with their miserable fantasies. Many of them had had years of unsuccessful psychotherapy and psychoanalysis. But they responded well to a few hypnotic sessions focused on teaching them how to distract their minds from obessions and dwell on more peaceful and productive thoughts. Self-hypnosis, in quite a number of these patients, proved to be an instrument of value. In follow-up studies, some of these people, who were considered resistant to therapy, have shown astonishing changes in total personality structure and in their adaptation to reality. These results far exceeded my clinical expectations. Hypnosis has proved particularly effective in treating certain hysterical symptoms, such as tics, contractures, spasms, paralysis, sensory disturbances, voice inhibitions (aphonia), visual disorders, amnesia, somnambulism, and wandering episodes with amnesia (fugue states).

One of the benefits of hypnosis is that a suitable method of treatment can be geared to removing a particular symptom. One case where this applied involved a patient of mine who suffered from paralysis of one leg. The paralysis had grown progressively worse over a period of years, and finally necessitated the use of a crutch. The symptom was obviously hysterical in nature, resulting from the loss of a valued job. Unable to support himself financially, the patient had relapsed into dependency on his relatives, who were openly resentful of their charge. It was decided to try symptom removal when it became obvious that the patient had no desire for extensive psychotherapy.

The patient was put into a trance and then given suggestions. The first step was to paralyze his arm. The purpose of this was to convince him that it was possible to have paralysis in another part of his body. Paralysis was then removed from his leg. Next, it was suggested that he visualize the two of us walking together, so that he would get a sensory impression of his capacity to ambulate. He was then regressed to the age of thirteen, an age at which he had walked freely. This was to show that he was capable of walking. He was then returned to an adult level, and the performance was repeated. Following this, suggestions were made that he would be able to walk through his own efforts. Reinforcing suggestions and posthyponotic commands that his paralysis would disappear were then given to him. Almost twenty-five years have passed since he underwent this treatment with me. With the exception of one relapse, which was treated in two sessions, there has been no return of paralysis or the development of other significant symptoms.

Symptom removal, judiciously employed, can serve a valuable purpose in carefully selected cases. The results are best when the symptom has a minimal defensive purpose and when there is a powerful incentive to be free of the symptom. Certain psychosomatic symptoms and habit disturbances, such as nail biting, insomnia, excessive eating, and inordinate smoking may be approached with hypnotic directives in symptom removal, since these problems incapacitate the person and usually have no great protective value.

Supplementary therapies are utilized where simple suggestions aimed at symptom removal prove insufficient. For example, alcoholism usually will require, in addition to hypnosis, such supplementary adjuncts as group sessions in Alcoholics Anonymous, and occasionally prescription of Antabuse. Drug-dependent persons need group approaches and intensive counseling. Sexual problems often yield to behavioral sexual therapy, which can be combined with hypnosis.

Results are most pronounced when the patient's only motivation for therapy is to get rid of his symptoms or to bring them under control. This is particularly true when he refuses to go into the genesis of his neurosis or to explore problematical interpersonal relationships.

The removal of a symptom, as mentioned before, may alter the total personality. A person who is handicapped by a disturbing symptom often loses his self-respect. He withdraws from people and becomes more and more involved with himself. The symptom develops into a major preoccupation around which he organizes his insecurity and inferiority feelings. For this reason, the removal of a symptom can alter his whole pattern of adjustment. A man addicted to alcohol, for instance, may suffer more from the social consequences of drinking than from its physical effects. Removing his desire for alcohol by hypnotic command may start a process of personality rehabilitation. A person with a hysterical tic may isolate himself because of embarrassment. Eliminating his tic can have an important influence on his social adjustment. A patient with a paralytic limb may be restored to economic productivity and benefit immeasurably from this restoration.

It should not be assumed from the above accounts that hypnosis is a substitute for long-term treatment in cases that require this approach. When it is deemed necessary and done well, long-term treatment may create a profound change in personality that proves rewarding. At the same time, benefits of short-term symptomatic treatment should not be minimized. This is especially true for those whose problems do not lend themselves to long-term exploration, or those who might become hopelessly ensnared in an interminable therapeutic quagmire because of personality needs. For such people hypnosis may contribute substantially to the short-term effort.

Not all symptoms yield themselves to hypnotic influence. The patient will often desperately cling to those that serve an important purpose in his psychological defenses and those related to deeply ingrained tensions with a defiance that resists the concerted skills of the hypnotist. Most patients can easily neutralize a hypnotist's intentions by resisting suggestions even in the deepest trance state. Yet sometimes a skilled hypnotist, by cleverly confusing the issues, can trick a patient who is emotionally very ill and a good hypnotic subject into compliance. Obviously, this is not good therapy, even though sometimes it helps the patient temporarily. More likely, the patient, lured by a camouflage, may then expose himself to dangers he has avoided through his symptoms. Liberated uncontrollable anxiety can, as a consequence, break down his psychological reserve. The selection of a good therapist who knows how and when to employ hypnosis is therefore a wise precaution.

Symptom removal need not block preparation for a deeper form of treatment. Efforts can be made to demonstrate to the patient the meaning of his symptoms. He may be shown how his distorted behavioral patterns contribute to his fears of the world and to difficulties with others. In this way, he may develop the motivation to explore the sources of his trouble. And here hypnosis, too, may prove beneficial.

Emergency Use of Hypnosis

Sometimes a neurotic symptom may be so destructive or so incapacitating that it constitutes a source of danger. Here the only course may be the use of symptom removal. At the same time, an attempt can be made to motivate the patient to accept deeper therapy, which, of course, he may refuse to accept.

I believe it is within a person's rights to retain a symptom if he really wants to do so. But when a patient comes to me for relief of a crippling symptom and tells me directly, or indirectly by relating his dreams, that he does not want to give up his symptom, I feel an obligation to help him reconsider his choice. Many patients who are forced by their physicians to consult me because of excess tension or improper life habits would like to get well. But they do not want to alter in any way their life style or the destructive patterns responsible for their problems. Sometimes they want me to force them to want to get well. Obviously, this is impossible with hypnosis or with any other technique. What I try to do is educate them to recognize for themselves the faulty thought processes that are responsible for harmful values and modes of behavior. But, in the long run, *they* must decide their own destiny and make a choice between damaging or destructive attitudes and those that will promote health.

In this category are people who are faced with the dilemma of smoking for pleasure while courting the disaster of emphysema, lung cancer, vascular diseases, or heart ailments. Many such persons come to the initial interview at the insistence of their doctors and have no real motivation to stop their destructive habit. A surface statement, "Doctor, I would like to stop smoking, but I can't," usually conceals the message "I am able to stop smoking, but I won't." In view of this obstinacy, it might seem little could be accomplished. But because proper suggestions given in the trance can alter motivation, a considerable number of these reluctant refugees from rationality can be persuaded to break their tobacco habit. With further suggestions they can avoid the equally harmful pastime of substitute overeating that would lead to obesity.

By reducing tension and influencing motivation, hypnosis can also be employed for the relief of other habits that have assumed destructive proportions, for instance, a penchant for fattening foods in dangerously overweight people, nail biting, hair pulling, and bed wetting. The benefits that result from the control of these habits need not be solely symptomatic: restored confidence may eventually produce other beneficial changes.

Insomnia sometimes reaches a point where it becomes an emergency. There are many reasons why people cannot fall asleep at night or, if asleep, awaken before they have had enough rest. Excitement brought about by the events of the day, distracting worries that preoccupy the mind, problems that seem insoluble, and random anxieties all prevent sleep. Generally, such insomnia is temporary, and ordinary sleep habits are resumed after a short period. But occasionally insomnia persists and soon becomes a major preoccupation, in which the sleepless person anticipates that he will remain awake and convinces himself he will be unable to doze off at night. Sooner or later, he indulges in sedatives, which compound the injury because they can become habit forming.

In chronic cases the inability to sleep is fueled by neurotic fears of dying during the might, or by terrifying dreams so upsetting that the individual protects himself from anxiety by insomnia.

Hypnosis may be eminently successful in dealing with milder forms of insomnia, particularly when a sleeping-pill habit has not become entrenched. But even in severe cases, hypnotic therapy may help, and self-hypnosis can often sustain restored sleeping. When unconscious conflicts plague the individual, it is sometimes possible to identify them by general or pointed questions during a trance state. Answers may be vague, or perhaps conjectural, but the mere acknowledgment and response may provide enough reassurance to relax his tensions at night and to divert him from keeping himself awake.

There are therapists, most notably in Russia, who report excellent results with hypnosis for the control of alchoholism. These therapists use special skills and have developed methods that seem to work with a problem so difficult that it defies almost every kind of treatment. But successful work with alcoholics is arduous. Generally, hypnosis is employed in chronic alcoholism to create an aversion to alcohol. In my experience, this has served as a means of motivating the person to go on Antabuse and join Alcoholics Anonymous, which, as mentioned before are the two best adjuncts for individuals with this disorder.

Hypnosis has been employed with success in some pediatric emergent conditions. Children respond well to hypnosis. Conceptually, they are often not motivated to take advantage of depth probings, and so symptomatic approaches are probably the only ones possible. A variety of disorders may be helped, including night terrors, self-imposed starvation, intense anxieties, hysterical reactions, and even behavior disorders. Dr. Norman H. Mellor, in an article, has written about the successful hypnotic treatment of thirteen out of fourteen children charged with juvenile delinquency. They were referred to him by a city police agency or county probation department. The one treatment failure was with a narcotic addict who had no desire or motivation to be helped.

In situations of physical emergency, such as the sudden development of a serious ailment, a tense and frightened patient may be materially aided by calming and reassuring induction of hypnosis. A good deal of the damage that occurs in emergencies is a product of an excited emotional state, which creates unnecessary tension and provokes distress. Relaxation helps to allay this reaction and in this way aids the mending process. It matters little whether the condition is surgical, medical, orthopedic, or neurologic.

Because hypnosis is so dramatic a phenomenon, it is easy to overestimate its potential. A great many things may be accomplished with a subject in a trance, even the temporary removal of psychologically determined symptoms that serve a purpose in adjustment. But almost immediately after hypnosis has ended, or shortly thereafter, the symptoms will return if the subject has a psychological need for them. For example, if a person has developed a weakness or partial paralysis of the right hand, we may be able to eliminate it, perhaps permanently, by showing him that his functions can be fully restored through hypnotic suggestions. His confidence in himself may accordingly be raised, and he will continue to use his disabled member with increasing assuredness. This most likely will occur when there is no advantage to the continuance of his symptoms.

Contrastingly, his trouble may have begun while he was working in a job that is disagreeable to him, perhaps after a slight injury to his hand. If his pay continues while he is at home, his mind may play tricks on him as well as on his employer. He may find that he cannot use his hand effectively: weakness and paralysis may continue, even spreading to his arm. It may not be conscious malingering. He may truly be convinced of his disability and feel and express great resentment against his employer and the world in general. Indeed, he may complain of great pain, consulting doctor after doctor in a futile effort to find relief. At the same time, however, he is compensated for his illness (secondary gains): he collects a weekly disability check; he does not have to expose himself to a loathsome job; he receives sympathy and reassurance from the people around him. Unconsciously, he says to himself, "Why should I be an exploited victim at work when I can be a hero at home and collect money for it?" In the long run, of course, he will pay the penalty of becoming progressively more helpless, dependent and sick, but this will only convince him all the more of his justifiable misery and martyrdom.

Quite often patients on disability compensation are sent to me by insurance companies for hypnotic examination and treatment. Almost invariably, these casualties cling to their symptoms with the desperation of a drowning man hanging onto a raft. I could undoubtedly help a good number of these anguished souls if they would undergo regular psychotherapeutic treatments, in the course of which I might introduce hypnosis. However, their motivation is lacking *until* a lump-sum settlement is made in their case, after which many of them have no further incentive to be ill.

There are other secondary gains a person may get out of holding onto his symptoms. The need to punish himself for his guilt feelings, the desire to abandon an adult adjustment and return to the protective blanket of infancy in order to be taken care of, and other subversive incentives, preconscious or unconscious, may make the retention of a symptom an important cornerstone in his adjustment. For all these reasons, simple suggestive symptom removal has a limited application and ideally should be combined with other psychotherapeutic approaches aimed at eliminating strong defenses. Symptoms do not magically vanish; they must be worn down. It is essential to replace them with productive habits.

Hypnosis and Behavior Therapy

A number of therapeutic methods have been lumped together under the term "behavior therapy," which is based on the theroy that all symptoms are the product of faulty learning and can be eliminated through the process of new and constructive relearning procedures. The re-educational process is geared to the specific symptoms involved. First, a detailed history of the subject is taken so that an analysis of the cause of symptoms (behavioral analysis) can be made. Then, specific methods are applied to break the connection between anxiety and unhealthy responses. Often the patient is taught how to control and eliminate his anxiety (systematic desensitization) by gradually facing his anxiety experiences, first in fantasy and then in reality (active graded therapy). He is also encouraged to recognize and feel the underlying anger and rage that he has been shunting away from awareness. Then he is taught to express these feelings openly and to assert himself aggressively (assertive techniques). By rewarding constructive responses through approval or other prizes (positive reinforcements) and by discouraging neurotic and unhealthy responses through negative reinforcements (aversive conditioning), it is hoped that new habits will be shaped to replace old, destructive ones. The methods work effectively with some patients, particularly those suffering from elaborate fears (phobias) and interpersonal timidity. As part of this technique, hypnosis may be used to reduce tension and provide a relaxing climate for desensitization fantasies.

In the desensitization technique, as in the "reciprocal inhibition" method elaborated by Dr. Joseph Wolpe in his book *Psychotherapy by Reciprocal Inhibition,* treatment is initiated by the construction of an "anxiety hierarchy." The patient is asked to prepare a list of situations to which he reacts with fear and anxiety. The items are ranked according to the intensity of anxiety they induce. The least anxiety-provoking situation is placed at the bottom. The most disturbing situation is put at the top. The remainder are listed in accordance with their anxiety-arousing potential. The patient is then hypnotized and relaxed as deeply as possible. In the trance it is suggested that he will imagine the least threatening item in the anxiety hierarchy. If he is capable of doing this without disturbing his relaxation, the next item on the list is presented, until anxiety is experienced. With each successive session, the ascending degrees of intense anxiety stimuli are dealt with during relaxation until "at last the phobic stimulus can be presented at maximum intensity without impairing the calm, relaxed state." At this point, the patient will presumably have ceased to react with his previous anxiety. He will be able to face in real life "even the strongest of the once phobic stimuli."

Dr. Edward Dengrove, a New Jersey psychiatrist, has prepared a leaflet for his "fearful" patients, which introduces them to the technique of systematic desensitization:

The type of treatment that is being offered to you is known as systematic desensitization. It is based upon scientific studies of conditioned reflexes and is particularly helpful to persons who are fearful. It makes little difference what these fears are: whether of closed places, or being alone, walking alone, driving or flying; or whether one fears loss of self-control, criticism by others, and the like.

Kindly list *all* of the fears that disturb you. Make the list as complete as possible. We will go over the list together and reduce it to its basic units. Treatment will be directed to each individual fear.

The next step will be to teach you how to relax. There are several methods by which this may be accomplished. The particular method that suits your needs will be chosen. This is very important, for the more relaxed you are, the more rapid your progress to health. You cannot be relaxed and remain anxious or fearful at the same time.

When you are completely relaxed—not partially, but completely—I shall present to your imagination a series of situations. These will be based upon your presenting fears. They will be organized in series, graded from the most mild to the most intense. Each forms a hierarchy.

As you visualize each scene in the relaxed state, you may find yourself unmoved by what you see. Or you may experience an uneasiness or restlessness (anxiety). This is a critical point in treatment, and must be signalled to me. No matter how slight, I must be made aware of it.

I may ask, "Do you feel relaxed? Do you feel at ease?" If you do, then move your head up and down ever so slightly. If you do not, move it from side to side.

This is a critical point, for we can only proceed as fast as you are able to accept these visualized situations with ease. I shall not push or prod you. It is only by the ability to maintain your relaxed state that you are able to overcome these fears.

The desensitization takes place gradually by getting you to cope with small doses of anxiety at first, then gradually increasing the dosage a small amount at a time.

With childern, desensitization is done in a less subtle manner. Consider a child who is afraid of dogs. The child is held by a trusted person who allows him to suck on a lollipop and point to a dog on a leash in the distance. A little later, the child, still held, is encouraged to view a dog through a pet-shop window. Still later, he is brought closer to a dog; closer still. With the pleasure of the food and security of being held by a trusted person, the child gradually overcomes his fear. At first there are pictures of dogs, then toy dogs, small, friendly dogs, medium-sized dogs, and so forth. At last he will be able to reach out and touch a dog.

This gives you a clue to a second part of treatment. You are to do the very things that you fear. One cannot overcome a fear by avoiding it, as you have done in the past, or by trying to drown it out with continued medication. Medicine is helpful, but only a crutch, to be reduced and gradually thrown away.

The same principles of gradual desensitization must be employed. You are not to attempt any activity that produces overwhelming anxiety. However, you can and should try those tasks that are only mildly upsetting, at the same time attempting to quiet yourself. If the anxiety persists, stop what you are doing, for this will only set you back. Instead, return to doing those things that you can do without getting upset.

With this approach you will find yourself gradually doing more of these tasks that you avoided in the past. One can get used to almost any new situation that is approached gradually.

Interestingly, as the milder fears are overcome, the more strong ones lose their intensity and lessen, much as the contents of a gum machine diminish with the discharge of each piece of gum. The more one attempts with relaxation, the more rapid the improvement. But one must keep in mind that these attempts deal only with those productive of mild anxiety.

A warning: everyone must proceed at his or her own pace. Some slowly, others more rapidly. There is no reason to feel guilt or shame if one's progress is slow. The process of desensitization cannot be hurried by rushing into highly anxious situations. You will not be thrown into the water and made to swim or sink on your own. At times, under the pressure of need or anger, a few of you will make large strides but this is the exception to the rule.

Consider the woman who is afraid to leave her home. Her first move is to step outside her front door and back again into the house. From there she gradually makes it to the street in front of her home, then around the house—by herself or with someone or while someone trusted is in the house. Each day this is extended until she is able to walk a house away, then two houses, then half a block; with someone, without someone, with someone at home, with no one there. Again, no new step is made until the previous step is mastered, and until it can be accomplished without any anxiety whatsoever. Each fear is attacked individually, daily or as frequently as this can be done.

Gradually you find yourself doing things without thinking about them. Sometimes it will be only after you have done something that you realize you have done it without forethought or anxiety. It may be that someone else will point out to you that you have done something you would not have attempted in the past.

A cooperative spouse is not only helpful and understanding but an essential part of this approach. He or she can be tremendously important to this undertaking. Marital problems tend to hold back progress and should be resolved.

It is by doing what you do for yourself away from the office, that will lead you to health. One or other of these techniques may be used alone, but when both are employed, progress is so much faster. Amaze yourself.

Another body of techniques involves "operant conditioning," in which a program of rewards is designed to influence the patient to change his habits and adapt to more balanced behavior. For example, presents such as money and candy are given for proper behavior and for giving up of unhealthy patterns. Operant conditioning has been effective with patients who are relatively inaccessible to verbal psychotherapeutic approaches—delinquents, autistic children, and psychotic individuals.

Another group of techniques involves the pairing of a painful stimulus, such as a small electric shock to a finger, with a fantasy or impulse that is harmful to the person. Thus, if a patient indulges in such practices as hair plucking, nail biting, and bed wetting, he is given or gives himself a shock the moment he starts the activity. In the case of bed wetting the shock apparatus is under the bed sheet and is activated by moisture. The aversive stimulus for alcoholism is hypnotically suggested nausea and vomiting that occur with the desire for or the attempt to drink alcohol. These techniques are grouped under the heading of "aversion conditioning." They have a relatively limited application since in most cases positive reinforcement for constructive behavior is more effective than aversive reinforcement for undesirable activities.

Behavior therapy is directed mainly at symptoms and destructive behavior and does not probe into the inconscious source of conflict. In spite of this, results can be substantial in motivated patients, particularly when the therapist is experienced and knows how to use hypnosis.

If the behavior therapist is psychoanalytically trained to probe the unconscious, he may be able to help people who are driven to act out their problems against all reason. For such people the rewards (reinforcements) that are offered in therapy may not be as important as the subversive gratification (like sexual excitation or masochistic self-punishment) they get out of indulging their neuroses. For example, when a well-to-do matron engages in compulsive shoplifting, it is difficult to find external reinforcements that will bring this compulsive behavior to a halt. In intelligent patients, a recognition of some of their unconscious motivations may enable them to practice the principles of operant conditioning for themselves.

A significant example of the success of operant conditioning involved an executive in a large business firm. Although he appeared to be happily married and well-adjusted, he would periodically visit prostitutes and have them strap him down to a bed and beat him unmercifully. As he struggled to escape from this humiliation, he would experience a strong orgasm. After these indulgences, his shame and guilt feelings, as well as his fears of being discovered, overwhelmed him to the point of depression and suicidal impulses. He sought to overcome his impulses with exercise, prayer, and involvement in charitable activities. But the intervals of abstinence from his desire for flagellation would be interrupted by strong sexual impulses, and he would go back again for another beating orgy. In studying his case, it was learned that one of his greatest joys in life was sailing in Long Island Sound, where he had a boat. It was felt that this activity could be used effectively as a reinforcement in controlling his masochism. However, before anything else, it was necessary for him to acquire some understanding into the meaning of his peculiar deviation. He agreed to hypnosis. From hypnotically induced dreams and free associations, it was determined that his aberration was related particularly to spankings from his mother during his childhood when he masturbated or was otherwise "bad." A fusion of orgiastic feelings with punishment apparently was the conditioning underlying his symptom. The origins of this association were repressed and could be restored best through analytic techniques. This knowledge gave him a new motivation to cure himself. A plan was organized whereby sailing was to take place only in the intervals of control. If a relapse occurred, and he indulged his masochism, there would be no sailing for a month thereafter. If he controlled the impulse during bad weather, he was to reward himself by taking a short sea voyage, which he enjoyed as much as sailing, to Bermuda. If he could conquer his compulsion during the winter, he was to take a sailing vacation in southern waters the following spring. Within a year of this regime, the patient's symptom was arrested. Whenever the desire returned, he was able to overcome it by reviewing the original causes of the symptom. As a result of his therapy and growth in self-knowledge, a better personal and sexual relationship with his wife was achieved.

Analytical Techniques for Symptom Relief

One of the most important contributions made by modern psychology to the understanding of human behavior is the idea that symptoms are not the product of disorganized forces, but rather that they follow scientific laws of cause and effect. When a person is victimized by fear, tension, and panicky feelings that seem to come from unknown sources, he may not be able to ascertain the meaning of his troubles. Sometimes he will attribute them to unpredictable, perhaps supernatural, forces. If he accepts the idea that nothing in the universe happens by chance, he may be reassured that he is not at the mercy of wicked, inscrutable forces over which he has no control, even though these forces are nightmarish in quality and make him feel that he is being manipulated by demons. If he is told by a person he respects that a matter-of-fact cause is responsible for his agony, he will feel much better. But accepting this explanation on faith is not enough. It is essential that he learn exactly how his symptoms become exacerbated in specific situations.

A man came to me for a consultation about the problem of passing a civil service examination, which was necessary for further advancement. He had evaded taking examinations for a number of years, feigning illnesses or inventing sick relatives as a way out. There had never been any explanation; he was simply terrified about taking examinations. He would get into such panic that he could not function. What he wanted me to do was to perform magic through hypnosis and give him the strength to take the next examination, which was to be held soon. I began treatment with the statement that if the patient really wanted to pass badly enough, he would master his tension sufficiently to permit his mind to work clearly during the forthcoming examination. In hypnosis I suggested to him that not only would he want to take the examination but he would also want to get at the basis of his fear so that in the future, if a similar challenge came along, he would be able to handle it. I suggested that his dreams would become more meaningful to him and that he would remember them so that we could explore them together. My purpose was to probe beyond the manifest screen of his symptoms into zones of basic needs and conflicts that might help us to understand what made him behave the way he did.

During the next sessions the main cause of his problem became more clear. The father was a self-made man who had advanced to a position of power in his community. He had come from a lower-status group, fighting his way up, and his ambition for his son in turn was great. If he could achieve his own success without money, he insisted, he expected his son to do better, since he would not have to spend precious time earning a living. Under these circumstances, he expected his boy to attain great distinction, perhaps even becoming governor of the state. These lofty aims, repeated over and over with dramatic emphasis, imposed obligations on the boy that he was unable to meet. When he brought home his marks from school, they were never considered good enough, and the father would confront him with variations on the following theme: "When I was eight years of age, I had to support myself selling newpapers. I fought my way up, and I don't want my son to have to go through what I was forced to face."

What the father failed to realize was that personal success is often related to a situation of deprivation. His son, not having experienced the same hardships, could not react in the same way. He might have done better if he too had to struggle for his education. But he had no motivation, since life had been made too easy for him. At the same time, the standards that were set for him were so far above what he felt he could achieve that he was frightened even to try. In addition, he harbored a great deal of resentment against his father for making unreasonable demands on him. Part of his impulse to fail was to prove his father wrong. He could get back at him best not by succeeding but by failing. This punishing tactic took its toll in guilt feelings. But his dreams clearly indicated the extent of his resentment. His father told him he was a failure; his mother told him he was a failure; he told himself he was a failure; so he was going to prove he was a failure. Whenever he faced an examination, he panicked. He seemed to find the idea of success threatening. As the years went by, all those below him were promoted in their civil service jobs, while he continued to occupy a mediocre position. People would say to him: "My God, you've been here ten years, and Joe Doakes, who's been here only for three, has reached a higher position than you have." This, of course, would make him feel all the more defeated, more helpless, and more panicky when he was asked even to think about examinations.

When such strong defense mechanisms are so deeply entrenched, it is very difficult to achieve symptomatic improvement on more than a temporary level. Something must be done with the underlying attitudes toward the self and the feelings about authority. What I did in hypnosis was first to help the patient obtain an awareness of the underlying dynamics and their source in his upbringing. This involved more continuing analysis of his dreams and their interpretation. Once he was able to understand his problem, we began behavior techiques, desensitizing him to fantasies in hypnosis. These involved successive exposures to situations involving examinations. After this, we launched into "assertive training," a form of behavior therapy, which helped him to stand up to authority, to recognize his anger, and to express it when justified by existing circumstances.

The patient improved rapidly and was able to take his first and subsequent examinations without difficulty. Not only did he advance his job, but his total adjustment was improved.

Whenever possible, an exploration of the meaning of symptoms in order to determine their dynamic significance is helpful. Long-term treatment may not be necessary, but a knowledge of the underlying mechanisms can help guide the patient beyond the immediate benefits of symptom relief. In some cases, all that is necessary is a relatively short-term form of treatment directed at symptom control. Results are excellent with people who have an essentially good personality structure, especially when the problems for which help is sought are of relatively recent origin. Should these brief measures not bring about the desired results, one may then go on to more extensive exploratory techniques which, as in the case above, may be combined with behavioral approaches.

11

The Recovery of Buried Memories

Once upon a time there was a theory that a neurotic person could be cured *solely* by the process of dredging up the buried memories of his past and by liberating his unconscious through insight. This alone would free trapped emotions that had been converted into symptoms. The only thing wrong with the theory was that it did not work. The most sparkling discoveries of the past succeeded only in adding more bulk to the individual's case history. Despite this exercise in futility, there are still some therapists who pursue the practice of burrowing into the unconscious with the hope that nothing more will be needed to open the doors to health. This is not to imply that a search for causes is irrational as an aspect of treatment. It sometimes can be very productive.

But instead of helping this search, the patient usually seems to block it by throwing up barricades of resistance to uncovering the sources of his trouble or, having uncovered them, refusing to use his insight toward changing himself. The therapist is almost entirely occupied in dealing with defensive maneuvers, for his patient seems to be working against himself in spite of his protests that he wants to get well. To manage such resistance requires a good deal of work and tolerance, and both may prove unsuccessful. It is at this point that the therapist may try hypnosis to cut through the resistance.

Hypnosis may prove itself to be singularly successful in overcoming resistance, exposing segments of the person's inner life that are deeply buried within him and which have hitherto evaded detection. And in rare instances this exposure of memories and experiences, as well as the related emotions, will result in the relief of a symptom. In my own work I have been able to remove isolated amnesias, motor paralysis, blindness, and anesthesias through the hypnotic revival of some earlier experience that resulted in these hysterical symptoms. This is what Freud did in his original work at the turn of the cntury, which resulted in his pioneer psychoanalytical discoveries.

A woman in her early fifties, who had developed a peculiar speech disorder that was very embarrassing to her and her family, was referred to me. As the woman talked, she would suck in air, producing a whining intonation and distoring her speech to the extent that it was scarcely comprehensible. This had been going on for more than five years. Two years of psychoanalytic therapy had had no effect on her symptom, and in desperation she had had twelve shock treatments, a course of intravenous "truth serum" (narcosynthesis), and then a period of supportive psychotherapy. All these efforts resulted in failure. At the initial interview with me she felt quite hopeless about her condition and confided that she was undergoing further therapy only at the insistence of her family.

During the induction process in the first attempt at hypnosis, she suddenly recalled a painful memory that involved conflicting emotions. She burst into hysterical crying, lamenting the death of a sister who had died immediately prior to the development of her speech difficulty. The violence of her lamentations can scarcely be described. As she explosively protested her bereavement, her speech became more and more clear. She had never, she confided, been able to cry before, because she did not want people to know how she felt. The sucking in of air and her inability to talk distinctly apparently were hysterical efforts to conceal her true feelings, which were a fusion of love for her sister, rage at being abandoned, and guilt for death wishes that she had always had toward her sibling. She had felt she must not show anybody how she felt. Her peculiar speech difficulty was the result of this denial need. With relatively short-term therapy, she was brought to an awareness of this problem. Unfortunately, she stopped treatments as soon as her speech returned to normal, which prevented her from working more intensively on the sources of her emotional difficulty.

Such immediate developments are rarely accompanied by real personality change. Usually by the time the patient has come to therapy his traumatic experiences have been structuralized in his personality, and the dramatic discoveries of the past serve merely to give information that has little or no effect on the patient's relationships with others.

One patient was referred to me because of persistent sleepwalking episodes, during which she would lock herself in a closet. In the morning she would be discovered there, asleep, by her husband, who was infuriated by her behavior and particularly by her inability to explain it. Hypnosis revealed that as a child she had locked herself in closets when she became angry at her mother, enjoying the hectic search for her. It was apparent to me that whenever she was angry at her husband, she was tempted to repeat this regressive, revengeful pattern in her sleep. The discovery of the roots of her symptom eliminated the sleepwalking but did not in the least influence her infantile dependency-hostility attitudes toward her husband.

There are still some practitioners who believe that the sole purpose of all therapy is to probe the secrets behind every illness through hypnosis, without connecting them in a constructive way to later behavior. After their subjects have been put into a trance, they proceed to cross-examine them, requesting that they signal by raising a designated finger when they have arrived at answers to pointed questions. The subjects are asked to return to the first glimmerings of a symptom and to relate the circumstances that originally brought it about. A search is conducted for the presence of similar symptoms in the past life as far back as childhood. Such approaches to psychotherapy may, of course, be challenged. Freud used and then abandoned them years ago. But the fact that the rationale behind these tactics may be wrong does not mean that the subject will not sometimes benefit from the activity of verbalizing fantasies and imaginings.

In my opinion, the successes of Scientology, Dianetics, and Primal Scream Therapy are the result of a cathartic release of emotion. The validity of the vehement material that is liberated must always be questioned, since fantasies are more rampant in hypnosis than in waking life.

I once had a patient who revealed in a trance the "cause" of her wry neck (torticollis). This condition had persisted for two years and defied the concerted efforts of internists, neurologists, and psychiatrists to cure it. When I asked her during hypnosis whether she had any notion of the cause of her sympton, she excitedly described a previous existence as a member of a royal family. She had been hanged in a public square by revolutionary rabble. Her wailing laments and fierce resentment seemed genuine enough, and after her exhausting account, she lapsed into a peaceful sleep from which she aroused herself with her head in a straight position. I did not discourage her by deflating her theory. Instead, we explored her story as we would a dream that was filled with significant symbols.

What she was telling me in a dramatic way was that she felt like an exploited, humiliated, and victimized member of her family. As the youngest child, she had been neglected by busy parents and tortured by an older sister, who resented her and often beat her on the neck. The present symptom of torticollis symbolized her need to "look away," and to deny her anger at her husband who was having an affair with a more aggressive and beautiful female. It was a significant symptom, a concrete token of her present humiliation and of having been "beaten on the neck" as a child.

The point I want to exphasize is that human problems can be quite complex and that while one may occasionally strike causative "pay dirt" directly with a hypnotic probe, it is necessary in most cases to take with a grain of salt the immediate trance outpourings, which often turn out to be nothing more than "fools' gold." This does not mean that the patient may not feel better as a result of his false revelations. The very fact that he has an opportunity to spill out his fantasies without restraint and to conjecture on the source of his difficulty in the presence of a kindly, nonpunitive authority may suffice to alleviate his symptoms. Even the labeling of an alarming symptom with a reasonable tag often reduces tension and diverts the individual from focusing on his troubles, thereby benefiting constructive adjustment. In this way, "insights"—true or spurious—can operate for the benefit of the sufferer.

On the other hand, there are instances when previous traumatic experiences have been so upsetting that they have been relegated to the oblivion of the unconscious. Yet these buried memories stir up constant distress in the here and now. Sometimes the trouble is in the form of headaches or nightmares, symptoms seen in war neuroses. In these cases the soldier or panicked civilian tries to bury the event of near death by acting as if it never occurred. Other symptoms, some very peculiar, are defenses to keep a memory bottled up when the person is unable to bring it to the surface. Here hypnosis may have a remarkable effect.

On a few occasions I have witnessed the permanent disappearance of symptoms following hypnotic recall of repressed memories and experiences. One patient came to therapy because of a doorslamming compulsion. He had a need to make certain that all doors through which he passed were closed, and to his great annoyance he had to return several times to make sure that they were not open. Regression and reorientation to a five-year level revealed an experience that apparently was the basis for this symptom. Shortly after the patient's fifth birthday, his younger brother smashed a toy that he especially treasured. He was filled with a rage so intense that it caused him to tremble. Instead of attacking his brother, however, he turned around and fled to his room, slamming the door shut as if to separate himself from his sibling. Thereafter, whenever he felt hostile toward his brother, he found himself slamming doors, an act that soon became compulsive, as though it served to neutralize his hostility. The patient's recitation of the original experience was accompanied by strong emotional feelings, by anger, weeping, and pounding his fists on the desk. He was asked to remember the original experience when he awakened. The door-slamming compulsion vanished from that day on.

In another case, a woman had developed a peculiar mannerism to which she resigned herself with a martyred calm. She would touch with her right fingers the outer surface of the first left finger, then the second, third, and the fourth fingers, repeating this motion again and again. During hypnosis it was possible for her to understand how the mannerism had developed and why it persisted. When she was fourteen years old, a girl friend told her the story of an Italian wedding at which an English priest had officiated. During the ceremony it was of course necessary for the bridegroom to put a wedding ring on the finger of the bride. However, both the bride and groom, because they could speak no English, were unable to understand what the priest had meant by the word "ring." Finally, in order to indicate the meaning, the priest brought the thumb and first finger of his right hand together and inserted in this circle the first finger of his left hand, working the imaginary ring up and down the finger. The bride blushed, looked at the ground, and muttered as if in anticipation: "Tonight, tonight."

The point of the story was the confusion of the priest's gesture with the idea of sexual intercourse. The movement of the patient's right hand across the fingers of her left hand signified a desire simultaneously for marriage and for sexual relations. Hypnotic regression furthermore revealed that as a child she had masturbated by use of the first finger of her left hand. A facial disfigurement, as well as an extremely puritanical upbringing, had helped to convince her that she could never marry, and her mannerism served as a substitutive mode of sexual gratification.

How hypnosis can recover the memory of a repressed traumatic experience is illustrated by the case of a man of forty-eight who came to me for therapy to relieve anxiety, and compulsive and psychosomatic symptoms. Although he was sexually potent, he had never been able to have successful sexual relations with his wife during the many years of his marriage. Disturbed by this fact, he was certain it was responsible for many of his symptoms.

During his first session the patient described some of his compulsive symptoms to me. He told of how, when driving a car at a high speed, he would feel the urge to close his eyes and see how far he could count. Another irrational impulse to count would occur when he was gargling hot salt water for a sore throat. He would find himself counting on his fingers while he gargled, obsessively repeating the ritual. Whenever he wrote a check, he would ask for it back after handing it in, pretending he wanted to make sure it had the correct date on it. Actually, he felt he had to check the amount again. If he had written a check for fifteen dollars, he would be afraid that he had put down fifteen hundred dollars, even though he knew he had not. But if he could not look at it again, he became very upset.

His principal complaints were tension, depression, dizziness, dyspepsia, and insomnia. He often took sedatives to get to sleep at night, but he felt tired all the time. Any action was an effort for him; he had to push himself to achieve even moderate success in his business.

When I asked him what he felt was the cause of all these symptoms, the patient admitted that his attitude toward sexual intercourse—which he felt was somehow wrong—was responsible. He quoted a line from a Kipling poem, "The Lady," which summed up his feelings about sex: "I wouldn't do such because I liked her too much."

The patient felt that there was much in his background to account for these feelings. His mother and father had been unhappily married. His mother suspected that his father was involved with other women, and she was very jealous. She would become hysterical on occasion, screaming accusations at the father, and waking up the patient and his sister in the middle of the night. When the boy became aware at the age of fourteen or fifteen of the nature of these suspicions, he found it hard to believe that they were true, and was never convinced of their validity. He did not relate well to his father until he was fourteen or fifteen, but from that point on he became very attached to him. His father died under tragic circumstances when the patient was nineteen.

The patient had been very close to his nurse, who had looked after him for many years. But when the boy was around eleven, she left. The father's business was suffering, and they could no longer afford to keep her. The family moved into a hotel at this point, and the patient shared a room with his sister. He had profound amnesia about this period in his life and could remember very little about his sister at this time.

We then discussed his marriage. He had been nineteen and his wife eighteen when they were married. There had been a great deal of parental opposition because they were so young. Nevertheless, the patient, who was deeply in love with his fiancée, insisted that they go through with it. Up until the time of his marriage, he had had only one sexual experience: he had gone to a house of prostitution with some other boys when he was sixteen, had been impotent during the experience, and had found the entire affair upsetting and disgusting.

The patient had always felt that he must suppress any feelings of sexual desire for his fiancée, and he suffered guilt when he thought of her erotically. On their honeymoon he was unable to have intercourse with her. Although he became sexually aroused, he could not perform. In all the years that followed, he had been able to have intercourse with her only when he was half asleep, in a state of semiconsciousness, and scarcely aware of who she was. Although he was sure he could have sexual relations with other women, he could not be unfaithful to his wife or leave her. They had discussed the problem, agreeing that their marriage was a happy one, except for their sexual relationship. Although the patient resisted the idea, he said that his wife did want to have sex with him. The problem was that he could not approach her at this level.

I then suggested to the patient that he undergo hypnosis in order to probe the reasons for his sexual problems with his wife. I felt there was a possibility that he was suppressing significant memories of past experiences and that hypnosis would be the best means of remembering them. During the next few sessions he was trained to achieve a deep trance, and we began to work on his dreams.

He had had a repetitive dream for many years, in which someone came toward him in a threatening way. He would try to shoot this person with a gun, but there was always something wrong with it, and it would never go off. Shortly after we had started hypnosis, he had a spontaneous dream, which he related to me. An elephant was chasing him. It came out of a building "like a mirage" and chased him through what appeared to be the backyards of the streets of Manhattan. As he was running, the patient saw a house that he felt he must run through in order to come out on Seventieth or Seventy-first Street. He ran in the back door. Inside, there was a man who was very pleasant to him and introduced him to his daughters. One was lying in bed, and he talked to her for a while. She was a young woman, and he felt attracted to her sexually. After a while, the girls suggested that they all play bridge. The patient liked the idea, but when he realized he would have to call his wife to tell her where he was, he felt sure she would not believe him. At that point, his dream ended.

The patient and I then began to explore possible interpretations of the dream. He explained that as a small boy he had called his father "Elly," which was short for elephant, because his father had been a large, stout man. But he could not explain why he felt the elephant was threatening him. I pointed out that an elephant is associated with a powerful figure and his father might have appeared to him very sinister despite his love for him. Another important aspect of the dream was the backyards and back doors figured prominently in it. Also, the elephant was pursing the patient from the rear. This suggested that the patient feared an attack from someone, possibly—as the symbols suggested—a homosexual attack. The fear of homosexual attack is often countered with a need to protect oneself. The patient's earlier dreams suggested this compulsion, particularly since his means of protection was a gun, which could represent the penis, or virility. Since the gun would never work in the dream, there seemed to be a feeling that his virility was defective.

Another important aspect of the patient's dream was that he wanted to go into the house near Seventy-first Street. Significantly, my office at that time was on Seventy-first Street. The man in the dream let him come in and was kind to him, and the patient was attracted to the man's daughter. The man in the dream obviously was I, and the fact that the daughter was sexually attractive to the patient suggested the fact that in coming to me he hoped to be able to cure his problem. Yet implicit in the dream was the fact that he had to get permission to have sexual relations with someone's daughter. This tied in with the patient's feelings toward his wife, with whom he had always had a relationship more like that of a sister and daughter than a wife. It also suggested that he might be repressing traumatic memories about his relationship with his sister.

In subsequent trances the patient was regressed to the period of his boyhood when he was living in the hotel and sharing a room with his sister. It was important, I felt, that he recapture the feelings and sensations he had at that time, which might revive what he had forgotten. Although, at first, the patient could recall upsetting episodes with his parents, he could not envision his sister in his memories. Apparently his repudiation of her was too strong to be easily overcome. At one session I suggested to the patient during a deep trance that he would experience an image of his sister the next day. I stressed that it was important that he remember his relationship with her to see if there were any residual fears and anxieties that prevented him from becoming a stronger and healthier person. At the next session the patient revealed that surprisingly he had been able to remember his sister during her childhood. He had had a glimpse of her in her nightgown. But after this revelation he entered a state of resistance that lasted for a number of days. It ended only with a dream that he described in a later session. "I remember being in a hotel room with this girl. I looked out of the window, and there was an awful storm coming up. Then I had sexual intercourse with her. I was sitting here on the edge of the bed, and I was partially undressed, and I had an erection, and all of a sudden the door opened, and several elderly women came in. One looked at me and uttered the most piercing scream. It was a horrifying scream; it horrified me. It was as though she had seen someone murdering somebody, or trying to murder somebody."

The patient insisted that the girl resembled a secretary who had worked for him years before. But he could not identify the woman who had caught him. At this point, I induced hypnosis and suggested that he try to remember more clearly the incidents of his dream. I speculated there was the possibility that they were related to events that had actually happened in the past. Then I told him that I was going to help him remember a significant word in a particular way. Every time I counted to five, I said, he would give me a letter in the word we were looking for. The letters he named were N, E, A, J, N, E, which when put in order spelled Jeanne. This was the name of the patient's mother. Next, I put a pencil in the patient's hand and told him that when he awoke from the trance, his hand would automatically move as if pushed by an outside force. I asked him not to pay attention to what his hand was writing. Upon awakening, the patient wrote "mtherscrmd," a condensation of "mother screamed."

A memory that the patient recalled in the next session involved an actual experience of sexual play with his sister, during which he had been interrupted and frightened by his mother. There is little question that he identified his wife with his sister and that his inability to consummate the sexual act with her masked an incestuous wish and fear. This was associated with guilt feelings and fear of punishment. In a dramatic way, hypnosis and automatic writing had helped this patient to bring to consciousness a painful memory that he had long repressed, which released his potency. At long last he was able to relate sexually to his wife.

A legitmate question may be raised concerning the permanent effect on the patient of recall of forgotten memories. The blotting from awareness of a traumatic incident or memory, as with war experiences or traumatic neuroses or in certain hysterical conditions, can create a number of symptoms designed to protect the individual from the implications of the traumatic event and the emotions associated with it. If the event is remembered and associated emotions are released, the symptoms that have functioned to reinforce repression usually disappear. This can happen in amnesia and in certain psychosomatic or phobic conditions. Apart from this effect the recall of memories does not seem to have any permanent influence. Nevertheless, the experience of recall may give the patient a motivation to inquire further into his interpersonal patterns and difficulties. If he can be convinced that his problems stem from hurtful past experiences, that present-day reality is constantly being influenced by what has gone before, that many of his existing concepts result from misinterpretations and fantasies of bygone days, and that his mind is a repository of anxieties rooted in past experiences, he may develop the motivation to change his attitudes toward life and people. The recovery of traumatic memories thus serves as a means of creating an incentive for change.

12

When Is Hypnosis Not Effective?

A young doctor asked me to hynotize him so that he could pass his state board examinations. He had recently completed an internship in a Midwest hospital, and had returned to New York to establish a practice that was being set up with the financial help of his parents. By scrimping and scraping, they had put their son through medical school, had supported him during his internship, and now they were about to realize their ambition of having him become a successful physician practicing near home.

Although he knew he had to take his state boards, he could find no time to study for them while interning, and, after leaving the hospital, he discovered that whenever he opened a book, his mind went blank. As time passed, he became more and more panicky, and when the examinations were only several days away, he became so agitated that he could scarely contain himself. He begged me to hypnotize him and remove by suggestion his mental block. He was quite certain that powerful pressures put upon him while he was in a trance would enable him to remember his medical studies and complete his examinations successfully.

Under ordinary circumstances, I would have refused to take

this assignment, but because he was so disturbed and there was so little time, I consented to try to put him in a suitable frame of mind for the examination. He co-operated eagerly and soon entered a deep trance, during which I regressed him to the period when he was at medical school.He recalled many details of his studies, of which he had only a faint recollection in the waking state. For instance, he was brought back to his anatomic dissection laboratory, and he painstakingly went through the motions of dissecting the radial nerve, explaining its course and distribution. In a similar way, he recalled many details of his other studies. I suggested that when he took his examination, he would recall everything he needed to know. On the evening before, he would retire early and sleep soundly during the night. He would awaken refreshed, with a clear mind and with enough energy and self-confidence to apply himself adroitly to the task of passing his examination.

On the evening before the examination, he telephoned me and asked if it might not be advisable for him to spend the night at a hotel instead of at his parents' house. He would be able to sleep better there, he said, and thus be in a better frame of mind. I agreed that this was probably advisable.

In the late afternoon of the next day, I received another telephone call from him, and he informed me in a calm and even droll manner that never before had he slept so soundly. As a matter of fact, he had just got up, having slept through the examination. There was no point now, he insisted, in taking the remainder of the tests. He volunteered to come to my office to talk things over.

When he arrived, he seemed to be in excellent spirits. There were no signs of tension or anxiety, and he even adopted a humorous attitude toward the incident. He considered it peculiar, however, that he had slept so long, since he rarely spent more than eight or nine hours in bed. He confided that there was no reason now why he could not go back west to visit a young lady in whom he had become interested while interning. His parents had opposed his marrying the girl, and because he felt he owed them a debt, he had given up his plan to settle in her home town.

He was obviously torn between love for the girl and loyalty to his parents, and his inability to study seemed a result of his conflict. He was unable to yield to his parents' wishes, and yet he did not want to incur their disapproval or rebuke. His inability to concentrate was a symptom of his repressed desire to go against his parents' plans to have him practice in New York. Guilt feelings, however, created anxiety and caused him to seek a desperate measure in hypnosis in order to break down this inhibition. Apparently, his guilt was so strong that hypnosis was successful. When he realized during the trance that he might be able to remember enough to pass the examination, his conflict again became dominant and eventually triumphed over my suggestions. His prolonged sleep was a means of escaping the possibility of becoming licensed in New York. He had obtained implicit permission from me to oversleep when I agreed to his plan to spend the night at a hotel. When these facts were brought to his attention, he laughed heartily and declared that he would deceive himself no longer. He was going to tell his parents they had no claim on him. He would repay them as soon as he was financially able to do so.

Many years have gone by since this incident, and he has established himself in practice in the Midwest. He is happily married to the young woman he went back to, and the situation with his parents resolved itself more or less successfully.

I cite this case as an example of how hypnosis indiscriminately applied can fail to achieve certain goals. It is essential for the therapist to understand what motivations lie behind the patient's desire for hypnotherapy. These may be so distorted that they discourage satisfactory results.

For instance, a young man came to me for hypnosis with a list of qualities he wanted to have injected into his personality. The first was that he would be masterful at all times, especially with women; the second, that he would always think clearly and speak effectively in a low, modulated tone; the third, that he would go to bed at 1:00 A.M. and wake up at 7:00 A.M. fully refreshed. His fourth request was that hypnosis give him the ability to be a success in life in spite of all obstacles. He had failed to gain these objectives after extended psychoanalysis, but he felt sure that hypnosis could succeed where psychoanalysis had failed. Many people have the misconception that hypnosis can correct defects and create aptitudes in a miraculous way. A number of persons have visited me for these purposes, including a seventy-five-year-old man who had become impotent, and a six-year-old mentally defective child who had never learned to talk. His mother had heard from her family physician that a cure was possible if hypnosis could be induced.

Failures in hypnosis can be divided into two types: those that involve failure of induction and those that involve failure to achieve a set therapeutic goal.

If the therapist has a good technique, induction failures are rare. But they do occur, usually because of the patient's fear of submission. In instances where there is terror of interpersonal relationships, and particularly a fear of yielding to an authority who is conceived of as destructive or dangerous, resistance that prevents the attainment of a hypnotic state may develop. The personality of the hypnotist and his experience are often determining factors in such cases. Resistance to induction can be successfully circumvented by adroit and perceptive handling.

One patient I treated demonstrated his ambivalence toward hypnosis by fighting treatment, while at the same time desiring it. He had asked to be hypnotized in order to learn mow to control his homosexual drives. During the process of induction, he clenched his teeth and his fists and almost physically tried to fight off sleep suggestions. As hypnosis proceeded, he panted violently, arose precipitously from his chair and cried, "I can't, I can't let myself go!" He then told me that he had experienced an orgasm and that he seemed to want to yield himself to a higher power, who would be able to possess him completely. He had incorporated hypnosis into the framework of his neurosis and had responded to the suggestions that I gave him as if I were virtually a lover whom he could not resist. Desiring both to yield and to resist suggestions, he experienced panic when he realized he was entering a trance state. When motivation of this kind is present, it is essential to work with it on a waking level so that the patient can accept therapy on a different, more rational basis. Should he refuse to do so, hypnotherapy may merely exaggerate rather than help his problem.

A proper motivation to be hypnotized is advantageous in facilitating induction. This motivation seems to be common, but sometimes, especially when a subject has severe emotional problems, it may not be present. However, an unconscious motivation to be hypnotizable may be stronger than the conscious desire to resist hypnosis. There are a number of persons who fight against entering a trance state, yet are unable to stay awake once the induction process has begun.

Failures in induction may be reduced to a minimum when the therapist recognizes the factors causing the patient's resistance. If, by his manner and attitude, he can also inspire trust, if he can clear up the patient's misconceptions about hypnosis, if he can mobilize the patient's healthy impulses to get well in order to realize certain ambitions and objectives, it may be possible to overcome the fear of hypnosis. For instance, when a patient spontaneously admits that he has a fear of yielding his independence, the therapist may assure him that no suggestions will be given without first gaining his consent. By openly expressing his feelings, the patient may feel more susceptible to trance induction. The hypnotic state may then be conducted in such a way that he vetoes or accepts the suggestions given to him in accordance with his own free will. The ability to modify the hypnotic technique to coincide with the patient's personality needs calls for an infinite amount of patience and ingenuity.

Even when hypnosis is induced successfully, therapeutic failures can occur for precisely the same reasons that they do in other kinds of psychotherapy. The most frequent reason for failure is a mistaken idea about the purpose of hypnosis. Some neurotic persons are particularly attracted to the hypnotic method because they want a magical formula and believe hypnosis offers a means of controlling themselves as well as the universe.

In some instances a distorted motivation of this sort, which is symbolically satisfied in hypnosis, may put an end to certain disturbing symptoms for a while at least. To illustrate, a man came to see me in order to learn self-hypnosis for the purpose of inducing skin anesthesia. He rationalized this peculiar request by saying that if he were seriously injured in an automobile accident many miles from town, self-induced anesthesia would prevent an awareness of pain. It seemed obvious that his desire for hypnosis concealed a much deeper motive, of which he was probably not entirely aware.

Before inducing hypnosis, I suggested that we discuss any

problems he might have. He refused to do so, contending that since his sole interest was to learn self-hypnosis, there was no reason for going into his various difficulties, one of which was a problem with his fiancée. As a matter of fact, he confided, he had already gone through a period of psychotherapy with a qualified psychiatrist and was sure he needed no further help.

Hypnosis was easily induced, and the patient rapidly learned the technique of self-hypnosis. In the course of training, through the medium of dream induction and other hypnoanalytic techniques, I hypothesized what fired his request for self-hypnosis. As a result of painful childhood experiences, the patient had developed a personality structure that used detachment as a primary defense. He had been able to manage his life successfully by maintaining a certain distance from people. His aloofness had kept him from becoming intimately involved with anyone. Outwardly he seemed self-contained and self-confident, capable of congenial relationships. But when a friendship began to develop, he became so fault-finding, demanding, and hostile that he had to end the relationship. A few months before he came to me, he had become seriously involved with a young woman, and for the first time in his life he had begun to experience the emotions of love, which disturbed him. He wanted to escape his feelings, but no matter what he did, his closeness to the young woman continued to stimulate feelings that he felt he could not handle. In desperation he conceived of a plan whereby he might possibly be able to function if he could get himself to a point where he could control and deaden physical sensation. Then he might perhaps be able to master his emotions. If he could manage this, his relationship with the young woman could continue without untoward reactions to her presence. These deliberations were not completely conscious. They were symbolically represented by his desire to control skin sensations and deaden them through will power reinforced by self-hypnosis. He had rationalized his wish to abnegate all feeling by convincing himself that his sole desire was to learn how to induce anesthesia in himself. I felt reasonably certain my theory was correct.

I presented these ideas to the patient during a trance and told him that he might not be able to accept them in the waking state.

However, I added, when he felt sufficiently strong within himself to tackle the deeper problems of his relationship with people and his need for detachment, he would be able to reach a point where he could rid himself of the many fears that prevented him from living realistically and productively.

This talk seemed to have little effect, since the patient gave no indication of remembering it. He seemed satisfied to have mastered the technique of hand anesthesia, and he practiced inducing anesthesia over various parts of his body. After five sessions, he said he had gained all he wanted from hypnosis.

Several months later he telephoned me. Self-hypnosis, he said, had made a new man out of him, and he no longer felt upset about his fiancée. However, it had suddenly occurred to him that his reason for wanting to learn self-hypnosis had been as much to control his feelings as his physical sensations. It was apparent from his conversation that the interpretations I made during the trance had been retained. He realized that he needed further help and shortly thereafter started psychotherapy with me.

Another reason for therapeutic failure with hypnosis is that some persons seek a rapid means of cure and are impatient with the prolonged time period required by traditional psychotherapies. Although it is true that hypnosis can often shorten the therapeutic procedure, it cannot immediately destroy habit patterns of an obdurate nature. A patient must work through his inner conflicts and external troubles, which may take time. His impatience to overcome his neurosis is quite understandable. However, when the complete rehabilitation of the individual in his functional relationships to life and to people is our aim, we cannot rapidly accomplish this objective. The patient must be helped to understand that therapy for reconstructive purposes will require time. If this is not made clear to him, he is apt to expect the impossible from hypnosis. And with the failure of his expectations, he may blame himself, adopting a completely hopeless attitude toward his illness. It is essential to understand that a few sessions of hypnosis cannot revolutionize all aspects of the personality. A patient does not acquire self-confidence and assertiveness overnight. He may begin to understand in therapy that he needs to develop these qualities, but their realization in the experience of everyday life may require a considerable period of time.

In order to better understand the reasons for therapeutic failure, it is necessary to define what we mean by therapeutic success. Success in therapy means that we have achieved a certain determined goal. As a matter of fact, therapeutic failures, as well as therapeutic successes, can be described only in the context of an explicit therapeutic goal. Once we have formulated a goal, we can determine whether we have achieved the desired results; then we are able to classify our effort as either a success or a failure. We may decide that because of inadequate time, or inadequate motivation, or for other practical reasons, we should reach for a limited goal, for instance, the removal of a disabling symptom. We may succeed in this goal with short-term psychotherapy. From the standpoint of our stated goal, then, we would say that our therapy is successful. However, we must admit that we have not markedly changed the personality structure of the patient, or altered his basic neurotic patterns. From another point of view, then, we would consider our therapy incomplete.

In the case of a neurotic patient who comes to therapy complaining of an inability to sleep and wants to be cured of his insomnia, we may be able to relieve or cure this isolated complaint through the medium of suggestion during the trance. However, because the neurotic structure itself is not touched, he may continue to suffer from habitual neurotic manifestations. Can we then rightfully speak of the cure of the patient's insomnia as a therapeutic success? If our goal has been merely to treat the symptom of insomnia, we may say that we have treated him successfully. However, if our goal is to reorganize his defenses and interpersonal relationships, we must admit that our effort should be classified as a failure. This does not invalidate the importance of what we have accomplished in treatment.

Another example may clarify this point. A patient was sent to me some years ago for hypnotherapy in order to recapture memories that he had been unable to bring to the surface in several years of psychotherapy. The therapist believed that through regression it would be possible to return the patient to a period in his life that he could not remember. Accordingly he would be able to recall and reenact experiences that might help to explain his homosexuality. When I saw the patient, it was apparent to me that he was markedly disabled in his relationships with people. He had been seeking a means of circumventing his anxiety and, through reading, became convinced that if he could get to a secret in his past, to some traumatic injury that had been inflicted upon him, it would explain and remove his fear of people, particularly of women. It was apparent to me that during his prolonged period of psychotherapy he had successfully evaded a close relationship with his psychiatrist and had spent most of his time attempting to single out elements in his past history that seemed to account for his difficulty. He had become progressively more and more frustrated as he discovered that memories of early difficulties had very little ameliorative effect upon his anxiety and interpersonal difficulties. He was convinced, thus, that all the early incidents he remembered were merely "cover memories," and that deeply imbedded in his unconscious was a memory so traumatic and devastating that it had successfully evaded all attempts to unearth it. He therefore wanted help in hypnosis in order to get to these basic hidden memories. Because the analyst petitioned me to try hypnosis, I consented to attempt it experimentally.

It was possible to induce a fairly deep trance, and through the medium of automatic writing in the regressed state the patient was able to recall an experience in which he had witnessed his parents having sexual relations. He relived the frightening experience of seeing for the first time the female genital organ, which he thought was mutilated. This incident had aroused deep fears of castration and a horror of observing female genital organs, since they suggested to him that he too might become castrated.

The recapturing of his early traumatic event and the emotions it inspired in him exhilarated him temporarily. But it did not alter in the least the customary patterns in his character or his fear of women. Obviously this entire recollection may have been fantasy. But this did not invalidate his reaction, which was as important as to a true past experience.

Stubbornly, he insisted that what he had recaptured was valid but that there was probably something even deeper than this, which, if discovered, would immediately remove his anxiety. In this patient's case, the goal of recapturing early memories had succeeded, but we had failed to produce any change in his neurotic behavior. From a therapeutic standpoint, his treatment would be considered a failure, even though this was not the fault of hypnosis. To consider it a success would be to subscribe to the generally mistaken notion that recapture of early traumatic memories can bring relief to a character disorder.

Another example of what I would consider a therapeutic failure is the case of an unusually disturbed psychopathic personality whom I treated. He had gotten into innumerable conflicts with the law as a result of episodic bouts of intoxication during which he signed worthless checks. His main reason for coming to me was to have something done in order to stop himself from signing blank checks when drunk.

Although he professed a desire for a better life, it soon became obvious that he did not want to abandon his disturbed and irresponsible ways of living, that he wanted only to avoid serious problems with the authorities after breaking the law. Therefore, therapy was begun with the object of establishing a conditioned reflex that would prevent him from passing bad checks. But I had another objective: trying to bring the patient to a gradual realization of his own destructiveness. This would make it possible for him to want therapy on a deeper level. During a somnambulistic trance, a conditioned reflex was set up: when he started to sign a worthless check, a spastic paralysis prevented him from doing so. This reflex was successful and with reinforcement sessions the patient found that he was not able to sign check, even though drunk. In later sessions, attempts were made to bring the patient to a better understanding of his neurotic problems and acting-out tendencies. This failed probably because enough motivation for change could not be brought about. The patient was inhibited in his attempts to sign worthless checks, but he continued to engage in bouts of drinking, which he rationalized with extreme ingenuity.

The conditioned reflex was successful for a time. Then, after several months, reports came to me that he had passed several more worthless checks. Upon questioning under hypnosis, the patient confessed that he had practiced signing his name with his left hand when he discovered that he was unable to use his right. A conditioning process then was set up which prevented him from signing checks with either hand. However, he soon found a way of circumventing this by getting one of his friend to forge his name. Therapy was then judged to be a complete failure. This case illustrates the fact that working with a patient in whom the motivation for therapy is inadequate is precarious, to say the least.

In attempting to define an adequate goal in therapy, it must be taken into account that what we strive for as an ideal is the complete rehabilitation of the person in his relationship to life. We seek to bring him to a point where he can derive pleasures from the creature comforts: food, sex, work, and relaxation. The capacity to satisfy these drives in conformity with prevailing mores is an important objective. So, too, is a realistic expectation of fulfilling needs in light of the existing resources and environmental opportunities. The patient must achieve a capacity for harmonious relationship with other people. He must have a balanced view of authority, one that lacks fear or rage, and, when necessary, be capable of assuming leadership himself. He must develop the ability to adapt to stress and frustration without resorting to childish forms of defense or fantasy. This involves the ability to withstand a certain amount of deprivation without anxiety, for example, when it is necessary to the welfare of a group or when the results of impulse fulfillment would cause inordinate pain. There must be a healthy regard for the self. This involves a capacity to face the past and to isolate anxieties related to childhood experiences from the present. Furthermore, there must be a realization of limitations and the ability to fulfill oneself within those bounds. Another objective is self-tolerance. Rarely does any one person achieve this fulfillment, for these goals are extremely ambitious. In many cases this balance cannot be attained for a number of reasons.

A principal cause of failure is that many people do not have a true sense of the extent of their difficulties. As a consequence, they suffer from inadequate relationships to life and to other people. Often they are unwilling to work with the type of technique that would make it possible for them to consummate worthwhile goals. Close relationships cause such intense anxiety that they are incapable of using their available strengths to work out an adequate solution to their difficulties. Sometimes a person derives many secondary gains from his neurosis that more than compensate for the anxiety associated with their fulfillment. Another cause of failure can be the mishandling of the therapeutic session itself. A therapist can asssume too authoritarian an approach, setting values for the patient, and then coercing or persuading him to adopt these values. While an anthoritarian manner has certain advantages, particularly in brief (short-term) psychotherapy, where partial goals are to be achieved, it can be a handicap when we seek extensive reconstructive goals.

When a patient comes to therapy, he usually assumes that he merely has to present his problem and the therapist will either get rid of it for him or tell him how he can get well. This assumption harbors considerable disadvantage, since the uncritical and complete accepting of direction and suggestions from the therapist may block some development.

The traditional conduct of the hypnotic session lends itself to the authoritarian demands that some patients make on the therapist. When the patient comes to the therapist for hypnosis, he immediately adopts an attitude of passivity. He assumes that he will be put into a suggestible state, that directions will be given him, and that through some magic he will be able to function in ways that will bring him health or success. The very fact that suggestions are proffered and that patients enter into a relationship in which they are submissive immediately handicaps some individuals, particularly dependent people.

Seemingly, we are confronted with an insurmountable contradiction. It will be said that induction requires passivity and that the patient's susceptibility to suggestion resembles a child-parent relationship. How then is it possible for him to achieve the goal of complete rehabilitation when the hypnotist is the commanding authority?

These objections are valid. In my opinion, the individual does not have the best opportunity of liberating himself from authority or of achieving the greatest posscble change in his character structure when the hypnotic situation is constantly conducted in an authoritative manner. Self-growth and the ability to become an independent, assertive individual are most effectively achieved when the patient is given the opportunity of working out his problems through his own capacities and resources. The entire conduct of the hypnotic hour, therefore, must be modified to a point where the patient no longer puts himself into a completely passive state and expects from the omniscient hypnotist suggestions that will direct him toward mental health. Achievement of the ultimate goal in thereapy—extensive personality rehabilition—requires the patient to abandon the notion that he can depend exclusively on direction and suggestions from the therapist.

One way of doing this is by couching suggestions in such a manner that the patient feels that he is participating in the induction process. This prepares the patient to begin assuming the responsibility of participating in his own growth process. Gradually, as he learns the technique of entering the trance state, the direction for this is transferred to him. He is told that, upon giving himself a certain command, he will be able to enter a trance and give himself suggestions to achieve certain goals through his own efforts (self-hypnosis). Thus the patient soon discovers that he can apply valuable hypnotic techniques to himself. The realization that he has the capacity to act by himself and work out his own problems has an enhancing effect on ego growth and frees the patient from the feeling that he needs the help of a stronger person.

13

Can Hypnosis Be Dangerous?

The grisly Sharon Tate murders in 1969 focused attention on Charles Manson, described in the press as a "master hypnotist" who had cast a spell on his family of assassins.* Susan Atkins, one of the defendants, testified that Manson's dominance caused her and the other members of the group to lose control of their senses. Many people found this a reasonable explanation for a bloody incident that no sane person could possibly have perpetrated. Hypnosis was again implicated as a potentially dangerous implement that could seduce people into committing crimes.

Newspaper headlines frequently accent this possiblity:

SCHOOLGIRL, 15, STUCK IN HYPNOTIC TRANCE

HYPNOSIS: THE CURE THAT CAN BE DYNAMITE

HOW HYPNOTIC POWER CAN TRAP YOUR MIND

*On August 7, 1969, Sharon Tate, a film actress, and six friends who were visiting her at her home in Benedict Canyon, Los Angeles, were brutally murdered. Charles Manson, the 36-year-old leader of a hippie group living in the Los Angeles area, and three women co-defendants were brought to trial for the crime in June, 1970, found guilty, and sentenced to death.

WORK FOR HOURS TO FREE CO-ED OF HYPNOTIC TRANCE: TEACHER SUSPENDED

DID SHE KILL WHILE IN A TRANCE? POSSIBLE, M.D.'S SAY

HYPNOSIS: ITS TREMENDOUS POTENTIAL AS A WAR WEAPON IS REVEALED HERE FOR THE FIRST TIME

These captions and stories that follow are based on the theory that human beings are like puppets who can be manipulated by sinister hypnotic forces to execute acts of evil design. In a James Bond movie shocker based on a book by Ian Fleming, a number of beautiful women are indoctrinated under hypnosis in nefarious ways of undermining their governments. As a thrilling fantasy the movie has many merits. But as a factual account of what hypnosis is all about the idea is preposterous, to say the least.

More disturbing is the fact that from time to time ominous admonitions about hypnosis are issued by a few respected members of the medical profession. For example, a reputable Danish psychiatrist, P. J. Reiter, has reported the case of a schoolteacher who was hypnotically enjoined by a hypnotist to shoot himself in the arm and to engage in several criminal acts. He reported another case of a man who, during a trance, was persuaded by an unscrupulous hypnotist to rob a bank, in the course of which he killed two people.

Whether these aberrations were the result of hypnosis, however, is open to question. There are persons who are so obedient to authority that they will do whatever is asked of them, even though the acts are foreign to their nature. During war many men in combat, who have been brought up to love their fellow men, willingly engage in slaughter at the behest of society and expect to be decorated rather than punished.

Compliance with the rules and obligations of society is the norm and more or less to be expected. What is singular is that there are people who have an implicit and unswerving trust in authority, no matter how irrational. A hypnotic subject realizes that the hypnotist wants him to perform in extraordinary ways; yet he remains certain that the hypnotist would not expose him to danger. Under these circumstances he will play-act. This is not to say that a criminally inclined person will not use the hypnotic situation as a cover to act out his lawless tendencies, and that a criminally inclined operator may not expose his subjects to real danger. But one does not need hypnosis to persuade people to carry out antisocial acts. Nevertheless, we may suspect that when a criminal act is actually carried out, other factors besides hypnosis are involved.

In a well-known experiment conducted by the psychologist P. S. Young (and described in the book *Experimental Hypnosis,* edited by L. M. LeCron), eight deeply hypnotized subjects were asked to throw nitric acid at an assistant and also to grasp what appeared to be a poisonous snake. In the second experiment, seven of the eight subjects handled the snake readily. In the first, acid was unhesitatingly thrown at the assistant, who was protected by an invisible glass partition. In the waking state the same subjects resisted the identical suggestion. Similar experiments were performed with the same results by psychologists L. W. Rowland and W. Lyon. The results of these experiments would seem to implicate hypnosis as the determing cause for this behavior. However, when M. T. Orne, a psychiatrist who has worked extensively with hypnosis, and F. J. Evans, a colleague, employed a group of unhypnotizable subjects and asked them to pretend being hypnotized, they carried out these same suggested "dangerous" tasks without hesitation. Moreover, a number of persons were told that they were to act as a "control group," and in the normal waking state they almost too eagerly performed the experimental assignments. The mere fact that they were part of an "experiment" and knew the experimenter, whom they felt they could trust, induced them to behave the way they did. On the other hand, if casually selected strangers had been asked to follow these suggestions, they probably would have resisted. The setting of an experiment would have been absent, as well as trust in the experimenter.

I once tested the latter hypothesis on a hypnotized subject who was trained to enter the deepest somnambulistic trance states. I instructed him to open his eyes and remain fully hypnotized. Then I told him that I expected a visit from a doctor friend who was evil and whose vile activities threatened the security of every person in the United States. This doctor had perfected viruses with which he planned to exterminate a good proportion of the population. He had, I insisted, already killed a large number of people. It was best to get him out of the way before it was too late. I asked the subject if he would co-operate with me in getting rid of the man. No one, I said, would realize that the man had been killed but if it did eventually become known, the subject would be hailed as a benefactor. The plot involved the subject's serving tea to the doctor and placing in the tea two lumps of sugar, which had an X marked on them. These, I insisted, were not sugar, but cyanide. The subject agreed to all this. Thereupon, I walked over to the sugar bowl and placed an X on two lumps of sugar. On signal the supposed victim entered the room, and the three of us began to talk. The subject, it was noted, was very irritated with the doctor and made a few biting, sarcastic remarks about people who put on a front. I suggested that we have tea, and the subject volunteered to make it. I notice that he carefully put the marked lumps into the victim's tea and passed the cup to him. The doctor drank the tea without effect, of course. I then called the subject to one side and mentioned there was probably some mistake, that we had not given the doctor a large enough dose of cyanide. Thereupon I gave him two capsules from a box marked "potassium cyanide" and asked him to put these in the next cup of tea. He immediately awoke from the trance. As long as he was playing a role, he was willing to follow suggestions. He knew very well that the lumps of sugar were not really cyanide. However, the possibility that there might be cyanide in the capsules brought him out of the trance.

Not even a criminal hypnotist can induce a person to execute a misdeed if a subject is not willing to co-operate. As long as the situation is a make-believe one, the subject will seemingly go along and put on an act. But when he senses that he is being requested to do something that violently opposes his values or acutely jeopardizes his safety, he will either refuse to comply or arouse himself from the trance.

Subjects who enter into experiments realize that the doctor must be assuming responsibility for what is being done, and they go farther than they ordinarily would, but only up to a certain limit. In Dr. Ernest Hilgard's laboratory at Stanford University in California the behavior of subjects who had been given bizarre commands in the trance state was studied. They were easily able to counteract instructions that they did not want to follow. Dr.

Hilgard noted: "Some said they deliberately did not pay attention; others said they used sheer effort or determination; and a few claimed they used autosuggestion to resist—but resist they did."

To the question, then, of whether it is possible for a deeply hypnotized person (one who is a somnambule and can open his eyes without coming out of a trance) to commit an antisocial act or to perpetrate such an act through posthypnotic suggestion after the trance has ended, we may answer theoretically, "yes." But it is equally possible for that person to do something criminal or outrageous in the waking state as well. In either case, the essential ingredient is *motivation*. If the person harbors deep desires for wrongdoing, he will easily rationalize any situation to justify his malefaction. He will allow himself to be persuaded to break the law if his impulses are in this direction; he does not need hypnosis to prod him into this acting-out. Some alarmists, however, find it intriguing to build up the power of hypnosis in order to picture it as an irresistible force that can convert a benign law-abiding citizen into a killer. The rash of stories that appear in the press from time to time seem to indicate exactly that. But when we examine the facts closely, we usually find that the relationship of hypnosis to the perpetrated crime is coincidental.

The majority of practitioners who have used hypnosis over a period of many years have never encountered a single subject who was harmed in any way or who could be induced to harm others in the trance state. A substantial amount of evidence has been gathered to lay to rest the idea that hypnosis can prompt a person to perform an antisocial act without his willing it.

Dr. Jacob H. Conn, of the Johns Hopkins School of Medicine, read widely through one hundred and fifty years of medical literature and case histories and found no proof of a single violent crime committed under hypnosis. There were three cases in which it was claimed that hypnosis was responsible for violent crimes. "In each case there was also found to be an extraordinarily intimate interpersonal dependent relationship beween the hypnotist and the subject over a long period of time, including homosexuality." On the bases of this pathological relationship each subject could have committed the crime of which he was accused without the formality of hypnosis. The fact the hypnosis had been practiced at one time or another gave the defendant a plausible-sounding alibi. "Outmoded Svengali-like theories in which the hypnotist inducts a zombielike trance in the subject who then becomes a passive, will-less tool of his master are clear out of nineteenth-century science fiction, [with] isolated instances of mismanaged patients by incompetent operators and the few cases in which undiagnosed pre-psychotic persons were hypnotized, then committed antisocial acts. . . . The facts speak for themselves. There are thousands of subjects who have been studied in laboratory settings and privately over a period of many years. Hypnosis probably has the fewest harmful or unpleasant side effects of any therapy in medicine."

The careful studies by Dr. Hilgard and his associates also cast a great deal of doubt on the contention that a person may be induced to harm himself during hypnosis, even to the point of suicide. Such speculations are fanciful and occur largely in novels and on the stage. If a subject has a great deal of faith in the integrity of a hypnotist, he may go along with a harmful suggestion, believing that the hypnotist is setting up a situation for mere play-acting. Thus, if a hypnotist hands the subject a glass of clear fluid and says, "Drink this," the trusting subject will do so. Should the glass contain a poison, it may be lethal to the subject. But we surely can discount such an eventuality. After all, when a patient goes to a surgeon for an operation, he confidently expects that he will not have his heart cut out while he is under anesthesia.

The behavior of a subject under hypnosis can be as sensible and adaptive as in waking life. He never loses control of himself. Indeed he may be able to refuse to comply with certain commands with an intensity not possible in the conscious state. His co-operation with the suggestions of the hypnotist are based on a mutual relationship that develops between the two. He never loses power to discriminate between right and wrong.

Untoward Reactions in Hypnosis

Because hypnosis is capable of easing repressions, some emotionally unstable or prepsychotic subjects may experience a release of emotions, with or without verbal content, either during induction or when they enter into a medium or deep trance. Angry expostulation, outbursts of fitful crying, fearful screaming, and other uninhibited behavioral manifestations may appear without the therapist's prodding. Individuals who react with such intense emotional catharsis have been living with barely controlled tension that has probably sought release but had no opportunity for it. Such release may be for the good.

In hysterical disorders certain symptoms are held in abeyance by intense repression. These may be liberated during hypnosis or posthypnotically because of the selective removal of repressions, either spontaneously or through analytic probing. Thus convulsive seizures may be observed on rare occasions during the trance. These seizures resemble epilepsy and may be the product of sexual and hostile impulses, formerly suppressed, assailing the nervous system. Paralytic phenomena, tics, muscle spasms, gait disorders, speech troubles, and somatic conversions such as pain, localized tenderness, sensory disturbances, visual field constriction, hearing problems, and other disorganizations of the special senses may develop. But these are so exceptional, and when they occur, so temporary, that they are of no concern.

In emotionally unstable persons temporary emotional outbursts may occur with hallucinations, amnesia, and fuguelike states. These symptoms may be so fleeting that they evade the attention of the operator and even the patient. Repressions usually return upon termination of the trance, or the reactions may persist for hours.

Certain transference reactions have also been reported. They take the form of voluptuous and erotic fantasies and impulses, and, because fulfillment is impossible, they may precipitate intense disappointment, resentment, aggression, and anxiety. The specific ways of expressing erotic and hostile impulses depend upon habitual resistances, the usual modes of gaining impulse gratification, and the reality situation. The hypnotist may become alarmed at the turn of events, thinking that his activities have stirred up a hornet's nest. Actually, these effects are to be expected in *any* psychotherapeutic depth situation. A proper recognition, handling, and resolving of transference are among the most important ways of bringing about reconstructive changes in the personality. The incidence of such reactions in hypnosis is no greater and probably less than in depth therapies.

Countering the idea that hypnosis may be harmful to some subjects, the experimenters in Dr. Hilgard's laboratory comment: "Out of the 1,000 inductions only about four or five people endured some curious disruption or emotion. . . . These adverse reactions to trance induction or after hypnosis were so rare that the experimenters had no evidence that experiments with hypnosis entail any more dangers than a variety of behavioral studies in the laboratories of psychology."

Sexual Seduction Through Hypnosis

I once received the following letter from a lawyer representing a physician in the Midwest:

> Dear Dr. Wolberg:
>
> I represent———. He employs clinical hypnosis in his practice. Last October a young housewife came to him complaining of pains in her abdomen. The doctor suspected a tipped or retroflexed uterus. He had her lie down on his examining table, covered her body with a drape, and explored the regions of her vagina, using two fingers of his right hand while his left was on her abdomen. He wore a rubber glove on his right hand. He confirmed his diagnosis and attempted to tip the uterus back into normal position. His patient complained of pain, and he then told her that he would try and relax her muscles and relieve the tension. He used hypnotic techniques and after about five minutes made another attempt to correct the condition. He was successful. The patient dressed, paid him, and left his office. About three days later, she became hysterical and told her husband that the doctor had "played with her sexual organs," producing an orgasm. She then took the matter to the state police and, after investigation, the doctor was arrested and charged with aggravated assault and battery. Such is a felony in this state, and he has been indicted by the Grand Jury for this offence and has furnished cash bail.
>
> I have conferred with a psychologist in a local university. He tells me that the patient's statement that she was conscious of everything that was going on but because of having been placed under hypnosis was powerless to prevent it is false. He says that in such treatment a hypnotic operation that goes against the moral grain of the subject

would immediately bring a subject out of her trance. He suggested that we try to obtain your opinion. He regards you as an authority on hypnosis and of course recognizes your great knowledge in the field of psychiatry.

My reply was:

Dear Mr. ———

Thank you for your letter. I do believe strongly, from the information in your letter, that Dr. ——— is being accused of an unfounded charge and that any reasonable jury should acquit him once the facts are brought out to them. The situation must be a very disturbing one for Dr. ———, but he should be reassured to know that sexual fantasies are common in women undergoing gynecologic procedures without hypnosis, and that hypnosis can provide them with a means of rationalizing guilt feelings engendered by enjoyment of medical manipulations, which normally can reach heightened excitation to the point of orgasm. This implies neither immorality on the part of the woman, nor aggressive sexual designs on the part of the doctor. Hypnosis employed for anesthetic purposes actually can lessen this common form of adventitious sexual release.

I quote the letter and my reply as an example of an incident of false accusation that is sometimes made against hypnotists. In rare cases, unstable and hysterical people are apt to claim sexual assault on the basis of projected wish fulfillment. While such accusations are extremely uncommon, the possibility must be kept in mind, and when a patient displays strong sexual fantasies, they must be explained to the patient in terms of deeper motivational patterns. The notion that every subject looks upon hypnosis as a symbolic sexual phenomenon is not borne out by facts. Indeed, it is extremely uncommon for the patient to conceive of it in this light, unless he or she regards all close contacts in terms of sex. There is no real danger that the person will act out sexual fantasies in a properly conducted hypnotic session.

Dangers of Dependency

It seems logical to assume that a hypnotized subject will become dependent upon the hypnotist or upon hypnosis itself and become addicted, as with a drug. Both of these assumptions are completely false. A person who is prone to dependency will become dependent on the most passive therapist. There is nothing in hypnosis itself that exaggerates inherent dependency or creates it where it does not exist. My patients rarely ask me to induce a trance, and when we carry on a session in the waking state, they are content to continue this way unless I suggest that we use hypnosis. Moreover, when self-hypnosis is prescribed, the problem is not addiction but getting the patient to practice regularly. Even when I simplify the process by making a tape recording that the patient can play by himself. he will often become more and more negligent about his practice sessions as soon as he feels better.

As far as the therapist's directiveness and heightened activity, which are an inherent part of trance induction and trance utilization, are concerned, this is completely subject to the patient's own interpretation. The patient will project his own needs to be led or dominated by the therapist, whether he is active or passive. I have had patients referred to me by psychoanalysts who practiced classical psychoanalysis, as well as by nondirective counselors. Their patients were figuratively clinging to the breasts of their therapists with the desperation of new-born kittens—to the dismay of both patients and therapists. On the other hand, I have also had patients who were in long-term therapy with Gestalt therapists, sensory-awareness therapists, hypnotherapists, behavior therapists, and others who purposefully assumed the most authoritative roles, often to a point of infantilizing their patients. In my opinion, the degree of induced dependency among patients with authoritarian therapists was no greater than those with the passive nondirective therapists. The crucial factor appeared to be the patient's need for a dependent relationship.

14

Who Should Do Hypnosis

He sat there looking like the lovable, cowardly lion in the movie version of *The Wizard of Oz*. In fact, he *was* that lion! Bert Lahr, the famous actor, had volunteered to appear with me as a subject on a national television hookup to demonstrate some of the medical uses of hypnosis. Our appearance was to be an epilogue to *Man in a Trance,* a play by Will Lorin. It was sponsored by "Kraft Television Theater" and dealt with the problem of amateur hypnosis. In the play a successful singer, acted by Julius La Rosa, had lost confidence in his voice and sought to regain his self-assurance by turning to an amateur hypnotist, played by Farley Granger. Hypnotism proved successful in restoring the singer's confidence, and he was able to perform once again. Flush with a feeling of power, this modern Svengali then tried to bring out the singer's feelings of competitivenss and repressed murderous resentment toward his older brother. The results were disastrous; La Rosa ended up in the office of a psychiatrist, played by Alexander Scourby. The actress Patricia Smith provided the romantic interest in the drama. The play was excellently performed and conveyed a dramatic message: HYPNOSIS SHOULD NOT BE PRACTICED BY AMATEUR HYPNOTISTS.

After the play Mr. Lahr and I had a brief conversation, during which we discussed some points that had arisen during the play. He seemed dubious that hypnosis could be used as an anesthetic for pain, and admitted that all his life he had been afraid of being operated on under anesthesia. When I mentioned that I might be able to help him with this fear, he agreed to undergo hypnosis on the program. Medical society clearance had been obtained.

I then proceeded to induct Mr. Lahr into a trance, during which we produced anesthesia of one of his hands sufficiently deep to permit me, as the television cameras zoomed in, to penetrate his skin with a sterile needle. There was no visible perception of pain on Mr. Lahr's part. Touching the other hand lightly with the same needle produced a withdrawal of the hand. On emerging from the trance, Mr. Lahr expressed great astonishment over what had happened and kept gazing with disbelief at the blood drawn in the anesthetized part. He was delighted that he had been able to withstand skin penetration without pain, and he expressed thanks to me after the performance for helping him deal with his fear.

The question posed by the play and the demonstration are relevant to the important question of who is qualified to practice hypnosis. Should stage hypnotists or amateurs be given permission? There are no general laws that prohibit any one person from hypnotizing another. In some states there are laws that try to prevent nonprofessionals from treating disease by any method including hypnosis. Not long ago the Texas Board of Medical Examiners brought suit in three major Texas cities against several hypnotists who were not doctors. The board sought conviction on the basis of a case in Fort Worth, Texas, in which a former diamond cutter was sentenced to a thirty-day jail term with a $5,000 fine for doing hypnotherapy.

Laws limiting the use of hypnosis do not exist in most states. Advertisements for hypnosis in newspapers and the telephone directory yellow pages promise phenomenal cures for almost any imaginable disease. "Foremost authorities," who possess neither professional qualifications nor modesty in their claims, offer courses in hypnosis to any person who has the price of tuition. Careers in a lucrative new field are promised. In a few easy lessons, they assert, their students can become "master hypnotists" practicing "rocket hypnosis," which qualifies a person to perform on the stage or to "treat resistant diseases" or even "to control beautiful women." Numerous books and records are also available for the same purpose.

Some people are natural salesmen and masters at ballyhoo. When they learn the technique of hypnosis, they wield their power among their friends, who accept them as inspired magicians and healers. These amateur hypnotists can do some good if they limit their activities to pure relaxation. Rarely, however, do they stop at this point. Because they themselves are impressed with their first successes, they often use hypnosis to probe into the psyche, to examine assumed sources of problems, and to make posthypnotic suggestions that can create considerable conflict in sensitive subjects. Having little or no knowledge of the dynamics of personality in health or illness, they plunge into the psychological matrix like a bull in a china shop, much as the hypnotist did in the play *Man in a Trance.* While most people, as a general rule, possess built-in safety devices that neutralize the hypnotist's ravages (which may be well-meaning although foolish), there is a considerable number of people whose psychological balance is so delicate that they may be harmed. Some particularly vulnerable persons may not even require pressures from the hypnotist to display upset and excited reactions. When the reactions are not handled appropriately, the subject may be propelled into a severe posthypnotic anxiety state that may continue unchecked for months. I have had referred to me not a few persons who were plunged into an upheaval because their amateur hypnotists were unable to deal with explosive emotions liberated in them by hypnosis. This is particularly true in borderline conditions. In the hands of a trained psychotherapist these responses are readily handled and even used for therapeutic purposes. Amateurs are totally unqualified to deal with this behavior.

Can Paraprofessionals Be Trained to Do Hypnosis?

There are many good, well-meaning people who are dedicated to helping others. Such persons, after some training, may be able to function in counseling roles under the guidance and supervision of professional persons. Distraught individuals, burdened by worries from within and vexations from without, frequently find relief through talking things over with a sympathetic, stable, and intelligent helper who has learned some principles of personality development and a few interviewing techniques. The training of such paraprofessionals has become standard in certain communities, particularly where the need for services overwhelms the existing professional resources.

It is to be expected that some paraprofessionals will try to expand their therapeutic horizons by going beyond the bounds of their training limitations, employing hypnosis for the purpose of psychotherapy, and justifying what they do on the basis of having taken courses in the subject. But no studies can replace the years of didactic and supervised clinical work essential for qualification as a professional hypnotherapist. A considerable amount of instruction above and beyond the training of a paraprofessional is necessary before anyone is equipped even to study how to do psychotherapy, let alone hypnotherapy. A degree in medicine or clinical psychology is preferable, followed by a considerable span of supervised clinical experience and training under qualified teachers. Even then the professional cannot hope to do good hypnotherapy without further supervised instruction in hypnosis.

The fact that hypnosis, even in the hands of an amateur, is relatively harmless for the average subject does not justify its use by nonprofessional persons. Nor do the extravagant claims of cures by unqualified persons lessen the necessity for caution. Even when the amateur does not use probing techniques to expose raw feelings and conflicts or gives no unusual suggestions to a subject, untoward reactions that need prompt handling by an expert therapist may occur. Admittedly this does not happen too frequently. But the fact that highway accidents occur only in a small percentage of driven vehicles does not allow us to relax our vigilance in driving.

I do not want to create the impression that hypnosis is a dangerous instrument. Drugs like hashish, LSD, mescaline, and psilocybin, widely used today, are much more likely to precipitate psychoses in unstable people. But drugs are not commonly used for their potential therapeutic benefits, although the users may deceive themselves into believing that "taking a trip" is revelatory of their latent potentials. (Certain drugs, like LSD, in the hands of highly trained psychiatrists are sometimes used for psychological exploratory or research purposes.) Hypnosis can also be a helpful aid in therapy, provided it is implemented by a properly trained professional. What should be emphasized is that there are some risks in exposing oneself to hypnosis performed either by an amateur or an improperly trained professional.

Stage Hypnosis

Watching such spectacles as a hypnotized man crawling in the belief that he is a dog, a woman jumping up on a signal to scratch at imaginary ants in her underwear, someone stretched out as rigid as concrete between two chairs, or an adult volunteer who is convinced he is a baby sucking on a bottle are as amusing to audiences as they are impressive. People go to theaters and resorts to be entertained, and hypnosis is a remarkably effective theatrical medium. I have heard that some resort hotels even have a staff hypnotist to ensure that the sources of diversion do not dry up.

I am often asked how I feel about stage hypnosis. I, too, am amused by the antics and histrionics of subjects obviously only too eager to exhibit themselves. I am impressed with the skill of the hypnotist in winning over a large audience, as well as his ability to select susceptible subjects. But, frankly, I find the demonstrations a somewhat undignified display. To me such presentations are in the same class as surgical operations on view for entertainment purposes. This analogy is not too farfetched: when the anesthetic nitrous oxide (laughing gas) was first discovered, it was also used in stage performances as indicated in the poster reproduced on page 230. This, however, is certainly not reason enough to prohibit the practice. The real question is whether hypnosis, as practiced by stage hypnotists, may not be harmful to subjects later on.

A stage hypnotist carefully selects subjects who are somnambules because he depends on posthypnotic suggestions for his effects, and these are possible only when there is amnesia for trance events. Since there are only from 10 per cent to 15 per cent of potential somnambules in an audience, it is essential to pick them out rapidly for demonstration purposes. Various techniques are employed to discover them. In general, the hypnotist delivers a talk designed to impress the listening group, or he performs magic or mathematical tricks with the same purpose in mind. He then lectures briefly on the powers of hypnosis and, to illustrate how it works, asks the members of the audience to clasp their hands together tightly. As he counts from one to five or ten, he emphasizes that their hands are getting tighter and tighter. He stresses that at the last count they will not be able to separate them, no matter how great the effort, until he gives the command to unclasp them. Most members will be able to separate their hands with some effort. Some will not; no matter how hard they try, only the hypnotist's command will release them. These are the people who are asked to come to the stage.

In every group there are excellent somnambulistic subjects who have had experience in entering a trance. Some are known to the hypnotist, having come to previous performances. These persons become models for the initiates on stage, most of whom easily follow the suggestions given them. An element of showmanship and exhibition is often involved, but the happenings are usually genuine, not contrived. If the subjects accept the suggestions willingly and with enjoyment, little harm is done. Problems arise, however, when some very susceptible subjects are lured into accepting an unrealistic situation as realistic, against their conscious desires, and then perform actions that embarrass them. I remember once attending a performance where a staid minister was given a posthypnotic suggestion to bark like a dog whenever the hypnotist scratched his left ear. To his amazement and great embarrassment, this dignified member of the church delivered yelps and other animal sounds as the audience was convulsed with laughter, some people practically rolling into the aisles. I later had an opportunity to talk with the minister about his reaction to the event. He felt that he had disgraced himself. One can see from this how a sensitive person can be upset or injured by an assault on his sense of propriety.

Let those now laugh, who never laugh'd before;
And those who always laugh, now laugh the more.

A GRAND EXHIBITION

OF THE EFFECTS PRODUCED BY INHALING

NITROUS OXIDE, EXHILERATING, OR

LAUGHING GAS!

WILL BE GIVEN AT *the Masonic Hall*

Saturday EVENING, *15th* 1845.

20 **GALLONS OF GAS will be prepared and administered to all in the audience who desire to inhale it.**

MEN will be invited from the audience, to protect those under the influence of the Gas from injuring themselves or others. This course is adopted that no apprehension of danger may be entertained. Probably no one will attempt to fight.

THE EFFECT OF THE GAS is to make those who inhale it, either

LAUGH, SING, DANCE, SPEAK OR FIGHT, &c. &c.

according to the leading trait of their character. They seem to retain consciousness enough not to say or do that which they would have occasion to regret.

N. B. The Gas will be administered only to gentlemen of the first respectability. The object is to make the entertainment in every respect, a genteel affair.

Those who inhale the Gas once, are always anxious to inhale it the second time. There is not an exception to this rule.

No language can describe the delightful sensation produced. Robert Southey, (poet) once said that "the atmosphere of the highest of all possible heavens must be composed of this Gas."

For a full account of the effect produced upon some of the most distinguished men of Europe, see Hooper's Medical Dictionary, under the head of Nitrogen.

The History and properties of the Gas will be explained at the commencement of the entertainment.

The entertainment will be accompanied by experiments in

ELECTRICITY.

ENTERTAINMENT TO COMMENCE AT 7 O'CLOCK.

TICKETS *12½* CENTS,

For sale at the principal Bookstores, and at the Door.

The Professional Person as a Hypnotist

We come now to the subject of who among the professional assemblage can work with the hypnotic method. Not all professional persons are equipped either with the conviction or skill to do hypnosis. Obviously those professionals who have suspicions about it and are fearful or critical of it because of personal prejudices will not be successful with the method, even though they are willing to experiment with the process. When they are of the opinion that it cannot do any good, it generally will not do any good.

In the field of research the term "experimenter bias" is used to describe the experimenter who is so eager to prove his point that he manipulates the situation to make the results come out in accordance with his expectations. He somehow communicates his bias by subtle cues. This bias applies to psychotherapists. We are not concerned here with a positive bias toward hypnosis, since this can cause the therapist to communicate such faith in what he is doing that his patients are affected by his confidence and motivated to succeed. Pragmatically, at least, this is useful and advantageous. We are concerned with a negative bias that can produce bad results. Unfortunately, there are some therapists who for various reasons are so bigoted against certain techniques that they use them in questionable ways to prove to themselves and the world that the techniques are valueless. During the past few years, a number of deprecatory articles about hypnosis have been written by people who are unskilled in its use but who want to discredit it in order to champion their own methods of therapy. The negative expectancies of such operators in hypnosis are only too easily communicated to their subjects.

Skill and temperament are other factors that are responsible for the degree of success a professional achieves with the technique of hypnosis. Psychotherapy is essentially a relearning experience in which old, maladjustive patterns are discarded, and new, more constructive ones acquired. There are many avenues of learning. We all possess highly selective and preferred modes of acquiring knowledge. Some of us emulate models with whom we identify and follow the example of authorities we respect. Others resist these identifications and launch out on their own personal trial-and-error experiments. Some people learn by carefully thinking things over and then applying their insights to everyday living. A moment of dramatic awareness can spark the beginning of constructive change that can become permanent if properly reinforced. Other individuals learn by doing, entering randomly into situations and activities, often acting impulsively. If the experience is rewarding, they will repeat it; if it is painful, they learn to avoid it.

For people in therapy the guiding hand of a skilled therapist is indispensable in all these learning processes. This is because the learner is constantly retreating from the pain or the fancied threat of his new adjustment. He incessantly seeks to return to the old, destructive yet familiar defenses of his past. Sometimes he is unaware of these patterns in his behavior. This is where the role of the therapist is valuable. He can help the patient understand how he is projecting into his relationships the same unhealthy drives that have caused him distress in the past. In this way, the therapist can help motivate his patient toward the development of healthier attitudes.

The therapeutic relationship operates as a prime learning medium. It is not enough that a hypnotist knows how to induct hypnosis. He must know how to blend it with his technical psychotherapeutic skills and how to adapt these techniques to the special needs and problems of his patients. This calls for a great deal of expertise acquired from extensive experience with a wide variety of problems and ailments.

The proficiency of the hypnotist in making the most of the subject's unique patterns of learning and response is crucial in working with a patient in the trance state. If routine methods that do not take into account the patient's individual needs and life style are forced upon him, the results will be limited.

The personality of the therapist, which can either enhance or minimize results, is probably the most important element in the complex process of hypnosis. Nobody has ever defined exactly what qualities make for a good hypnotist, or psychotherapist, for that matter. But a number of characteristics have been found to be important and valuable:

1. sensitivity to the patient's needs, with an ability to detect the areas of difficulty that can be expediently handled;
2. flexibility in approach, which will permit the use of selected techniques designed best to help the existing problems;
3. empathy toward the patient and an ability to communicate one's understanding of his struggles and suffering;
4. capacity to handle one's own personal shortcomings and biases without projecting them onto the patient.

There are therapists who are able to do satisfactory psychotherapy but lose their therapeutic poise when they do hypnosis. Some become so excited about their influence on the patient that they tend to overestimate what hypnosis can do or fail to admit its limitations. Hammering away with authoritative suggestions, they force some patients to comply with what is expected of them. Although the patient yields under duress, there is no way of knowing what personality complications may occur later on. Therapists who manifest this need to prove the invincibility of hypnosis constitute a small but vocal group that carries on a constant quarrel with its more conservative colleagues.

In addition, other personal limitations or faulty reactions can limit a hypnotist's effectiveness. For instance, some therapists become upset by the emotional upheavals in very disturbed patients, although such occurrences are an essential part of the hypnotherapeutic process.

The supernatural quality that some subjects invest in the hypnotic procedure sometimes influences the hypnotist as well. This feeling may be related to an unconscious desire to be a controlling or omnipotent parent figure. On the other hand, some therapists' fear of using hypnosis or resistance to it may reflect a dread of exercising magical powers that they do not trust themselves to handle.

An analogy to surgery is helpful here. If a patient with a severe abdominal complication is looking for a surgeon, he certainly will not go to a doctor who cannot stand the sight of blood. The same is true for hypnosis. If a patient has the motivation to overcome an emotional problem, and reasonably good reparative powers, the X factor in restoring him to health is the skill and intergrity of his therapist.

Professional help may not be cheap. In shopping around, one will inevitably find therapists with different fee scales. The fee is not necessarily an index of competency. But if there is a choice between a good therapist whose reputation is endorsed by the professional society of his speciality or by other competent practitioners and a therapist with questionable qualifications who charges less, one should not trade his health for a bargain.

The story is told of a man who went for some dentures to the best dentist in his community. The dentist, after a thorough examination, told him that the work would be difficult and expensive, costing $1,000. The man replied that that was too much. "I'm going to find a competitor," he promised himself, "who will be more reasonable." He went to a second dentist who said he could do the job for $750. That, too, in his opinion was excessive. He continued to look and finally found a dentist who said he would be willing to do a complete restoration for $200. That sounded reasonable. "Can you give me any references from people whom you've treated?" asked the man. The dentist gladly referred him to a former patient. It took several weeks for the prospective client to track this man down. "Yes," avowed the latter, "the doctor did do dental work for me, quite extensive and reasonable." "What kind of a dentist is he? Is he any good?" queried the prospect. "I can only answer that with a story," was the reply. "I am a skindiver by hobby. One day, a half-year after my dental work, I went skindiving off the Bahamas. I was swimming around deep down looking for a submerged vessel. I saw this vessel, and as I drew close to it I suddenly realized that there was a shark after me. To my horror, the shark snapped at my heels, and I tried to get away. But when I was trying to escape, an octopus hiding in a roll of barbed wire near the ship reached out and with one of his tentacles grabbed hold of my leg. Then the shark charged again. And you know, that was the first time in six months that my mind was off those teeth."

It simply does not pay to go to an incompetent doctor just because he charges low fees. The question of where to find a competent hypnotherapist will depend on two factors: one's community and the available resources. When advice is needed, a local social agency or medical society may be of help.

PART TWO

15

Common Questions and Misconceptions

Many ideas about hypnosis are traditionally accepted at face value as unquestionably true. Yet, when we examine them critically, we discover that, first, they are apocryphal and their origins uncertain; second, they are dogmatic, and repeated over and over again like canons by those who dare not challenge their seeming authoritative stamp; third, they do not hold up under sober investigation. Yet fictions about hypnosis keep cropping up constantly in the popular literature and are repeated even by sophisticated workers in the field of mental health.

In this chapter we shall deal with some questions about hypnosis that have not been answered fully in previous sections. Over the years I have tabulated inquiries, and I am including those that seem to puzzle people most.

Why do some doctors have doubts about hypnosis?

Hypnosis is a much misunderstood phenomenon. For centuries it has been affiliated with spiritualism, witchcraft, and various kinds of mumbo jumbo. It is a common tool of quacks, who have used it to "cure" every imaginable illness, from baldness to cancer. The exaggerated claims made for it by undisciplined persons have turned some doctors against it. Some psychiatrists, too, doubt the value of hypnosis because Freud gave it up seventy years ago and they themselves have not had too much experience with its modern uses.

Can hypnosis be used for lie detection or cross-examinations?

Newspapers sometimes publish accounts of cross-examinations under hypnosis of persons who presumably are capable of remembering forgotten facts or of testifying to their guilt or innocence regarding a crime. I have always found it amusing that material elicited from a subject in a trance state is accepted as factual even by sophisticated interrogators. In hypnosis the fantasy life is extremely vivid, and subjects are apt to fabricate stories quite inventively and artistically, following leads from the hypnotist or pursuing their own imaginative flights. They may also willfully lie or conceal incriminating data. Hypnosis, then, is an unreliable instrument for lie detection.

Periodically one reads about a hypnotist who is accused of sexually seducing a subject in a trance. Is this possible?

A subject who succumbs to hypnotic seduction is not an unwilling captive. Sexual fantasies may be active during hypnosis and are usually responsible for accusations of rape. When a situation is not acceptable to a subject, or creates anxiety, he or she will come out of the trance. It is the hypnotist who is being seduced if he believes that hypnosis lowers moral standards.

Does hypnosis have any relationship to spiritualism?

Spiritualists presumably use self-hypnosis to transport themselves to the spirit world so they can communicate with the dead. Good mediums are somnambules who sincerely believe that their trance experiences are manifestations of powers beyond mortal capacities. The fact that they have amnesia for their revelation from spirits of the departed convinces them and their clients of their inspired gifts. I have treated a number of mediums, and I can attest to their naïve sincerity. There are also frauds, of course, who try to impress their customers with the playing of musical instruments, levitation of objects, rappings, and other mysterious goings-on that only spirits could indulge in. Photographs of ectoplasm are also produced as evidence, and sometimes it is difficult to explain how these were obtained. Some spiritualists in a trance convince people that they have the power to diagnose disease and to prescribe the proper cures, which they claim can rectify incurable ailments. We are reminded here of the work of Edgar Cayce, whose revelations have had wide publicity.

What about the cases of people reliving their previous lives during hypnotic regression?

I am convinced that no element of fraud exists here, because the subjects truly believe in their productions. And if the hypnotist also believes in reincarnation, he may be convinced of the truth of his subjects' revelations. I have listened to dramatic outpourings of previous lives in many of my patients, and in each instance I was able to trace the tales to forgotten impressions of early childhood, which had been experienced by or told to the subjects. The subjects' need to recall these events and to adorn them dramatically became a focus for treatment that proved highly revealing.

Why was the book **The Search for Bridey Murphy** *so popular?*

I suppose man's eternal quest for immortality makes him grasp at any evidence that can guarantee his eternal existence. I know there are many people who do not agree with me. When my viewpoint on Bridey Murphy (Ruth Simmons) was published in *Life* magazine, I received a number of letters contesting what I said. Some of them questioned my point that the solution to Bridey's claims lay largely in Ruth Simmons' childhood and background. The solution could just as easily be found in my—and others'—personal history, they said, and thus, by implication, in the life of someone who had lived before us. Some readers questioned the ability of science to interpret factual knowledge with absolute certainty. They pointed out that science also deals with the unknown and has to make allowances for the inexplicable. By and large, those who disagreed with my interpretation of Bridey Murphy tended to be sympathetic to the idea of reincarnation, or receptive to mystical and supernatural theories.

Is there any relationship between "miracle cures" and hypnosis?

In both religious healing and hypnosis certain allied processes operate. Many religious healers actually invoke a trance state in their subjects and then proceed to give suggestions. The famous Pierre Janet once said that he could effect a miracle cure in his office with hypnosis and thus save his patients the cost of trips to Lourdes.

Would you say that hypnosis is a form of faith healing?

Not exactly, although faith is an aspect that enters into it. Faith is a powerful force in all human affairs. It can bring about many changes that seem miraculous, including an extraordinary control over emotions and organ systems. To some extent, the acceptance of the hypnotist's suggestions is contingent on the faith of the subject in the hypnotist or in the methods he is employing. The subject, on the basis of his conviction that proper reponse is inevitable, may invoke latent capabilites not available to him under any other circumstances. Only the subject has the ability to produce the effects associated with the trance, not the hypnotist. The subject's desire to surrender himself to the designs of the hypnotist or to the force of his methods is of immediate importance. As hypnotic effects take place, the subject credits them to the hypnotist's words. This further enhances his faith in the omnipotence of the hypnotist and encourages continuing altered preceptions of himself and reality. Faith may operate in the same way outside hypnosis. The phenomenon of religious healing offers substantial testimony to how strong an influence there can be on physical functions without the formality of hypnotic induction.

How deeply into a trance does one have to go to get benefits from hypnosis?

If hypnosis can be conceived of as a spectrum of awareness that stretches from waking to sleeping, it will be seen that some aspects are close to the waking state and share the qualities of being awake; some aspects are close to sleep and similar to a light sleep. But over the entire spectrum suggestibility increases, and this is what makes hypnosis potentially beneficial, provided we put suggestibility to a constructive use. The depth of hypnosis is not always proportionate to the degree of suggestibility. In other words, even if one goes no deeper than the lightest stages of hypnosis and is merely mildly relaxed, one will still be able to benefit from its therapeutic effects. It is possible with practice to go more deeply into a hypnotic state, but that is really not too important in the great majority of cases.

Is there any special way in which hypnosis works?

The human mind is extremely suggestible. It is constantly being bombarded with suggestive stimuli from the outside and with suggestive thoughts and ideas from the inside. A good deal of suffering results from "negative" thoughts and impulses that invade the mind from subconscious recesses. Unfortunately, past experiences, guilt feelings, and repressed impulses and desires are incessantly forcing themselves into awareness, directly or in disguised forms, sabotaging happiness, health, and efficiency. By the time one has reached adulthood, "negative" modes of thinking, feeling, and acting have been established and persist as bad habits. And like any habits, they are hard to break. In hypnosis, we attempt to replace these "negative" attitudes with "positive" ones. But it takes time to get rid of old habit patterns. One must not be discouraged if there are no immediate results. With continued practice, changes will eventually take place. Even though there may be no obvious difference outwardly, a restructuring is going on underneath. An analogy may make this clear. If a batch of white blotters is held above the level of the eyes so that only the bottom blotter can be seen, and drops of ink are dribbled onto the top blotter, nothing different will be observed for a while. But after enough ink has been poured to soak through the entire thickness, the ink will eventually appear at the bottom. Nothing seemed to happen for a while, but penetration was going on. If the process had been stopped before enough ink had been poured, the process might have been considered a failure. Suggestions in hypnosis are like ink poured on layers of resistance; one must keep repeating them before they come through to influence old, destructive patterns.

Are not hypnotic drugs a valuable aid, helping one go more deeply into a trance?

Experience shows that drugs are usually not necessary. Often they complicate matters. If medications are required, the therapist may use them, but this is extremely rare.

If hypnosis is valuable, shouldn't it be employed in all psychological or psychiatric problems?

Most psychological and psychiatric problems respond to treatment by skilled therapists without requiring hypnosis. When blocks in treatment develop, a therapist skilled in hypnosis may be able to use it effectively. But only a qualified professional person can decide whether this is necessary or desirable. When hypnosis is used by a therapist who knows how and when to employ it, it can catalyze the therapeutic process.

Can self-hypnosis be helpful?

Indeed it can. Throughout the ages people have resorted to relaxation methods and meditation to calm themselves down. The Eastern philosophies, such as Yoga and Zen Buddhism, promote exercises that are self-hypnotic in essence. Constructive suggestions made to oneself while in a self-induced trance can help neutralize negative and upsetting thoughts and feelings.

What harm can come from self-hypnosis?

I have never seen any harm done, nor have any of my colleagues who have trained their subjects. The reason for this seems obvious when one considers that the state of self-hypnosis is similar to falling asleep. Of course, some people have nightmarish dreams during normal sleep, and such persons may also have nightmarish fantasies during self-hynposis. These fantasies can be significant if the person is in analytic psychotherapy and the therapist searches the subconscious for dynamic material.

Do people get addicted to self-hypnosis?

No. The problem is usually getting them to practice it regularly when needed.

Can a person use self-hypnosis to explore his own unconscious?

It is advisable that this be done only when a person is in therapy with a trained psychoanalyst and in relation to a total treatment plan.

Is group hypnosis ever practiced?

Yes, and it can be highly effective in the addiction problems: food, tobacco, alcohol, and drugs. It is also valuable in prenatal training.

Has hypnosis any effect on dreams?

Hypnosis may stimulate memory in those who claim they do not dream, or in those who do have dreams but forget them. Suggestions are given to the subject that he will be able to remember his dreams, or that he will find himself dreaming during self-hypnosis and will be able to recall what he dreamed when he is awake. In instances where insights are fragmented, it may serve to unite unrelated segments into a meaningful fabric.

Is the hypnotic relationship the key factor in producing hypnotic effects?

Yes. In hypnosis the person often feels soothed because of the relationship. He feels a flow, a bond between himself and the hypnotist, which comforts him; in this protective milieu he is able to face up to certain experiences and feelings from which he fled before. This situation prevails, of course, in any kind of psychotherapy, but it take a great deal longer to develop this bond in the usual psychotherapeutic relationship. It is often established immediately in hypnosis. In many instances the very induction of hypnosis will release a flood of emotional feelings with ensuing relief. This has temporary therapeutic value in reducing tension. It does not cure, because the basis for the generation of burdensome emotions is still there. Nevertheless, it helps the patient to get things off his chest, to develop and consolidate a relationship with the therapist. The fact that he begins to reach into deeper layers of feeling helps liberate repressed ideas and memories, sometimes quite spontaneously.

Why did Freud give up hypnosis?

Freud turned away from hypnosis for a number of reasons. First, he believed that not enough people could be deeply hypnotized to recover significant forgotten (amnesic) data. Second, he minimized the permanence of suggestions given the patient by the therapist, and he presented material that seemed to indicate that when a patient lost confidence in the hypnotist his symptoms returned. Third, he believed that hypnosis by-passed resistances and that they remained intact, continuing to cause problems. Actually, when we examine his writings, we see that what Freud was inveighing against was not hypnosis as a technique but the suggestive use to which it was being put. We must remember that hypnosis in Freud's time was dedicated to the search for traumatic memories. Since the memories Freud considered significant could not be brought back, or, if memories did occur, they were often found to be fictions, Freud assumed hypnosis was not effective. Actually, it merely had failed to fulfill Freud's hopes. We do not restrict hypnosis to this use any longer. Freud himself predicted that hypnosis would eventually return as a respectable form of treatment, particularly as a means of shortening treatment methods.

What about the contention of many analysts that hypnosis is effective only as long as the dependent relationship between the therapist and the patient continues, and that as soon as this relationship is over the patient relapses?

This is the original idea Freud voiced in the early 1900's. He said that as long as a positive relationship exists, a patient retains his gains; the moment a negative element enters, gains are lost. But not all gains in hypnosis are the result of a positive relationship, that is, if the therapist has been doing his job. The basis for Freud's early premise does not take into account the broad extensions of therapeutic hypnosis to which we are now dedicated.

Why do some psychiatrists continue to say that when you remove a disturbing symptom, the underlying anxiety will come out, or some other symptom will arise to take its place?

Again, they are repeating folklore. A hypnotist's influence is not so powerful that he can eliminate symptoms by forceful suggestions if these symptoms are important in maintaining a good balance. And if he is fortunate enough to help the patient overcome a symptom, it may never return. In fact, the elimination of a symptom often means a better general adjustment. The exceptions occur when certain symptoms are removed by forceful methods in some borderline patients who happen to be peculiarly susceptible to suggestions. This is rare, and when it happens, it indicates a poor technique.

Some practitioners suggest that schizophrenics or borderline psychotics should never be hypnotized. I'm wondering if in your experience you have some ideas about contraindications for hypnosis?

Some therapists are unable to treat schizophrenic patients, with or without hypnosis. There are some who are not able to treat drug addicts. There are some who find that they cannot work with neurotic children, or with psychopaths, or with alcoholics, or with obsessive-compulsives, or with homosexuals. Difficulties will appear when the therapist does not like a patient or feels uncomfortable with him. We all have our likes and dislikes, our personal prejudices, and our particular areas of interest. We find that we can work better with some patients and not so well with other patients. I know some therapists who do remarkably well with schizophrenics; they are able to work on various levels with them, even analytically. Why? Because they like their patients, and the patients know it. They want to help their patients. Patients perceive this and can have a better relationship with such empathic therapists. Under such conditions, one can work with schizophrenics, borderline cases, obsessive-compulsives, homosexuals, and so on, on hypnotic or nonhypnotic levels. I treat psychotics, psychopaths, borderline patients, and homosexuals—even paranoids—with hypnosis, and I have experienced few problems. If a patient feels a therapist does not like him or is not too sympathetic, he will interpret hypnosis as an attack on him, and he is apt to become upset. The inability to treat certain patients with hypnosis has nothing to do with the fact that they fit into designated diagnostic categories. Of course, if a therapist used hypnosis with hostile intent or humilates or frightens a patient with it, the latter will get upset. A patient with a weak ego may respond with disintegrative tendencies. I have found that in cases where unconscious conflicts come up in hypnosis, as repression is released and the patient becomes momentarily disturbed, he can nonetheless pull himself together easily if we have a good relationship. His calm is restored with reassurance or with suggestions to repress and to forget. This exposure to traumatic experiences tends to strengthen him ultimately. I have often observed how a patient will go back voluntarily to these conflicts, as if he wants to resolve them. Dreams also reveal that the patient is developing a progressive mastery in coping with his defense mechanisms.

Doesn't hypnosis upset paranoid patients and convince them that their ideas of being persecuted or influenced are genuine?

Yes, if the therapist does not have the proper relationship with them. Paranoids are difficult patients, but it is possible to work with them if one has their confidence. I have used hypnotic treatment with a number of paranoid patients, including several whose chief delusion was that somebody was trying to hypnotize them. I cannot say that my results were always brilliant, but using hypnosis to get them to relax and to want to take phenothiazines certainly helped them above and beyond the influence of drugs.

Do you use hypnosis with alcoholics?

Yes, but hypnosis alone is not particularly successful with alcoholics. That does not mean it should not be used. There are some psychiatrists who claim that it is a prime source of help. But I find that Antabuse and Alcoholics Anonymous are the most effective means of dealing with alcoholism. On top of this, psychotherapy with or without hypnosis may be effective.

Have you had any success with sexual difficulties in a short-term therapeutic approach? Can you cite an example?

Sexual difficulties, interestingly, seem to clear up rapidly in hypnotherapy, often without relapse. Impotence responds more easily than frigidity. I teach self-hypnosis to patients with sexual disorders. In the case of impotence, a lack of self-confidence is generally involved and an equation of low self-esteem with poor performance. In any kind of biological function, whether this involves sleeping, eating, or sexuality, using it for any purpose other than for its biological aim is bound to bring trouble, particularly if the person is trying to prove himself through the exercise of this function. I try to get my patients to accept the fact that they must approach sexuality for whatever pleasures they can derive from it, not caring whether they succeed or fail. If they have given up sexual relationships, I advocate resumption of sex, without undue anxiety about failure. I encourage them to employ self-hypnosis, to recondition themselves to accept a different attitude toward sex. I may want to talk to the wives or husbands to enlist their co-operation and to get details of other problems in their relationships. One case I treated, for example, involved a man who had been impotent for fifteen years. It started off in the usual way. He was tired one evening, and his wife was irritated at him when he approached her sexually. She used this opportunity to goad him into trying to function "like a real man." When he was unable to retain an erection, she reviled him for his inability to perform. This reinforced his feelings of ineffectuality; he then began to approach sex with anxiety, wondering whether it would work or not. His wife did not help matters any with her deprecatory attitudes. In desperation, he tried other women, but his anxiety was too strong to enable him to function. Finally, he gave up sex completely, but years later, upon reading an article on hypnosis, he decided to explore its possibilities. We had eight sessions, during which I taught him self-hypnosis, enjoining him to practice daily and warning him that it might require a good deal of time before all the results revealed themselves in a better performance. It took almost three months of constant work for himself to restore his potency. It is important, therefore, not to give up if results are not immediate.

Can hypnosis be used on adolescent delinquent-type boys?

Adolescent delinquents are often intrigued with hypnosis and usually make excellent subjects. The delinquent is often looking for a powerful authority figure; he wants to identify with somebody who is stronger than himself, whose disciplines and injunctions he cannot challenge. Hypnosis creates the impression of this powerful authority. Of course, one cannot trust this illusion, or relax with the patient's temporary improvement. He will challenge the hypnotic authority after a while. Nevertheless, hypnosis is a way of establishing a relationship with a delinquent or young psychopath, which may very well open the way for therapeutic work.

How do you account for the fact that a person may be given a suggestion in hypnosis and yet not follow it until years later?

I believe the person did not really ignore the suggestion entirely. It may have been too much for him at the time, or it may not have had any particular meaning for him when it was given. A suggestion made to a subject prematurely is often repudiated by him. But years later he may come around to it, having worked it through the layers of his defenses. He gradually comes to suspect that the suggestion may have a validity for him. Then he tests it and finds it does have validity. Of course, certain suggestions and interpretions can be wrong; then they do not have too much meaning for the individual.

Since the hypnotic state is not a loss of consciousness, but rather a heightened state of consciousness, what are the possibilities of developing insight with or through hypnosis?

Let us say that hypnosis is altered consciousness, selectively heightened in certain instances and selectively lowered in others. If, in hypnosis a subject's attention is focused on specific aspects of his experience, he will get a heightened awareness of some of its elements. He may be able to enlarge on things he was not able to talk about before, and this heightened awareness may persist in the waking state. One may be able to get a person to dream, and this may increase his insights. While he is in hypnosis, one may be able to get him to perceive himself in certain roles with people and clarify certain kinds of emotional responses that he could not understand before.

Shouldn't hypnosis, then, be used in all cases?

Hypnosis may expedite the learning process, but one does not have to use it for this. Most people are able to work on their problems without hypnosis. It should be used for special reasons and only as part of an intergrated treatment program.

Will hypnosis remove resistance to therapy?

Yes, in some cases it can. Resistance may be a reluctance on the part of the individual to relinquish primary or secondary gains of his neurosis; he clings stubbornly to the difficulties he has, even though they cause a continuing maladjustment. He may find more security in his neurotic tendencies than in normal values and will be filled with anxiety whenever he tries to give up some of his neurotic problems, arduous though they are to sustain. Consequently, in working therapeutically with patients, resistance to change in some form can be expected. And this includes therapy with hypnosis. Resistance may even take the form of no longer being hypnotizable. However, in my experience, hypnosis can help work through many forms of resistance.

Hypnosis is considered by some to be a regressive manifestation. Wouldn't a completely psychoanalyzed person then lose his ability to be hypnotized?

Since there is no such thing as a completely psychoanalyzed person, the question answers itself. But even assuming that we could find a "monster" of complete normality, I am sure he would be able to be hypnotized. I consider this ability an inborn characteristic—like sleep.

Is research being done to determine what hypnosis is all about?

A great deal of folklore continues to influence ideas about hypnosis. These are promulgated chiefly by uninformed persons. However, some sincere practitioners also espouse essentially unsound ideas, which are residues of the historical fusion of hypnosis with the occult. In order to introduce a scientific perspective, psychologists have conducted controlled experiments that attempt to distinguish between fact and fiction. But it is difficult to do accurate research in areas that investigate what people think and how they behave. Among other obstacles, a good deal of bias, conscious or unconscious, exists among many experimenters. This can interfere with what should be an essentially scientific attitude. Moreover, the prejudices of subjects themselves interfere drastically with their reports. When we try to perform an experiment using hypnosis, the subject is apt to respond in order to please the experimenter, or to frustate him if he feels so inclined. He may decide to act dramatically, since the hypnotic situation lends itself to histrionics. He may deduce what is expected of him from explicit or roundabout suggestions and comply obligingly in order to be a "good" subject. Or he may decide to oppose the experimenter, whom he may confuse in his mind with an authoritarian parental figure, and act out an oppositional role. One of the problems in an empirical approach to hypnosis is the difficulty of defining reliable and conceptually meaningful data. There are problems in identifying significant variables that constitute data under observation. The ambiguities inherent in the concept of hypnosis itself must also be taken into consideration. We do not yet have a clear picture of what psychological and physiological elements constitute the hypnotic state per se. This should not hamper us in the attempt to define and explore its nature or phenomena. But we should not deceive ourselves into thinking that this is a simple task.

Can a researcher with a bias influence results?

The hypnotist may have so strong a need to prove his theories that he will consciously or unconsciously select compliant subjects or suggest to them his own solutions to tasks that he sets forth for them. This, of course, holds true in all experiments, but it is especially true in hypnosis, where the subject is susceptible to a need to please the operator and where there is a high degree of suggestibility. On the basis of a hypnotist's predilections, then, he may make observations about his experiments that seem to substantiate his biases. For example, some hypnotherapists are constantly reporting experiences in which their patients attempt sexual seductions or resort to violence. Others never do. We may suspect in the first case that the hypnotist arouses sexual and hostile impulses in the subject because of his own personal drives and needs.

Can hypnosis itself be used as a means of research?

Hypnosis can be used as a means of research to investigate some complex aspects of mental activity, such as dreams, cognitive organization, reactions to anxiety, symptom formation, and other unanswered questions of thinking, feeling, and behaving. But it must be employed with humility and with the realization that there are difficult problems in any research involving the mind.

Doesn't hypnosis make the patient more dependent on the therapist?

Peculiarly enough it does not. A penchant for dependency is inherent more in the characterologic make-up of the individual and because of existing personality needs than in any techniques employed, including hypnosis. On the contrary, hypnosis, properly implemented, with the teaching of the individual the ways he can utilize self-hypnosis, will often lead to greater self-sufficiency. Some therapists dictate a cassette tape with relaxing suggestions that the patient may use by himself to promote relaxation and to reinforce ego building suggestions. In follow-up studies with patients using such tapes, I have never discovered a single case that has become addicted to the tape. Indeed the problem is the reverse. After feeling more relaxed and more self-confident, the patient often forgets to play the tape or deliberately stops using it.

Isn't hypnosis always beneficial?

Since hypnosis acts as a catalyst it will enhance not only virtues in technique but also it will exaggerate errors. It will not correct deficiencies or imperfections in the conduct of psychotherapy. Its applications must be limited to a therapist's areas of competence and expertise.

Doesn't hypnosis mobilize sexual feelings in patients that will interfere with the therapeutic relationship?

An erotic transference is possible in any kind of psychotherapy where a strong relationship develops between patient and therapist. If handled properly it need not interfere with the therapeutic process. One is reminded of the experience of Freud in his first uses of hypnosis. In speaking about a patient with whom he had secured excellent results using hypnosis by tracing back to their origin her attacks of pain, he wrote: "As she woke up on one occasion, she threw her arms around my neck. The unexpected entrance of a servant relieved us from a painful discussion, but from that time onwards, there was a tacit understanding between us that the hypnotic treatment should be discontinued. . . . I felt that I had now grasped the nature of the mysterious element that was at work behind hypnotism. In order to exclude it, or at all events to isolate it, it was necessary to abandon hypnotism." Freud believed that hypnosis was a state of being in love and was "based entirely on sexual impulsions that are inhibited in their aims . . ." This idea has long been repudiated. In my own experience with hypnosis, I never got the impression that the erotic transference was an especially prominent event, but I would assume it might come up with certain repressed hysterical patients. If it did arise, it could certainly be managed therapeutically.

Can hypnosis control or eliminate the smoking habit?

Success in smoking control has been modest with all treatments including behavioral methods, stimulus satiation, group methods, pharmacological aids, psychotherapy and hypnosis. Hypnosis may be employed to reduce tension and to enhance the patient's resolve to overcome the habit, and some therapists find an ego-building tape useful for this purpose. Many methods have been employed with varying success. What is probably best is a multi-dimensional approach tailored to the patient's needs.

Is there any correlation between personality structure and hypnotizability?

Generally no. However, I have noticed that highly imaginative artists (such as actors who can readily assume roles) and deeply religious people or those who were in childhood immersed in religion often make excellent hypnotic subjects.

Can hypnosis accomplish anything that cannot be achieved in the waking state? In other words, can people be made to perform better by hypnosis?

With proper motivation an individual may achieve in the waking state anything he could achieve in hypnosis. But hypnosis is an easier route to suggest proper motivation for certain tasks. People sometimes transcend their usual capacities when they have a latent potential to excel, but never beyond this potential. Suggestions in hypnosis may stimulate a greater incentive to achieve one's potential, but this can also be done by properly motivating the subject in the waking state.

Do deep trance states accomplish more than light or medium ones?

Deep trance states are important to therapeutic successes only in certain situations, such as symptom removal in hysteria or suggested analgesia in severe pain syndromes. In most cases psychotherapy can be facilitated with light or medium hypnosis. Indeed in some instances deep hypnosis with posthypnotic amnesia may inspire a protective resistance in patients who need to retain control. On the other hand, patients who have doubts about their ability to be hypnotized may block themselves from benefiting from the effects of hypnosis unless they can be convinced (by amnesia or through posthypnotic suggestions they cannot control) that they have entered a deep trance state.

Can a lightly hypnotized subject experience hallucinations?

Hallucinations related to touch and smell may sometimes be easily induced, but it is more difficult to produce auditory hallucinations and visual hallucinations. Hallucinations may under certain conditions be experienced in the waking state by suggestion or self-suggestion where the need for such a sensory experience is great. Thus, during a seance a person wanting to hear the voice of a departed person may be able to do so.

How about pain relief through hypnosis as compared to a placebo given in the waking state?

Studies show that there is a difference in the degree of analgesia achieved in favor of hypnosis.

Are suggestions given during mere relaxation less effective than if given during hypnosis?

Suggestions given in the waking state can be highly effective in some persons. Yet in the same individual the identical suggestions during hypnosis may be more strongly acted on. Paradoxically in some cases the reverse is true. The reason for this is that patients who have a powerful need for control may fear losing control during hypnosis and consequently they will act more oppositional as they enter the hypnotic state than when they are fully conscious. The crucial element is the *meaning* to the person of the proffered suggestions. If the subject has the motivation to execute a suggestion he is likely to do so in both the waking and trance states. Where a suggestion creates too much anxiety on the other hand it may not be effective. What helps a subject tolerate an anxiety-provoking suggestion is the protective relationship with the hypnotist. Where the subject trusts the therapist and has confidence in him, where he has a need to win the approval of the therapist, he may excute even anxiety-provoking suggestions like probing for past traumatic experiences and recalling anxiety dreams. There is a limit of course to the extent of tolerance of anxiety or the accepting of untoward, guilt-inspiring or criminal suggestions even if there is trust in the hypnotist. One's critical judgement is never suspended and usually will neutralize suggestions. On the other hand, where no warm relationship exists with the hypnotist and there is little trust and confidence in him, anxiety-provoking suggestions are likely to be vigorously resisted.

How would you distinguish deep relaxation from hypnosis?

This may be difficult because there are few reliable differential signs except in very deep hypnosis where hallucinations or regression and revivification can be evoked. In light or medium hypnosis one may have to rely on the subjective statements of the patient: "I felt not quite myself," or "my body felt disjointed," and other comments related to distortions of the body image. Some therapists gradually deepen relaxation by progressive suggestions, with step-by-step arm levitation. When the subject's hand touches his face they assume he is in hypnosis. Actually there is a difference between relaxation and hypnosis insofar as the depth of alteration of consciousness is concerned. Whether suggestions are more effective in hypnosis than in relaxation will depend on how the patient interperts the suggestions and on their meaning to him during both states.

Is hypnosis useful in criminal investigations?

Where a subject is likely to incriminate himself by confessions, he may resist revealing information. He may bring up false phantasies or deliberately lie even in deep hypnosis. On the other hand, where the subject trusts and has confidence in the operator he may decide to relieve himself of guilt and tell the truth, even revealing suppressed or forgotten experiences. Facts brought up during hypnosis have to be scrupulously tested because phantasies are move vivid in this state than in the waking state.

16

The Nature of Hypnosis

The question is often asked: Exactly what is hypnosis? Here are some answers given by a variety of laymen and professional people:

"A healing miracle"

"A theatrical performance"

"A profound happening similar to a religious experience"

"A peaceful siesta"

"A journey into the unknown"

"A *folie à deux,* during which we cannot tell who is being hypnotized, the subject or hypnotist"

"A decrepit old tactic in new trappings"

"A charismatic menace"

It is not surprising that these responses are so contradictory, since they describe a phenomenon which has been misunderstood. In hypnosis there are complex, puzzling elements that are present in a number of other kinds of human interaction, such as religious conversion, faith healing, natural childbirth, and yoga systems. Hypnosis probably occurs when a mother lulls her child to sleep, when the advertiser breaks through the sales resistance of a customer, when the police interrogator elicits a confession, and when the politician implants propaganda in the minds of his constituents. One reason for the confusion about hypnosis is that no one has ever been able to give an exact and complete definition of what constitutes the hypnotic state. In fact, there are those who even deny the validity of hypnosis as a distinctive, identifiable state.

Actually, it is difficult to pinpoint the nature of hypnosis because it assumes so many varying forms in different people. Attempts to define it are often influenced by differing interpretations of how people behave under hypnosis or by beliefs of what is supposed to take place. Moreover, a subject's reactions may change at different times according to his prevailing mood. For instance, when a subject is happy and calm, he is apt to respond differently from when he is upset and despondent. A further complication is that trance characteristics will sometimes be influenced by the method of induction as well as by the immediate relationship that is developing between subject and operator. Finally, the subject tends to comply with what he imagines is demanded of him at the moment.

This does not mean that he is a puppet of the hypnotist. The subject at all times remains in control of what he will do, and he may easily resist any suggestions that he interprets as threatening. Of course, if he is a person who ordinarily lacks control over his impulses and emotions, he may not be able to hold himself in check. But he will also display a lack of restraint under other circumstances, for example, in drinking or becoming involved in an upsetting human relationship.

How Can One Tell If a Person Is Hypnotized?

A solution to the problem of the nature of hypnosis would be more readily forthcoming if it could be established without question that a person in a trance state is going through something totally different from any other state he has experienced. The difficulty here is that one is never really sure of this, either by observing the behavior of a person or by asking him whether or not he has entered a trance. It is easy for a subject to simulate hypnotic behavior if he knows in advance what is expected of him. For that matter it is also simple to pretend being asleep. The deep breathing, the inertness, and the occasional snoring that we associate with sleep are readily assumed by a person who wishes to put on an act of dozing. However, in the case of sleep simulation it is possible to spot impostors by attaching an encephalographic apparatus to the skull and studying the brain waves. These waves are different in sleep. We have no such objective test for hypnosis, because the electroencephalographic tracings are generally the same as those in waking life. Of course, with the refinement of instruments in the future, it may be possible to develop new techniques to detect or determine hypnosis. To date, however, we have no such methods. One of the factors that complicate any definite interpretations of the nature of hypnosis is that most people after they have come out of a true hypnotic state believe that they were faking. This makes it difficult to accept the statements of a subject at face value. Yet an experienced hypnotist will be able to tell from the reactions of his subject, with a reasonable measure of certainty, whether or not he has induced hypnosis.

An important finding confirmed by experimenters over and over again is that hypnosis does not release any truly unique reactions that cannot be brought on by other means. For example, if a person is able on suggestion to imagine he sees a tiger during a trance and cannot do so with the same suggestions in a condition of full consciousness, we would be inclined to credit his perceptual aberration to the hypnotic state. However, we would be wrong to assume that hallucination is an exclusive property of hypnosis. For if the same subject were to be sealed off in a dark soundproof room with no stimulation of any kind, he would sooner or later, through sensory deprivation, have imaginary perceptions, even though he was fully awake. Or if he were lost in a desert for days, subject to parching thirst and hunger, he would probably see an oasis in the distance as part of a mirage. By the same token, we fail to show that any other behavioral manifestation brought about through hypnosis is exclusive to the hypnotic state. This is what makes it so awkward to set up objective criteria that tell us whether a person has entered a trance.

Most people assume that it is relatively easy to tell when a person is in a waking, conscious condition. He is alert, his eyes are open, he reacts to stimuli around him, he answers when spoken to. But these signs are not always reliable indications, because good subjects (somnambules) can be hypnotized and remain in a trance with their eyes open. They can be alert, react to whatever stimuli impinge on them in a normal way, and converse with persons around them. I have done this dozens of times experimentally, and people in contact with the subjects could not discern that they were in a trance. The subjects themselves, brought out of hypnosis, could not remember the interlude during which they were presumably conscious.

Asking a subject if he has been hypnotized is of little help. Generally, the subject will deny having been in a hypnotic state, even when he has achieved the deepest somnambulistic trance. An example of this is a subject who insisted on proof that he had been hypnotized. He asked me to produce anesthesia, to penetrate his skin with a sterilized needle, then wake him up with the needle still in his flesh. This was done, and even though the subject seemed momentarily convinced, he still could not entirely accept the fact that he had been hypnotized. He insisted he must have fallen asleep and that I may have injected his skin with Novocaine so that he would feel no pain.

It has always been amusing to me how rarely patients will admit having entered a condition of hypnosis. Sometimes this is a psychological defense to deny their fear of yielding control to another person. Usually it is that they expect something quite spectacular and supernormal from hypnosis. When they experience no other sensations than that of mild relaxation, when their minds wander off spontaneously, when they remain in complete communicative contact with the operator, and when they realize they could resist any suggestion they consider unreasonable, they assume that they are not hypnotized. I have often tried to circumvent this resistance by explaining before induction exactly what phenomena will occur, debunking the conventional ideas that a hypnotized person loses control, automatically obeys, and forgets what has taken place. My subjects will seem to understand what I say, but upon awaking, they continue to express disappointment that they could hear everything I said, that their minds wandered off from time to time, that they could have opened their eyes if they wished, and that they remembered everything or almost everything that had taken place. Even when, to their delight, they have responded to posthypnotic therapeutic suggestions, they continue to believe that they were merely relaxed, not hypnotized.

Nonetheless, we have come to regard a number of conventional signs as significant for hypnosis. Since these signs are not unique to hypnosis, we may say that what hypnosis does is merely to facilitate or catalyze the emergence of certain responses latent within the individual.

We may now proceed to examine some of the conventional theories about the nature of hypnosis. It is understandable that adherents of different schools interpret hypnosis within the framework of their own special way of looking at behavior. Psychoanalysts advance the idea of hypnosis as a regression to a more primitive type of personality operation, reminiscent of childhood, with enhanced dependency, suggestibility, and desire to identify with an authority model as well as to take over power from him. Role theorists regard the individual undergoing hypnosis as playing a role and behaving as he believes a hypnotized individual should behave. Behavior therapists look on hypnosis as a phenomenon of conditioned learning. There are many other hypotheses advanced by authorities with special interests.

All the present-day theories are highly speculative. It is difficult to evolve a sound theory of hypnosis for a number of reasons. The most important one is that there are gaps in our understanding of brain mechanisms and psychodynamics; we do not yet have the tools by which we can examine hypnosis scientifically. What we observe in hypnosis must be questioned carefully. It is difficult to differentiate a person's reactions toward hypnosis from the hypnotic state itself. We must remember that hypnosis is filtered through a screen of the individual's own personal prejudices, demands, and needs. What we observe in the hypnotic state is more likely to be the individual's unique responses *to* the trance rather than manifestations *of* the trance state itself. This, of course, should not inhibit us from examining hypnosis and attempting to apply our tentative understandings empirically to the phenomena that emerge.

Physiological Theories

There are a number of theorists who insist that hypnosis is a purely physiological manifestation that, while covered with a psychological overlay, can be explained adequately in nonpsychological terms. This theory essentially states that a real physical change occurs in the nervous system during hypnosis. The nature of this change has never been demonstrated, but there are various speculations that locate alterations in the white substance of the brain, in the connections between the nerve cells (synapses), in the arteries feeding the brain, which produces a temporary anemia, and in the autonomic nervous system. In the main, these theories put hypnosis into one of four categories: first, a special kind of sleep; second, a hereditary immobilization mechanism found in many animals (animal hypnosis); third, a split off from customary activities (dissociation); fourth, a copy of an organic reflex altered by conditioning (conditioned reflex).

Hypnosis and sleep

Is hypnosis sleep or perhaps partial sleep? This viewpoint is a popular one and seems to be supported by the observable behavior of the subject, who, during hypnosis, becomes drowsy and apparently ready to enter sleep while responding to the verbal commands of the hypnotist. That the brain is never completely inhibited, even in deep sleep, is apparent in the fact that people in slumber are attuned to selective stimuli. A train may roar by outside the sleeping chamber without awakening a mother who arouses at the slightest sounds of her crying baby. A dog conditioned to expect food at the sound of a trumpet will doze through an entire range of instruments, but awaken immediately when the trumpet is blown. In the sleeplike state of hypnosis, also, the brain is keenly perceptive of sounds and other stimuli.

According to the great Russian scientist Pavlov, there is actually a close resemblance between hypnosis and sleep insofar as the physiology of the brain is concerned. Modern Pavlovians continue to uphold his theories about brain activity and have done some interesting work in attempting to substantiate them. The operations of the brain, they contend, are sponsored by different clusters of cells, some of which excite the organism while others inhibit it. In waking life the excitatory subdivisions predominate. In sleep, areas of inhibition spread widely, overwhelming the excitatory zones and bringing the individual to a state of slumbering repose. During hypnosis there is a partial inhibition—spheres of inhibitory cells surrounding the excitatory cells and virtually isolating them—which produces a "dissociation." A "watch zone" of alert cells continues to function, however, accounting for the rapport with the hypnotist. The induction of hypnosis, say Pavlovians, follows the laws of the conditioned reflex: the original stimulus that lulled the individual to sleep was provided by the mother who rocked the infant and supplied him with rhythmic soothing words and songs. The hypnotist in essence becomes a new mother who does the same thing with his chanting during induction. The Pavlovian theory of hypnosis has been criticized because it does not explain variables that are operating in the hypnotic process. Moreover, accounting for hypnosis by a physiological sleep theory is not supported by physiological studies.

The brain is subject to intrinsic electrical rhythms that can be recorded by electronic devices (electroencephalograms). Through the use of such instruments it is possible to detect when a person goes to sleep. For instance, in sleep, slow high-voltage waves (delta waves) that differ from the rapid low-voltage waves of waking life can be observed. In hypnosis, such slow waves are not in evidence. Furthermore, measurements of electrical skin resistance (galvanic reflex), basal metabolic rate, respiration, knee jerk (patellar reflex), cerebral circulation, and heart action are more like those in waking than sleep. Of course, if a person should slip off into sleep from the hypnotic state, which sometimes happens, particularly when suggestions to become drowsy and to sleep are made, the findings will be more characteristic of sleep. In general, there is little evidence to classify hypnosis in the category of sleep. Indeed, it is possible with nonconventional methods to induce hypnosis in subjects who continue to be wide awake and alert, and who mainfest none of the drowsy sleeplike manifestations found in persons inducted through the traditional fixation and relaxation techniques.

Hypnosis as a hereditary trait

Various species of invertebrate and vertebrate animals assume under certain conditions, such as restraint or sudden stimulation, muscular rigidity and immobility that ranges from several seconds to several hours. Among such animals are beetles, scorpions, spiders, cockroaches, frogs, crabs, lobsters, opossums, alligators, octopuses, crawfish, rabbits, lizards, guinea pigs, rats, chickens, owls, and monkeys. The reasons for this phenomenon are baffling, but it has been assumed that it is a form of "animal hypnosis" which serves some adaptive purpose. Darwin credited the reaction to death-feigning in the face of mortal danger, a kind of hereditary self-protective reflex.

There are those who believe that man is nothing more than a complex animal and that the special quality which sets him apart from other animals is more a matter of degree than of kind. They insist that once the psychological cover is removed in human hypnosis a basis is found similar to that in animal hypnosis. Hypnosis is regarded as a regressive hereditary trait developed in the course of evolution, the residue of an immobilizing reaction used by lower animals as a means of survival.

These ideas are provocative ones, and there is much to be learned by studying them. However, most authorities do not believe that animal and human hypnosis are at all alike, even though some neurophysiological reactions in man resemble those of animals. When we compare animal hypnosis with human hypnosis we find that the differences are much greater than the similarities.

Hypnosis as a form of dissociation

During the syndrome commonly known as sleepwalking (somnambulism), one moves about at night capable of performing complicated acts like telephoning or writing letters and reports and has no recollection of these occurrences in the morning. In unusual cases, a person may, during the daytime, for a brief or prolonged period, suddenly engage in activities that are at variance with his usual behavior, and then revert to his previous activities with no memory of things done during the interlude. He may wander off far afield from his customary habitat (fugue state) during the spell or engage in immoral actions that he may deny upon returning to his usual self. The latter reactions are classified as forms of hysteria.

In hysteria of this type, a number of unconscious memories and activities, usually repressed in the normal waking state, temporarily appropriate the stream of consciousness and function autonomously. The French psychologist Pierre Janet attributed this phenomenon to a splitting off of an important group of memories and ideas from the mainstream of recognition. He realized that dissociated strivings, even though subconscious, were able to influence behavior. Because it was possible under hypnosis to induce phenomena that resembled the symptoms of hysteria, and because the individual could perform complicated mental feats involving thinking and judgment, Janet looked upon hypnosis as a species of somnambulism, analogous to hysteria, in which intellectual processes could function simultaneously and independently through dissociation.

For many years the theory of dissociation was regarded as the key to hypnosis. Depth of hypnosis was presumably related to the degree of dissociation. Both hysteria and hypnotic susceptibility were considered dependent upon an aptitude to dissociate in hypnosis. The various functions governed by the brain were split off from each other by suggestion. The dissociation hypothesis was particularly suited to the idea of hypnosis as a form of automatism. This notion had its origin in the early theory that there are two distinct levels of behavior: one, a level of purposeful, volitional striving; the other, a level of reflex activity. Since hypnosis appeared to abolish volition, a reflex kind of behavior would automatically come into being. The latter was dissociated from consciousness, particularly in the posthypnotic state.

Although posthypnotic amnesia would seem to bear out the

fact of dissociation of a complex group of memories, investigation has revealed that the amnesia is an artificial one, being more apparent than real. It has been shown that there is no real barrier between two apparently isolated and dissociated groups of mental activity. Instead of dissociation, there is actually a very high degree of co-ordination in hypnosis.

Dissociation apparently serves an important function, and it may be looked upon as a form of motivated behavior. The dissociative tendency can be enhanced through suggestion, particularly during the hypnotic state. This, however, does not prove that hypnosis is basically a state of dissociation. Nevertheless there are some modern authorities who have elaborated on the dissociation hypothesis and still consider it the key to hypnosis.

Hypnosis as a conditioned reflex

Learning by verbal conditioning is a fact of life, and all kinds of responses may be linked to words presented in proper sequence. Experiments have shown that involuntary physiological reactions may be brought about by certain words. For example, flashing a light into the eye produces a contraction of the pupil. If a bell is simultaneously rung as the light is flashed and this action is repeated a number of times, eventually the bell itself, without the light, can produce pupillary contractions. The effect is even more pronounced and more permanent if the word "contract" is repeated with the light flash instead of the bell. For a period of time, depending on the degree of reinforcement, *i.e.*, repetition of the experiment, the word "contract" alone will be accompanied by contraction of the pupil. This fascinating phenomenon goes on entirely outside the consciousness of the individual.

The conditioning of physiological reactions to words has absorbed the attention of experimenters for a number of years. For a long time it was believed that the organs of the body were outside voluntary control. It has been discovered, however, that by simple techniques involving speaking, or even thinking certain words, almost any organ can be excited or inhibited. Thus the blood vessels of the skin can be conditioned to (1) contract with the word "cold or "snow," if such words are paired with plunging the hand into ice water, and (2) dilate with the word "hot," if the water is of high temperature. It has been shown that merely thinking about using certain muscles can start action currents in these muscles and that these currents can be measured.

By the same token, the words uttered during the induction of hypnosis are said to stimulate physiological reflexes and reactions that constitute the basis of hypnosis. The sleeplike condition, say the proponents of the conditioned-reflex theory, is thus only secondary to a plunge into a regressive state in which the subject gives up inner controls and abandons himself compliantly to direction by the hypnotist.

While the conditioned-reflex is an intensely interesting theory and undoubtedly accounts for physical reactions and even for certain psychologic reactions during hypnosis, it does not explain many important and complex phenomena of the hypnotic state. In itself, it is not a complete answer to the problem of the nature of hypnosis.

Psychological Theories

There are a number of theories which contend that hypnosis is dependent on factors other than physiological, namely, suggestion, role playing, and the revival of early child-parent relationships. Any physiological reactions are considered secondary to these basic psychological aspects. As with physiological theories, none of the psychological theories has been able to stand up under intensive scrutiny. Elements of each theory are nevertheless relevant to an understanding of some of the phenomena that may be observed in hypnosis.

Hypnosis as a form of suggestion

Because the suggestibility level is generally higher in hypnosis that in the waking state, there are some theorists who classify hypnosis as a form of suggestion. They maintain that the subject believes he can uncritically accept the pronouncements of the other partner in the hypnotic relationship. Even if this were true—and there are many reasons why it is not—it would not be a unique situation. There are many other areas in life where people uncritically accept mandates and ordinances. A person convinced of the power of a plenipotentiary or political official, or the wisdom of the religious leader or healer, will subject himself to regulations and directives with little or no contradiction. Soldiers in battle will face death at the command of an officer. A man convinced of the authority of the Bible will tend to live according to its precepts. There seems to be a built-in suggestibility mechanism in all people that works for both good and evil.

Suggestion, then, is not unique to hypnosis, even though it may operate to a higher degree in the trance than the waking state. We cannot characterize hypnosis by classifying it as a mere state of generalized or selective hypersuggestibility. That would be the same as saying that eating is a condition of increased salivation or gastric secretion simply because these physiological functions are increased during the intake and digestion of food.

Actually, the heightened state of suggestibility in the trance can easily be neutralized by a subject who is unwilling to accept some of the hypnotist's exhortations. This was dramatically illustrated to me by one of my subjects, a man who had come to a rehabilitation center with the complaint of intractable pain in his back. The surgeons whom he had consulted insisted that this pain was psychological in nature, possibly hysterical. It was for this reason that hypnosis was suggested as a diagnostic aid. At our first meeting I quickly induced a trance and then remarked that the subject would be relieved of the pain in his back but would experience pain in his right arm. This suggestion was readily accepted. I then gave him a posthypnotic suggestion to the effect that he would continue to have pain in his right arm but would have no pain in his back after he emerged from the trance.

We tested this after hypnosis was terminated. With great astonishment he said he ha- no back trouble. But he complained bitterly about pain in his arm. I then rehypnotized him and gave him the same suggestions, this time telling him he would feel pain in his *left* arm. He refused to obey this command. When he opened his eyes, he seemed flushed. Complaining of tension, he shook his head and said, "I refuse." When I asked what he refused to do, he replied, "I refuse to have pain in my left arm." He then told me that his father had died of a heart attack, and one of the preceding symptoms had been pain in his left arm, a result of angina pectoris. Even though he had gone into a somnambulistic trance, he refused to obey a command that provoked anxiety.

The suggestive element in hypnosis is relative. No matter how deep the trance may be, the subject is capable of selecting those suggestions he wishes to obey and rejecting others.

Hypnosis as a form of role playing

Some theorists contend that hypnosis does not occur in isolation. It exists, they say, as a consequence of a relationship in which the subject focuses on the words of the hypnotist. Accepting them as true, he is willing to act on them. What the subject does, then, is to fulfill roles prescribed by the hypnotist's explicit and/or implicit structuring. These roles alter the way the individual looks at himself and the world. Some role theorists regard hypnosis as a form of acting, during which the subject achieves the greatest success in his role if he accurately perceives what he is supposed to do and has an aptitude for role playing.

However, critics of role-playing theories point out that some of the phenomena of the trance cannot be explained solely on the basis of acting a part. To refute these theories, they point to induced anesthesia, deep enough to permit major surgery, and age regression, during which the subject revives childish patterns and experiences of which he is not conscious in waking life. Additionally, role theories cannot account for trance states produced in the absence of a hypnotist, such as involuntary "highway hypnosis" during night driving.

Hypnosis as a regressive phenomenon

Some early psychoanalytical theories, advanced between 1900 and 1910, held that hypnosis was a special kind of relationship in which the hypnotist attempted to wrest from the subject control over his volition and actions. The peculiar susceptibility of the subject to these designs on him by the hypnotist was regarded by Sigmund Freud many years ago as the result of the subject's unconscious desire for regressive gratification.

Sandor Ferenczi, a contemporary of Freud, expanded this idea around 1910, explaining that hypnosis was a reactivation of the subject's infantile attitude of blind faith and implicit obedience based on both love and fear of his parents. The authority with which the hypnotist was endowed was thus a projection of repressed infantile impulses, which made the subject regard the hypnotizer as the authoritative parent (transference). The hypnotist with an imposing presence was often successful because he resembled the stern all-powerful father who expected the child to obey and imitate him. A situation in which the mother-child relationship was repeated might also be conducive to hypnosis. Soft, monotonous words spoken to the subject during the process of induction simulated those of the tender mother lulling the child to sleep. Although the feeling of awe for the parents and compulsive need to obey them implicitly disappeared as the individual matured, there nonetheless persisted within each person, Ferenczi explained, a need to worship someone. This need was realized in the hypnotic state, and the subject actually looked upon the hypnotist as a revived image of the parent.

The hypnotic situation thus reanimated unconscious desires and fantasies that existed during the early stages of the child's development. In a later study, *Group Psychology and the Analysis of the Ego,* published in 1922, Freud pointed out that the emotions experienced during hypnosis and the state of being in love were similar. He also stressed the fact that feelings of helplessness in the face of a superior power might be aroused, provoking a passive masochistic yielding to the hypnotic trance.

Some authorities continue to subscribe to these early psychoanalytic theories, which regard hypnosis as a regressive kind of masochistic surrender to a power figure. Others, while accepting the validity of transference as a key element in hypnosis, elaborate on it in terms of an "ego subsystem." They define this transference as a process in which a part of the self remains reality-oriented. Hypnosis in short is said to be an "altered ego state," from which the individual may reap certain benefits. As long as these benefits continue, the subject will comply with the demands made on him by the hypnotist. There are certain theorists who believe that in hypnosis the subject escapes the condemnation of his conscience (superego) under the wing of the omnipotent hypnotist, who in effect gives him permission to do so. The subject surrenders his responsibility to the hypnotist for gratifications he ordinarily would not allow himself to indulge in.

Applications of Theory to Practice

All these theories demonstrate that there are areas of disagreement as well as agreement among different theorists about the nature of hypnosis. Although hypnosis has been practiced for over two centuries, no one has yet been able to define it precisely. This is not surprising, since our knowledge of the workings of a single body cell is still fragmentary. Yet every year brings new scientific developments and the refinement of our measuring instruments, which enable us to learn more and more about the chemistry, physiology, and psychology of waking life, of sleep, and of conditions of altered awareness, such as the trance state. Gradually, the shadowy parts are being illuminated by research. There is a good chance that in the not too distant future we may be able to describe more accurately what happens during hypnosis. Today many of the conclusions about the nature of hypnosis are derived from relatively unreliable data. The resulting theories are accordingly vague, none of them explaining satisfactorily the phenomena we observe, and none of them truly testable. For the present a complete explanation of the mysteries of the trance is not possible. But we can be reassured by the knowledge that though we cannot define all the dimensions of hypnosis, we can take advantage of its beneficial effects. After all, we also use electricity, although we are largely ignorant of its exact nature.

17

The History of Hypnosis

> And the Lord God caused a deep sleep to fall upon Adam, and he slept; and he took one of his ribs, and he closed up the flesh instead thereof;
>
> And the rib, which the Lord God had taken from man, made he a woman, and brought her unto the man.
>
> Genesis 2:21, 22

The story of hypnosis constitutes one of the strangest chapters in the history of medicine. The early writers of the Bible undoubtedly were aware of the powers of induced sleep, as the passage in Genesis quoted above indicates. The miraculous nature of divine intervention during sleep is repeatedly recorded in the inscriptions of the ancients. Thousands of years before Christ, the priests of Egypt and Greece built sleep temples dedicated to healing the troubled and afflicted. A man tortured by pain or anxiety could find refuge here from the vexations of his everyday life. An assigned priest or priestess would listen to his complaints and then arrange for the appropriate rites and rituals. Under the injunctions of the attendants, the troubled pilgrim would retreat into a soothing repose from which he might periodically arouse himself to relate his dreams. These were analyzed for clues of spirit infestation, for which specific remedies were prescribed.

The pilgrim was fed, bathed, massaged, and given essential potions, poultices, emetics, and clysters. Assurances were proffered that he would get well, and in this temple of tranquillity surcease from suffering often came about.

In the reaches of recorded history, priestly authorities were credited with special powers of healing. For instance, hieroglyphics thousands of years ago show Imhotep so influential with the sick that his very presence banished disease. The Ebers Papyrus mentions the "laying on of hands," a practice that presumably reduced fever, removed inflammation, eliminated pain, and banished physical and mental abnormalities.

With the advent of Christianity, suggestive healing was regarded as a miraculous working of the Deity. The powers of Christ in curing the diseased and afflicted are legendary. The chants, prayers, and invocations voiced by ecclesiastics, who patterned themselves on the example set by Christ, scored beneficial results. During this early period of Christianity, disease was ascribed to demoniacal possession. Accordingly, the religious healer directed his suggestive efforts toward the casting out of demons.

But the demons continued their ravages, and epidemics of hysterial illness and hysterical behavior, such as frenzied dancing and flagellation, broke out repeatedly among masses of people, stimulating more concentrated healing efforts on the part of the clergy. Prayer was sometimes reinforced by other suggestive measures like the laying on of hands. Because royalty was believed affiliated with divinity, special healing powers were credited to a king's touch. Somewhat less effective powers were residual in a queen's touch and in the touch of lesser nobility. The cures effected by King Pyrrhus, Emperor Vespasian, and various kings of France are legendary. During the London plagues incredible successes were reported through use of the touching miracle.

There was no question in the minds of people that the cures were due to divine intervention. However, around 1530 Philippus Paracelsus, a controversial physician, considered by some a genius and by others a scoundrel, advanced a theory that human health and well-being were influenced by emanations of a magnetic fluid from the stars and other heavenly bodies. Not long after this an eminent scientist, Jean Baptiste van Helmont, expanded this idea by claiming that not only were people bombarded by extraterritorial rays, but that they themselves radiated a magnetic field which could be directed by will and could gain control of the mental and physical lives of others. Individuals who claimed healing powers were undoubtedly possessed of powerful fields of influence. Periodically, practitioners appeared who with great confidence in their magnetic powers cured diseases by stroking with the hand. A particularly effective operator was Valentine Greatrakes of Affane, in the county of Waterford, Ireland, who around the middle of the seventeenth century applied himself with such great proficiency that he was reverently called "The Stroker." He was reputed to be able to eliminate the "King's Evil," scrofula, actually a tubercular involvement of the lymph glands. Thousands of afflicted souls from all parts of England applied to "The Stroker" for cures, and his fame spread throughout England. Such eminent scientists and theologians as Robert Boyle and Ralph Cudworth endorsed his successes. Regressive ideas about the nature of healing continued to appear during the next century, particularly the crediting of disease to demoniacal possession, which required rigorous exorcism through prayer. Perhaps the most noted of the "exorcists" was the Roman Catholic priest Johann Joseph Gassner of Swabia, whose talents in destroying devils made him world famous. His "cures" around the middle of the eighteenth century brought hordes of people to his chambers to receive the benefits of his supernatural powers.

In 1646 a German mathematician and scholar, Athanasius Kircher, published a book that proposed a force in nature responsible for the creation of disease and for its cure. He called it "animal magnetism." Influenced by this idea, an obscure Scotsman named Maxwell developed around 1665 a theory of magnetotherapeutics, which purported that living things emitted rays from their souls. These emanations came from a vital spirit, a universal substance that bound all bodies to each other. Even animal and human excreta contained this spirit. It could thus be used to cure diseases. Apparently the practice of applying urine or feces to wounds, which incidentally is still employed in some parts of the world, stems from this theory. Disease could, it was believed, also be transferred from one individual to another, either by direct touch or through intermediary objects.

It will undoubtedly be recognized that many of these early theories and practices have their modern counterparts, not only among primitive but among civilized peoples. The idea of divine meddling with the fortunes of mankind, of spirit possession and the need for exorcism, and of planetary and stellar influences on health and personality (e.g., astrology) are rampant in universal belief systems. One need only observe how effectively the evangelist Oral Roberts banishes symptoms on a national television hookup to realize that the laying on of hands is not a defunct therapeutic method. The belief in transferring disease by touch is still not dead in some areas. When I was a schoolboy in Rochester, New York, there was a widespread neighborhood practice of rubbing a coin over a wart and throwing it over one's shoulder to transfer the wart to the unwary person who retrieved the coin.

The Impact of Mesmer

Franz Anton Mesmer (1734–1815) is often credited with having been the first to claim hypnosis as a scientific branch of medicine under the label of "animal magnetism." Actually, Mesmer originated neither the term nor the concept of animal magnetism. He lifted it from the work of a number of persons before him. Indeed, his doctor's dissertation was liberally plagiarized from the treatise *De imperio solis et lunae in corpora humana et morbis inde oriundis,* written by an English physician, Richard Mead, in 1704. The thesis of his dissertation, "The Influence of the Stars and Planets as Curative Powers," presented in 1773, was that there were gravitational tides in the atmosphere that influenced everything on earth. Thes tides issued from the planets in the form of an impalpable, invisible gas that filled every crevice of the universe. Unknown mechanical laws governed the ebb and flow of this field. In some ways the substance had properties similar to those of magnets. Indeed the magnetism within some persons was so powerful that it could even at a distance be transferred to animate and inanimate objects. This force Mesmer called animal magnetism.

As a physician Mesmer applied himself to the treatment of disease with his theory, and on one occasion he achieved a cure of hysteria in a young woman by holding magnets close to her body. This confirmed his idea that magnetic forces could cure diseases by restoring a harmonious distribution of nervous fluid. A succession of patients responded favorably to Mesmer's magnets, their cure often being preceded by a convulsion that Mesmer called a "crisis," a sign to him that magnetism was working. These successes convinced Mesmer that a universal fluid did exist in which all bodies were immersed.

Mesmer did not always succeed in curing his patients, and he explained his failures by saying that some individuals had an undefined neutralizing force within their bodies that could negate the effects of animal magnetism. But where it was accepted, animal magnetism issuing from a person especially charged, or from things this person touched, could directly cure diseases of nerves and indirectly all other maladies.

Mesmer's chief contribution was not his theories but his method of inducing a trance state, which he associated with sleepwalking. He recognized that therapeutic work could best be accomplished in a trance, but he wholly misinterpreted its powers or nature. He wrote:

> In this state of sleep or trance the patients can foresee the future and represent to themselves the remotest past. Their senses expand to all distances and in all directions, without hindrance. It appears as if all nature were present to them. But these capacities differ in different individuals. The most common phenomena are to be able to see the interior of their own bodies and those of others, and to recognize not only the disease, but also the course it will take and the means which will cure it. But these capacities are seldom found united in one and the same individual.*

Mesmer was forced to leave Vienna because of the hostile attitude of the medical profession. He took up residence in Paris, where he founded with Deslon a clinic for the "Mesmeric" treatment of varous diseases. Mesmerism became a fashionable fad, and throngs of wealthy followers filled his apartments to receive the magical nostrum. His impressive manner, the lush surroundings, his mystical passes and strokings, the slow music and the expectation of benefit all contributed to the effect. Patients were placed in a *baquet,* or large wooden tub, which was filled with

* Many of Mesmer's ideas continue to be espoused by those who posit the existence of supernormal phenomena such as clairvoyance, telekinesis, and paranormal perception. Edgar Cayce has written what are probably the most popular materials along these lines.

water, iron filings, bottles, and iron rods. These were then applied to the patients' various ailing parts. Mesmer himself appeared in a long silk robe carrying an iron wand with which he touched his patients. Several such treatments sufficed to cure a variety of disorders.

Mesmerism attracted a great many charlatans who, as "magnetizers," made extravagant claims for the efficacy of this treatment. Many of them professed supernatural powers that made it possible for them to detect lesions deep within the patient's body. Common expressions were, "This patient's stomach is full of pimples. . . . I see a ball of hair blocking the bowel. . . . Your chest is all grazed inside, and you must not sing for several days; it looks as if it had been scraped with a knife, and your lungs are full of dust."

The cult of animal magnetism, with its promise of dramatic cures, swept through France. Charges of fraud and quackery from most of the medical profession prompted the French government, in 1784, to launch an investigation through a committee of nine eminent scientists, among whom was Benjamin Franklin. The king of France also appointed a separate commission of physicians to conduct a separate study. It was easy for both groups to prove that animal magnetism was a powerful force only when its power was imagined in the mind of the patient. For example, where a patient was told that a tree had been magnetized, even when it had had no contact with Mesmer or his followers, a convulsion followed. On the other hand a tree than had been "magnetically charged" by a mesmerist had no effect when patients were not informed of this fact.

A secret subsidiary report condemned magnetism on the basis that it facilitated sexual seduction.* The commissioners then

* This idea has still not died out. The seduction theme of hypnosis was perhaps best popularized in George du Maurier's novel *Trilby,* in which the hypnotist Svengali overpowered a helpless female and inspired her, not to sex, but to musical accomplishment. A novel of the Victorian underground printed in Moscow in 1891, *The Power of Mesmerism,* condenses most of the distortions about hypnosis in one highly pornographic unit. There are some writings on hypnosis that advise a hypnotist for his own protection never to induct a woman into a trance without a third party being present as a witness. While it is possible for a lady to be sexually tempted during hypnosis, she is not imperiled to act this out or to accept indecent proposals unless she finds it difficult to maintain her virtue in the waking state.

unanimously concluded that "there was no proof of the existence of an animal fluid and that the violent effects (such as convulsions) observed in public clinics are to be attributed to the touching, to the aroused imagination, and to the mechanical imitation which leads us in spite of ourselves to repeat that which strikes our senses. . . . the sight of these crises is likewise dangerous because of the imitation which nature seems to have imposed on us as a law. . . ."*

Mesmer denied the validity of these statements, and he stubbornly continued to insist that animal magnetism was a physical fact and that the imagination had little or nothing to do with his therapy. Interestingly, in spite of the condemnatory report, he continued to attract students and colleagues who published many books and pamphlets on the wonders of animal magnetism. This is testimony to man's unquenchable penchant for the mysterious.

The Post-Mesmeric Period of Animal Magnetism

Truth, however delayed and piecemeal it may be, somehow vanquishes superstition. A tiny ray of light illuminated one aspect of trance behavior through the work of one of Mesmer's followers, the Marquis de Puységur (1751–1828). While applying magnetism to a young peasant, the marquis discovered that he produced a sleeping trance without the conventional "crisis," the violent, often convulsive paroxysm hitherto considered an essential part of magnetic treatment. He found too that he could cause physical and emotional changes by proffering suggestions, which up to this time had not been made during the magnetic interlude. Moreover, the subject could talk in the trance and after

* Benjamin Franklin laconically wrote: "There are so many disorders which cure themselves and such a disposition in mankind to deceive themselves." What the commissioners observed was what we continuously see even today, namely that people in their trance behavior imitate the actions of those around them. What we often classify as phenomena of hypnosis are patterns copied by the subjects, and which they believe are inevitable. The more suggestible the individual, the more faithfully he will model himself after the examples around him.

awaking not remember what had happened until he had again been magnetized. This condition Puységur called "artificial somnambulism," which we now recognize as the deepest form of hypnosis occurring in from 10 per cent to 15 per cent of subjects.

Puységur still maintained the idea of a vital fluid flowing from the mind of the operator to the subject and controlled by the operator's will. Indeed, he often practiced magnetism by magnetizing an elm tree in his yard in Buzancy, around which his patients were gathered. By touching it they presumably obtained therapeutic benefits. Puységur overestimated the powers of magnetized persons, believing that they became clairvoyant, possessed telepathic capacities, were capable of diagnosing their personal maladies as well as those of others, and could prescribe for these the proper treatments. These fallacious notions still persist among some credulous persons. In spite of Puységur's naïveté he did contribute many significant observations. For instance, he found that no person could be magnetized against his will or be made to do anything in conflict with his critical reasoning.

The error perpetrated by Puységur was the idea that the magnetizer not the subject was responsible for somnambulism. It remained for a follower of the marquis, a Portuguese priest named José Custódio de Faria, to place a new emphasis on the subject's psychic impressionability and not on any magnetic force. However, he offered a most astonishing explanation for what happened when suggestibility produced somnambulism: the subject's blood thinned out! We can forgive this creative man (who incidentally died a pauper) for his lack of medical knowledge, since the richness of his discoveries about methods of induction and trance behavior prepared the way for the next advance in the understanding of what Faria termed "concentration" rather than "animal magnetism." For example, he described how through "concentration" (*i.e.*, hypnosis) pain could be lessened ("mesmerica anesthesia") permitting surgery. His astute observations were mixed with a number of confused theoretical concepts published posthumously. The contributions of this gifted priest influenced many magnetizers away from the dead-end theory of Mesmer. Perhaps the most important professional person who followed Faria's original path was the physician Alexandre Bertrand (1795–1831), who wrote an interesting volume titled *Du Magnetisme Animal en France* in which he proposed suggestion as the principal force in magnetism, a crucial discovery that was unfortunately not considered valid until many years later.

Around this period (the early 1800's) a great controversy raged over what phenomena constituted the trance and whether or not Mesmer (even if he was a charlatan) had discovered a new vital fluid in animal magnetism. Articles and books, pro and con, medical and nonmedical, flooded the marketplace. Magnetizers throughout France, Prussia, and England participated in a heated debate and published an extensive literature and many bibliographies. Even students in the humanities and arts became involved, and animal magnetism became the theme of books and plays. Some persons, including physicians like Justinus Kerner of Prussia, believed in miracles that could be brought about through animal magnetism. Kerner presented as evidence his work with a stigmatized nun, the "Seeress of Prevorst." One of the most inspired poets of the Swabian period, Kerner published his findings in 1829 in a famous work, *Die Seherin von Prevorst, Eröffnungen über das innere Leben des Menschen und über das Hineinragen einer Geisterwelt in die unsere.*

A new commission was appointed in 1825 by the French Academy of Medicine, which studied the evidence carefully for five years and then reversed the decision made forty years earlier by what had obviously been a more scientifically minded group. Endorsing the existence of animal magnetism, it insisted that subjects in a trance could predict months before it happened the exact time to the minute that a convulsion would occur. It also maintained that some subjects could even see with their eyes closed. The commission terminated this monstrously unscientific proclamation with the softening statement that magnetism had a place in medicine and that the academy should support further research.

Prior to the discovery of chemical anesthesia there was a great deal of interest in any measure that could dull pain for surgical and dental procedures. There was considerable excitement over the claims of magnetizers who were heralding magnetism as a useful anesthetic. It was inevitable that the academy would again launch an investigation of magnetism. The new commission in

1837 examined the evidence for clairvoyance and telepathy under magnetism, as well as the ability to perform such supernormal acts as reading written messages when notes were placed against the abdomen. Its conclusions were the reverse of the previous commission's, and it wrote a strongly negative report about the virtues and even the existence of magnetism, denying any validity in Mesmer's theories or methods.

It was obvious to the commission that the "cures" which were being produced, as well as the manifestations of magnetic interchanges such as convulsions, were entirely due to suggestion. The patients anticipated and expected these effects; their faith was sufficiently strong to bring them about. To Mesmer, however, it was the physical impact of animal magnetism that was curative, and he believed so strongly in his magnetic powers that he insisted he had helped patients whose illnesses had been found impossible to palliate by other physicans.

Even after Mesmer was discredited, and years after his death, magnetism flourished in Europe, particularly in Germany, Russia, and Denmark. Its healing value was applauded by some dignified members of the medical profession and by the clergy. In the United States, New Orleans became the center for magnetic practices. A monument was placed at Mesmer's grave at Morsburg by Berlin physicians. Influential magnetizers with a dedication to the mystical continued to believe in the clairvoyant and telepathic virtues of the trance, which now had taken the title of "electrobiology" instead of "animal magnetism." This is not extraordinary since even today, one hundred and twenty-five years later, there are practitioners who continue to fuse hypnosis with spiritualism. At any rate, magnetism underwent a revival, and many physicians continued to believe that a healing magnetic fluid issued from their bodies into the bodies of their patients. This notion was combined with more or less weird concepts of astrology, phrenology, and the curative effects of metals and magnets. A psychological explanation for the trance was submerged by a tidal wave of fallacious ideas, which were grouped under the pseudoscientific label "odylic force," a term invented by the Baron Karl von Reichenbach. This doctrine convinced the more sober elements of the medical profession that magnetism was a fraudulent and superstitious concept. Feeling ran so high among medical men that any physician who experimented with magnetism was regarded with suspicion and considered a quack.

While most of the activity and controversy was taking place in France and Prussia, a few physicians were working with magnetism in England. One of the earliest professional practitioners was John Elliotson (1791–1868), a professor of medicine at the University College in London, who resigned his appointment when magnetism was forbidden at the University College Hospital. Elliotson took up the cause of magnetism against the opinion of almost the entire medical profession. His activities cost him dearly in reputation and income. He was discharged from his position at the University College Hospital for choosing magnetism as his subject for the Harveian Oration of 1846. Despite the fact that he was branded a charlatan, Elliotson and his followers started the *Zoist,* a journal dealing with mesmerism and cerebral physiology. Under the influence of Elliotson, Mesmeric institutions were formed in various parts of the British Isles. At the institution in Exeter, a magnetizer named Parker claimed to have mesmerized twelve hundred persons and to have performed a total of two hundred painless operations.

Contributions of James Braid

The rise of the natural sciences in the early 1800's, along with a repudiation of any mystical orientation ultimately diverted attention almost completely from magnetism. Its practice was largely left to laymen who continued to use it for healing purposes against the advice of the medical profession.

A feeble attempt was made later to revive animal magnetism in England. When in 1841 the French magnetizer Lafontaine conducted some magnetic experiments in Manchester, James Braid, a Manchester physician, became interested in the phenomenon. He was able to prove that it was not brought about by any special force or magnetic fluid; instead he avowed that it was the product of forces within the individual himself. Braid coined the word "hypnotism," which he derived from a Greek word meaning "to put to sleep." He used it to describe the physical condition created within the individual through the manipulations of the operator. Braid published several treatises on his work, the best known of which was *Neurypnology,* released in 1843. In it he attributed the effects of hypnotism to fatigue of the nervous system. A second book, *Magic, Witchcraft, Animal Magnetism, Hypnotism and Electro-Biology,* published in 1852, described the details of painless surgical operations under hypnosis.

Since Braid was a more scientifically oriented person than Elliotson, and because he offered a physiological explanation for the phenomena of magnetism, he was not subjected to persecution by his colleagues. His experiments soon convinced him that psychological rather than physiological forces were principally responsible for hypnotic effects, and he stressed the importance of suggestion as the dominant influence. Actually, Braid rediscovered what Bertrand had stressed years before, namely, that the individual who was magnetized was in a highly suggestible state. Essentially, his behavior was influenced by the operator and by others around him.

Around this period James Esdaile (1808–1859), a Scottish surgeon working in India, was achieving great success in the use of trance anesthesia. He performed over one thousand minor and three hundred major surgical operations, which were completely painless. Esdaile's influence was short-lived, however, for two reasons. First, chemical anesthesia was discovered around 1848, and the administration of chloroform proved to be a swifter and more reliable method than hypnotic anesthesia. Second, the public's revived interest in spiritualism included hypnotic phenomena. As a result, scientific groups associated hypnosis with black art. This prejudice still exists to some extent today.

Pre-Freudian Period

Although interest in hypnosis declined in France during the last part of the nineteenth century, there was excitement over the work of A. Liébeault (1823–1904). Liébeault, a physician who shied away from publicity, used hypnosis successfully in his treatment of patients, most of whom were so poor that they paid him no fee. The medical profession remained skeptical about his claims, so much so that when he published a book on hypnosis, scarcely a copy was sold. Liébeault, like Braid, subscribed to

Bertrand's theory that the operator exerted his influence on a subject largely through suggestion. Physiological explanations, he insisted, were invalid. However, Liébeault tended to exaggerate the powers of hypnosis, which he believed could influence favorably not only functional but also organic diseases. It could even, he imagined, cure cancer and might also act as an antidote to poisoning. He claimed cures for anemia, intermittent fever, pulmonary tuberculosis, menstrual difficulties, neuralgia, and migraine.

Liébeault's work would have gone unnoticed had it not been for the physician Hippolyte Bernheim (1840–1919), a professor at the Nancy Medical School, who became incensed by Liébeault's claims and decided to visit his clinic to expose him as a quack. Bernheim was piqued because in 1882 Liébeault insisted that he had cured a patient who had been treated for sciatica without success by Bernheim for six years. But Bernheim's investigation of Liébeault's methods had surprising results. Not only did he accept this cure, but he became so intrigued by Liébeault's work that he undertook a study of hypnotism. Soon he became one of its most ardent devotees, publishing a book in which he claimed cures for hysterical paralysis and the loss of the capacity to speak (aphonia), hysteroid crises, gastric difficulties, loss of appetitie, "depression of the spirit," pains, tremors, "fixed ideas," sleep-walking, and a number of other complaints associated with functional diseases.

A puzzling chapter in the history of hypnosis was contributed by the most famous neurologist of his time, Jean Martin Charcot (1825–1893), of the Paris Hospital of Salpêtrière. Charcot, fascinated by hypnosis, experimented with a few hysterical patients and then arrived at a completely erroneous idea of what was taking place. Since he was an organicist, he attempted to explain hypnosis as a pathological state. He completely misinterpreted what was happening to his hypnotized patients. He even believed a magnet could transfer induced paralysis from one part of the body to the other. Charcot finally concluded that hypnosis was an abnormal condition, possible only in persons with an unusual nervous constitution. He devised several singularly peculiar tests for hypnosis, which he linked with hysteria.

Another false physiological exposition was given by the eminent physiologist R. Heidenhain, a professor at Breslau. He believed that fixation of the eyes temporarily paralyzed the functions of the higher brain and made the subject the victim of automatic actions. Both Charcot and Heidenhain were so influential in their day that their conclusions were difficult to dispute, let alone reverse.

Among those who dared to do this were Bernheim and his associates at the Nancy school. Disputing Charcot's findings, they disagreed that hypnosis was a pathological condition, insisting it was a state that could be induced in normal subjects through suggestion. A violent quarrel between the Salpêtrière and the Nancy schools was eventually settled in favor of the more experienced observers of Nancy, who, against Charcot's score of a handful of hysterical patients, had worked with thousands of subjects.

It was Pierre Janet, director of the Psychological Laboratory at Salpêtrière, who finally explained the errors of his chief on the basis that Charcot had never hypnotized a single subject but had instead accepted the conclusions of younger, more inexperienced physicians. Charcot nevertheless did a service to hypnosis by confirming its respectability as a practice and by interesting such persons in the phenomenon as Baron Richard von Krafft-Ebing and Sigmund Freud.

Because of the renewed interest in hypnosis around the end of the nineteenth century, a committee was appointed in 1890 by the British Medical Association to investigate the validity of hypnotism as a medical procedure. Among the committee members were Daniel Hack Tuke, the eminent psychiatrist, and many other distinguished physicians, who completed their report in 1892. Not only was hypnotism acknowledged as a useful phenomenon, but its use was warmly encouraged for insomnia, pain, alcoholism, and many functional disorders.

Freud and Hypnosis

Sigmund Freud became interested in hypnosis early in his career. In 1885 he visited Charcot at Salpêtrière, and in 1889 he worked with Liébeault and Bernheim at Nancy in an effort to improve his technique. His goal, like that of his teachers, was symptom removal through hypnotic suggestion. Freud's friend and colleague, Joseph Breuer (1842–1925), on one occasion described to him a unique way of using hypnosis. While treating a hysterical patient, Anna O., whose illness was precipitated by her fear and shock at discovering that her father had developed a lung abscess, he was confounded by the fact that in spite of all hypnotic efforts, her symptoms became progressively worse. She was incapacitated by distressing physical symptoms and alternating states of consciousness.

Breuer accidentally discovered that when Anna was induced to speak freely under hypnosis, she exhibited a profound emotional reaction and thereafter experienced a decided relief from her complaints. He learned from the things she said that the states of somnolence into which she lapsed each afternoon were repetitions of the vigils she had held at her sick father's bedside when she nursed him in the early stages of his illness. Although Anna's general condition gradually improved, she continued to exhibit alternating states of consciousness, and she was indolent, moody, disobedient, and at times actively hallucinated.

One afternoon, during a period of intense heat, Anna suffered from great thirst, but to her dismay she found that she was unable to swallow water. For six weeks thereafter she quenched her thirst exclusively by eating fruit, especially melons. During a hypnotic session, she revealed in a fit of anger that, to her great disgust, a former governess had permitted a dog to drink water out of a glass in her presence. Out of politeness, she had not protested at the time. Following this revelation, she surprised Breuer by asking for a drink, which she imbibed without hesitation, awaking from hypnosis with the glass at her lips. There was no further recurrence of her refusal to drink. It was Breuer's belief that the act of recalling the experience of the dog drinking from a glass caused the symptom to vanish.

Breuer then attempted to associate all of his patient's peculiar habits with damaging or disgusting experiences in the past. During the morning sessions Anna was hypnotized and asked to concentrate on a particular symptom. As she talked, her observations were jotted down. In the evening, during the day's second hypnotic session, she elaborated upon the events that had been mentioned previously. In this way, there was a gradual working back of situations to their primal causes. Only when the basic cause was discovered did the symptom disappear. It usually required a considerable amount of work to arrive at the basic cause. For instance, Anna gave one hundred and eight reasons for her failure to hear a person enter the room before she revealed the real explanation, which involved her father. The discovery finally removed the symptom.

Gradually, Anna recalled under hypnosis all the events associated with the development of her hysteria. In July, 1880, when her father had first become ill, she and her mother shared the task of nursing him. On one occasion when her mother was away, she was awakened from her sleep by a sense of foreboding and great anxiety. She hurried to her father's sickroom and sat near his bed, holding her right arm over the back of the chair. As she began to doze, she imagined she saw a black snake coming out of the wall toward her father as if to bite him. She had an impulse to drive the snake away, but her right arm seemed paralyzed and asleep. She looked at her fingers with dread and noticed that they had changed into small snakes with skulls. She wanted to pray, but her anxiety was so great that the words refused to come. Finally, she remembered an English nursery rhyme. Only in the English language was she able to think and pray. The blast of a locomotive, however, interrupted her reverie. Next day, while outdoors, a bent twig evoked the snake hallucination, which in turn automatically brought about a contracture of her right arm.

Anna's inability to eat was traced to the constant feeling of anxiety during her father's illness, when she lost her appetite. Her deafness first appeared when she attempted to block out the sound of her father who was having a choking attack. Her visual disturbance, too, was associated with her father. Once as she sat near him tears filled her eyes. Her father asked her for the time, and because her vision was blurred, it was necessary to bring the watch close to her eyes. Anna also had difficulty speaking. During a quarrel with her father she had to suppress a sharp retort, and her throat contracted. This spasm repeated itself later on. By going back and discovering the experiences associated with the first appearance of all these symptoms, Anna "related away" her loss of feeling, cough, trembling, and other complaints. Finally, her entire hysterical attack came to an end.

The importance of Breuer's work lies in the change of emphasis he gave to hypnotic therapy. Instead of simply trying to remove the symptoms, he tried to get at their causes. Although there is evidence that Janet simultaneously arrived at the technique of liberating emotions that had been repressed ("strangulated affects") and that were associated with traumatic memories, Breuer traditionally has been given credit for the discovery.

There is some indication, too, that Breuer's work gave Freud the ideas that resulted in his monumental work on the unconscious. He was so impressed with what Breuer was doing that he devoted a good deal of his time to hypnotic experimentation. With Breuer he published in 1895 *Studien über Hysterie* that set forth a theory of neurosis with early traumatic experiences as the basic cause. "We found at first to our greatest surprise, that the *individual hysterical symptoms immediately disappeared without returning if we succeeded in thoroughly awakening the memories of the causal process with its accompaning affect, and if the patient circumstantially discussed the process in the most detailed manner and gave verbal expression to the affect.*" Breuer and Freud concluded that hysterical symptoms developed as a result of experiences so damaging to the individual that they had been pushed out of awareness. The "mental energy" originally associated with the experience was blocked from reaching consciousness by the mechanism of repression. The energy was then converted into bodily symptoms. Under hypnotic treatment, the release of these repressed emotions into normal channels of consciousness made it unnecessary to convert the energy into symptoms. Because this technique seemed to remove a great deal of damaging emotion in the unconscious, it was called the "cathartic method."

Another important modification in hypnotic technique was instituted by Freud. In attempting to hypnotize a young woman, Lucie R., who complained of depression and constant peculiar odors, he was unable to induce the somnambulistic trance essential for cathartic treatment. Remembering an experiment by Bernheim, who, by persistent urging, had caused a patient to remember in the waking state her experiences during a somnambulistic trance, Freud placed his hand on the patient's forehead and asked her to repeat everything that came to her mind. Recollections and fantasies that the patient thought too insignificant to mention were by this process of "free association" brought to the surface. Freud was thus able to recapture important pathogenic experiences without recourse to hypnosis.

Perhaps more significant was Freud's discovery of the motives and resistances involved in the process of forgetting. Because many memories were inaccessible to hypnotic recall even in the somnambulistic state, Freud concluded that there were forces that kept memories from entering consciousness, and he discovered that it was necessary to neutralize the repressing forces before recall was possible. An effective way to overcome this resistance was to permit the patient to relax and to talk freely about any idea or fantasy that entered his mind, no matter how trivial or absurd. Freud could observe in this "free association" a sequential theme that was somehow related to the traumatic event. Other important ways of discovering traumatic episodes were in the interpretation of the patient's dreams and the irrational attitudes and fantasies the patient developed about the physician, a phenomenon Freud called "transference." He concluded that hypnosis was ineffective in the face of resistance, and he consequently abandoned the trance as a means of uprooting repressed memories.

In continuing his psychoanalytic work, Freud laid less and less stress on the repressed emotions of early traumatic experiences as the chief cause of neurosis. He became more and more convinced of the protective nature of the symptoms, and, in 1926, he revised his theory of neurosis drastically, claiming that symptoms were not only manifestations of repressed instinctive strivings, but also defenses against these strivings. Essentially they were techniques to avert anxiety. By pointing out that symptoms served a defensive function in the psychic life of the individual, Freud veered further and further away from using hypnosis for removal of symptoms.

Freud's discoveries, as well as the widespread disappointment in hypnosis as a permanent cure for hysteria, almost succeeded in dealing hypnosis a death blow shortly after the turn of the century. Whereas thousands of scientific articles and books on the subject had been published annually up to this time, the number of publications thereafter dwindled to several dozen. A few authorities, nevertheless, proceeded with hypnotic research. The most notable among them—Pierre Janet in France, J. Milne

Bramwell in Great Britain, and Morton Prince and Boris Sidis in the United States—published on the subject. However, the growth of the psychoanalytic movement and the development of other forms of psychotherapy reduced hypnosis to a place of relatively minor importance. Hypnotism again, as in the previous century, became subject to attack by the medical profession on the basis that it was allied to quackery and a source of moral danger. Even Bernheim, who had done so much for hypnosis, no longer defended it.

Janet, however, continued to believe in hypnosis as a most effective treatment for neuroses provided one could accept its limitations. He warned that hypnotic suggestion could produce no action beyond the power of the normal will. Indeed, because neurotic persons suffered from "defects of the will," he contended that the physician should be satisfied if hypnosis produced actions no greater than those encompassed by the average will.

In the eyes of most physicians, nevertheless, hypnosis was absolutely abandoned as a relic of the past. Although it was given a passing nod in psychiatric textbooks, it was considered to belong in the category of such ancient practices as cupping, leeching, and bloodletting.

There are psychiatrists who still disavow hypnosis on the basis of Freud's original arguments against it. Yet Freud's theories about hypnosis were biased, despite his usual great objectivity as an observer. He came to the conclusion that hypnotic symptom removal was always temporary or accompanied by substitutive symptoms, that results were entirely dependent on the maintenance of a positive relationship, that the trance was a regressive libidinal manifestation, and that not many patients could be hypnotized deeply enough to make the effort worthwhile. All these ideas had a damaging impact on the popularity of hypnosis. We now know that these assumptions are not correct. Yet there are those who still uphold their validity, as they support many other early hypotheses of Freud that he himself later revised or abandoned. Actually, Freud never repudiated hypnosis; he put it aside for what he believed was a more effective method of working with neurosis. He even wrote that it had a place in medicine which could be of great value.

There were other important contributions to hypnosis during the early years of this century. Morton Prince (1854–1929) in the United States published fascinating accounts of his work with hysterical patients suffering from multiple personalities. Prince used hypnosis as a way of reintegrating the alternating discordant personalities.*

Clark L. Hull (1884–1952) attempted to give hypnosis scientific validity by setting up a number of experiments with controls in order to validate the many assumptions that had always been accepted at face value without challenge. Hull's book, *Hypnosis and Suggestibility*, published in 1933, set forth his theory of hypnosis. Like all other theories to date, it has been challenged.

Actually, the hypnotic state, like the conscious state and the sleeping state, is extremely complex and involves so many physiological, psychological, and interpersonal factors that no one theory has yet been able to account for all the intricate operations that take place within its range. This does not at all hinder our practical employment of this interesting method. In medicine we utilize many remedies and procedures because they work, even though we may not know exactly why and how they work. Every year, research adds more data to our fund of knowledge, providing an empirical foundation for our pragmatic superstructure.

The Revival of Hypnosis

During the First World War, a large number of victims suffered from muscle spasms, paralysis, and amnesia, as well as other symptoms caused by the trauma of war. Because of the shortage of psychiatrists, an abbreviated form of therapy was needed. Hypnotherapy was revived and used both for direct symptom removal and the release of traumatic memories. During the Second World War there was an even greater employment of hypnosis as a short-term therapeutic procedure. Success in the treatment of war neuroses created a new wave of enthusiasm for

* In recent years, the movies *Three Faces of Eve* and *Sybil* popularized the syndrome of dissociated personality, which is among the rarest of hysterical symptoms.

hypnotherapy, which has persisted to the present. However, in the immediate postwar years confusion about methods and reasons for success and failures made the application of hypnosis in medicine a hit-and-miss procedure.

To deal with the problems posed by the use of hypnosis, a number of clinicians and researchers organized two scientific societies in the United States, the American Society of Clinical Hypnosis and the Society for Clinical and Experimental Hypnosis. It was largely because of the work of these societies that hypnosis has continued to gain a respectable foothold in research and psychiatry.

Interest in hypnosis has also been steadily mounting among members of the medical profession in fields other than psychiatry, as evidenced by the increasing number of articles appearing in nonpsychiatric medical periodicals. These have dealt principally with the control of pain and discomfort in acute and chronic medical and surgical conditions, and with the use of hypnosis as an anesthetic aid in obstetrical procedures and minor surgery.

In 1953 the British Medical Association appointed a subcommittee of the Psychological Medicine Group Committee of the association to investigate the virtues of hypnotism in medical practice. It was asked to issue a statement about the nature and uses of hypnotism, its affinity to medical science and to psychologic medicine in particular, the proper attitude of the medical profession toward the inevitable popular interest that hypnosis arouses, the place it should occupy in the medical curriculum, and the advisability of making available to those training for certain specialties a fuller knowledge of its phenomena.

The report of the subcommittee stated that hypnotism was a valuable aid in psychiatry and as a means of inducing anesthesia and analgesia for surgical and dental operations, as well as for the effective relief of pain in childbirth. It recommended that (1) a description of hypnotism and its therapeutic possibilities, limitations, and dangers be given to medical undergraduates, (2) the clinical uses of hypnotism be taught to all medical postgraduate students training as specialists in psychological medicine, and possibly to interning anesthetists and obstetricians, so that they might understand when and how it should be applied, and (3) there be further research into hypnotism, since this could benefit medical science.

In 1956 the Council on Mental Health of the American Medical Association undertook a study of the medical use of hypnosis. The report of the Council endorsed hypnosis, stressing the need for competent professional training in its methods. The report concluded: "General practitioners, medical specialists, and dentists might find hypnosis valuable as a therapeutic adjunct within the specific field of their professional competence. It should be stressed that all those who use hypnosis need to be aware of the complex nature of the phenomena involved. . . . Certain aspects of hypnosis still remain unknown and controversial, as is true in many other areas of medicine and the psychological sciences. Therefore, active participation in high-level research by members of the medical and dental professions is to be encouraged. The use of hypnosis for entertainment purposes is vigorously condemned." Later, the American Psychiatric Association published its report, which accepted the proper use of hypnosis as an important aid in therapy.

During the 1960's and 1970's, hypnosis experienced a spectacular revival largely as a product of experimental work with this method as an adjunct to psychotherapy. Much of the interest has been due to the activities of a dedicated group of professionals who have worked diligently to provide a scientific base for the procedure. Among these are Milton Erickson, Margaret Brenman, Mertin Gill, Andre Weitzenhoffer, Martin Orne, Jerome Schneck, Herbert Spiegel, Milton Kline, Ernest Hilgard, Erika Fromm, Theodore X. Barber, John Watkins, Harold Crasilneck, Leon Chertok, and others. The most prolific worker was Erickson, one of whose unique endowments was his ability to perceive the specific learning capacities of his patients and to design interventions suited to their idiocratic styles of acquiring and utilizing information. His modes of dealing with resistance were perhaps his most trenchant contribution to the therapeutic process.

Modern uses of hypnosis embrace its employment within the matrix of a number of paradigms, such as social influence, dissonance reduction, indirect meta-communications, employment of paradox, imagery evocation, double binds, and a variety of other interventions. Most recently the dramatic innovative techniques of Milton Erickson have been re-examined and analyzed by Haley, Rossi, Grinder, Delozier, and Bandler with the object of distilling from them strategies that can enhance the therapeutic process. Some new ideas have emerged from this work including "neuro-linguistic programming" through which subjective experience is reorganized to specify and achieve desirable behavioral outcomes. It is apparent from this work that hypnosis can be employed in practically all forms of psychotherapy as a catalyst to technique.

Present-Day Trends

It is obvious that any therapeutic procedure which arouses as much cyclic enthusiasm as hypnosis does must have some intrinsic values. Yet obviously there are certain elements inherent in the practice of hypnosis that cause its periodic demise. What these factors may be certainly merits exploration, if for no other reason than to assign to hypnosis a more secure place in the catalogue of accepted therapies. Research and carefully evaluated studies might conceivably help to avert the imminent discrediting of hypnosis, for there is no reason to assume that the present favorable trend toward its acceptance will not be followed by another decline in popularity.

There are many rifts and areas of disagreement about the virtues, limitations, and modes of application of hypnosis to the field of medical and psychiatric treatment. However, the dissension among its practitioners is by no means greater than in most other divisions of psychotherapy. Problems that arise over the uses of hypnosis are based more on the personalties that employ it than on the method itself. There are some untrained persons who practice with few or no qualifications. There are others who utilize hypnosis not only for purposes of therapy or research but also as an outlet for their own neurotic designs. Lacking the modesty and prudence required to practice within the limits of hypnotherapy or to serve the needs of their patients, these practitioners may make of hypnosis an ineffectual method or convert it into an instrument of potential harm.

These professionals who are fearful of hypnosis as a therapeutic aid or who exaggerate its virtues either have never used hypnosis in a properly applied manner long enough to test the method, or else are victims of superstition, prejudice, or a naïve magical expectancy. Unfortunately, a number of self-appointed spokesmen for hypnosis, some writing extensively, help discredit it in a number of ways. They overdramatize the process, exaggerate its virtues, participate in and publish results of poorly conceived experiments, engage in naïvely organized therapeutic schemes, and offer theoretic formulations that violate the most elementary precepts of dynamic psychology.

Serious workers in the field, however, are gradually undermining rampant prejudices against uses of hypnosis in the field of medicine. Through their efforts hypnosis is being freed from its superstitious associations to take its rightful place in the family of sciences.

Bibliography

Bandler, R., and Grinder, J.: *The Structure of Magic: A Book About Language and Therapy*, Vol. 1. Palo Alto, Calif., Science and Behavior Books, 1975.

Barber, T. X.: *Hypnosis: A Scientific Approach*. New York, Van Nostrand Reinhold, 1969.

Brenman, M., and Gill, M.: *Hypnotherapy: A Survey of the Literature*. New York, Wiley, 1964.

Breuer, J., and Freud, S. E.: *Studies in Hysteria*. New York, Basic Books, 1957.

Chertok, L.: "From Liébeault to Freud." Historical Note. *Am. J. Psychotherapy* 22:76–96, 1972.

Conn, J. H.: "Is Hypnosis Really Dangerous?" *Int. J. Clin. Exp. Hypnosis* 20:61–76, 1972.

Crasilneck, H. B., and Hall, J. A.: *Clinical Hypnosis*. New York, Grune & Stratton, 1975.

Erickson, M. H: *The Practical Application of Medical and Dental Hypnosis*. New York, Julian Press, 1961.

Esdaile, J.: *Hypnosis in Medicine and Surgery*. New York, Julian Press, 1957. Originally published in 1850 under the title: *Mesmerism in India*.

Fromm, E., and Shor, R. E.: *Hypnosis: Research Developments and Perspectives*. 2d ed. Chicago, Aldine-Atherton, 1979.

Gill, M. M., and Brenman, M.: *Hypnosis and Related States*. New York, International Universities Press, 1959.

Hilgard, E. R.: "Pain: Its Reduction and Production under Hypnosis." *Proc. Am. Philosophical Soc.* 115:470–476, 1971.

Janet, P.: *Psychological Healing*. New York, Macmillan, 1925.

Kline, M. V.: *Freud and Hypnosis*. New York, Julian Press, 1958.

Orne, M.T.: "Can a Hypnotized Subject Be Compelled to Carry Out Otherwise Unacceptable Behavior?" *Int. J. Clin. Exp. Hypnosis* 20:101–117, 1972.

Rossi, E., ed.: *Collected Papers of Milton H. Erickson*. New York, Halsted Press, 1980.

Spiegel, H.: "Is Symptom Removal Dangerous?" *Am. J. Psychiatry* 123:1279–1283, 1967.

Watkins, J. G.: "Antisocial Behavior under Hypnosis: Possible or Impossible?" *Int. J. Clin. Exp. Hypnosis* 20:95–100, 1972.

Weitzenhoffer, A. M.: "The Nature of Hypnosis II." *Am. J. Clin. Hypnosis* 6:40–72, 1964.

Wolberg, L. R.: *Medical Hypnosis*. New York, Grune & Stratton, 1948.

———: *Hypnoanalysis*, 2d ed. New York, Grune & Stratton, 1964.

Glossary

Affect: A feeling, mood, or emotion.
Amnesia: Loss of memory; inability to recall past experiences.
Analgesia: Diminution or absence of pain.
Anxiety: An extremely unpleasant emotional reaction characterized by panicky feelings and physical distress often brought about by inner conflicts. It is to be distinguished from fear, which is related to identifiable danger situations.
Apperception: Awareness of the contents of one's mind.
Automatic writing: Messages communicated in writing that are elaborated without conscious participation from dissociated aspects of the personality.
Behavior therapy, behavior modification: A form of therapy that deals with the patient's symptoms and complaints through desensitization and reconditioning methods rather than insight.
Body image: Awareness of one's body as an object in space.
Caesarian operation: Surgical removal through abdominal incision of the newborn child.
Catelepsy: Extraordinary maintenance of fixed postures.
Catharsis: Emotional unburdening through verbalization.
Conditioned reflex: The result of a form of learning (conditioning) whereby a neutral stimulus produces the same response as that of a primary stimulus.
Conflict: A clash between two or more opposing impulses, needs, or ideas, leading to tension, anxiety, or neurotic behavior.

Countertransference: The therapist's attitudes and feelings, mobilized by the relationship with patients, that are products of the therapist's deeply ingrained personality disturbances or past experiences.

Defense mechanisms: Unconscious processes that serve to give relief from emotional conflicts. Common motives that activate these mechanisms are anxiety, guilt, disgust, and shame.

Depersonalization: The process of losing one's identity or sense of reality of oneself.

Depression: A mood of sadness and despair. In its intense form it constitutes a clinical syndrome.

Dissociation: A defense mechanism through which emotion and affect are separated and detached from an idea, situation, or object.

Experimental conflict: An artificial situation created by suggestion during hypnosis to study a subject's response to conflict.

Free association: Unrestrained and undirected verbalization of everything that passes through one's mind.

Fugue, fugue state: A temporary flight from reality in which the individual performs complex acts, followed by amnesia for these events.

Hallucination: A sensation occuring in any of the senses that is perceived without any external stimulus.

Hypnoanalysis: A form of psychoanaytic psychotherapy that employs hypnosis to explore the unconscious.

Hypnosis: An altered state of consciousness in which suggestibility is greatly enhanced.

Hypnotherapy: Psychotherapy aided by hypnosis.

Hypnotic regression: The return by suggestion during hypnosis to an earlier period of life.

Mirror or crystal gazing: Projecting visual hallucinations into a mirror or a crystal ball.

Neurolinguistic programming: The manipulation of unique individual thought processes to effect changes in behavior and feelings.

Pathology: The science that deals with the nature of disease.

Phobia: A persistent and intense fear of an object or situation.

Placebo: An inert substance or technique whose effect is achieved by faith in the measure and expectation of success.

Posthypnotic suggestion: A suggestion, made during hypnosis, that is carried out later in waking life.
Psychoanalysis: (1) A theory of human development and behavior, (2) a means of exploring repudiated and repressed memories, and (3) a technique for correcting existing emotional difficulties and promoting reconstructive personality change.
Psychoanalytic psychotherapy: An active form of treatment for emotional problems that contains some of the ideas and techniques of psychoanalysis.
Psychodynamic: Pertaining to mental forces in action that are responsible for thoughts, ideas, emotions, and behavior.
Psychopathic personality: An individual with a personality now described as antisocial.
Psychosomatic: Commonly used to refer to disorders whose physical symptoms are brought about and sustained by emotional factors. These may also be called psychophysiological disorders.
Psychotomimetic drugs: Drugs that produce psychotic-like alteration of the mental processes.
Rapport: A harmonious relationship.
Rationalization: The process of justifying an attitude, idea, or behavior that is otherwise illogical or unreasonable.
Regression: The partial or symbolic return to a more infantile or childlike stage of behavior.
Resistance: An oppositional response, conscious or unconscious, to therapeutic interventions.
Revivification: The process of reliving a (usually) traumatic or conflictual past event or situation.
Somnambule: A subject capable of achieving somnambulism.
Somnambulism: The deepest form of hypnosis.
Symbol: A disguised representation of an object.
Trance, trance state: hypnosis, the hypnotic state.
Transference: The projection by the patient to others of thoughts, wishes, and feelings that were originally associated with important people (such as parents and siblings) in the patient's early life.
Working through: The joint exploration by patient and therapist to understand and resolve a problem.

Index

Addiction
problems, 243
to hypnosis, 222
Alcoholics Anonymous, 175, 178, 247
Alcoholism, 175, 178, 184, 247
Altered ego state in hypnosis, 270
American Medical Association, 8, 293
American Psychiatric Association report, 293
American Society of Clinical Hypnosis, 292
Amnesia, 19, 70, 71, 110, 174, 220
Analgesia, 90, 158
Anesthesia, 16, 90, 159, 163
Animal
hypnosis, 264
magnetism, 274, 275
Antabuse, 178, 247
Anxiety, 120, 128, 178
Aphasic disorders, 15
Aphonia, 174
Assertive techniques, 187
Astrology, 275
Automatic writing, 35
Aversive conditioning, 181, 184

Bandler, Richard, 291, 296
Barber, Theodore X., 293, 297
Bedside manner, 135, 159
Beecher, Henry K., 159
Behavior
disorders, 179
therapy, 21, 141, 155, 180-186
under hypnosis, 40-42
Bernheim, Hippolyte, 284, 288, 290
Bertrand, Alexander, 279, 283
Bleuler, Eugen, 105
Blister formation, 86
Borderline conditions, hypnosis in, 226, 245
Boyle, Robert, 274
Braid, James, 282
Brain-wave studies (electroencephalography), 89-90
Bramwell, J. Milne, 290
Brenman, Margaret, 293, 297
Breuer, Joseph, 286
Bridey Murphy, 41-42, 239
British Medical Association, 8, 292
Bronchoscopy, 17
Bruxism, 166
Burns, 16, 167

Caesarian operation, 160
Cancer, 167
Cardiac conditions, 15
Cardiovascular effects, 85
Catalepsy, 80
Catharsis
verbal, 136-137

emotional, 193, 220
Cathartic method, 288
Cayce, Edgar, 239, 276
Charcot, Jean Martin, 284
Chertok, Leon, 293, 296
Childbirth, hypnosis in, 161-164
Children, hypnosis with, 178
Circulatory phenomena, 88
Clairvoyance, 276
Conditioned
learning theories, 266
reflex theories, 266
reflexes, effect on, 94
Conflict induction, 9
Conn, Jacob H., 218
Constipation, 13
Contractures, 174
Contraindications to hypnosis, 246
Conversion hysteria, 167
Convulsive
phenomena, 81
symptoms, hypnotically liberated, 220
Crasilneck, Harold, 293, 296
Creative imagination, effect on, 9
Crile, George, 160
Criminal investigations, hypnosis in, 255
Criminality during hypnosis, 215-219
Cross-examinations, 238
Crystal gazing, 91
Cudworth, Ralph, 274

Dangers of hypnosis, 214, 223, 226, 227
Darwin, Charles R., 264
Debilitating disease, 15
Delinquency, hypnosis in, 248
Delusions, induced, 95
Dengrove, Edward, 181
Denial of hypnosis, 260
Dentistry, hypnosis in, 15, 164-166
Dependency
and hypnosis, 245, 251
reactions, 222-223
Depression, 98
Depth of hypnosis, 27
and results, 254
Deslon, Charles, 276
Detachment, helping, 144
Diagnostic uses, 17
Dianetics, 193
Die Seherin von Prevorst, 280
Disability problems, 179
Dissociation theories, 264
Dreams
hypnotic, 243
induction of, 68-69
interpretation of, 19
posthypnotic, 44
recall of, 146
Drug dependence, 175
Drugs, hypnotic, 242
Du Magnetisme Animal en France, 280
Dumping syndrome, 13

Ecker, Herbert, A., 161
Eclecticism, 155
Eczema, 13
Effectiveness of hypnosis, 3
Electroencephalographic findings, 78, 259, 263
Elliotson, John, 282, 283
Emergencies, 176
Emotional problems, 14
Endorphin, 158
Enuresis, 13, 18, 177, 184
Episiotomies, 163
Erikson, Milton, 97, 168, 293, 294, 297
Esdaile, James, 283, 297
ESP. *See* Telepathy.
Estabrooks, George H., 110
Evans, Frederick J., 216
Experimental
neurosis, 107
uses of hypnosis, 8

Failures in hypnosis, 8, 201-213
Faith healing, 240
Faria, José Custódio de, 279
Ferenczi, Sandor, 269, 270

Franklin, Benjamin, 276, 278
Free association, 67, 145, 288
Freud, Sigmund, 5, 191, 238, 244, 245, 252, 269, 270, 285
Frigidity, 13, 247
Fromm, Erika, 101, 293, 296
Fugue states, 174, 220, 265

Gait disturbances, diagnosis of, 18
Gassner, Johann Joseph, 274
Gastric ulcers, 12
Gastritis, 13
Gastrointestinal problem, 89
Gill, Mertin, 293, 297
Goals in therapy, 208, 211
Greatrakes, Valentine, 274
Grinder, John, 294, 296
Group hypnosis, 243
Guided imagery, 21

Habit disturbances, 174
Hair pulling, 177, 184
Haley, Jay, 294
Hallucinations
  hypnotically liberated, 220
  in light hypnosis, 254
  negative, 92
  producing, 67, 91
Hallucinogens, 42
Headaches, 18
Hearing
  disturbances, diagosis of, 18
  effect of hypnosis on, 91
"Heartburn," 13
Heidenhain, Rudolf, 285
Helmont, Jean Baptiste van, 273
Hiccuping, 13, 18
Highway hypnosis, 269
Hilgard, Ernest R., 26, 31, 217, 218, 219, 220, 221, 293, 296
History of hypnosis, 272, 295
Homosexuality, 172
Hull, Clark L., 291
Huxley, Aldous, ix
Hyperamnesia, 94
Hypersuggestibility, 81-83
Hypertension, 13
Hypnoanalysis, 20, 32, 35, 91
Hypnotists
  amateur, 225
  limitations of, 233
  qualifications of, 231-234
Hysterical disorders, 92, 174, 178, 220, 265

Imagery, 21
Impotence, 13, 172, 247
Induction of hypnosis, 47-77
  failures in, 205
  reactions to, 36
Insight, 126, 152, 190, 194, 249
Insomnia, 15, 14, 177
Intellectual functions, effect on, 93-96
Irritable colon, 13

James, Stanley L., 163
Janet, Pierre, 240, 265, 285, 289, 290
"Jumpers," 41
Juvenile delinquency, 179

Kerner, Jestinus, 280
Kircher, Athanasius, 274
Kline, Milton, 293, 297
Krafft-Ebing, Richard von, 285

Lafontaine, Charles, 282
Latah, 41
Laying on of hands, 273, 275
Learning process, effect on, 94
LeCron, Leslie M., 216
Lie detection, 238
Liébeault, Ambroise Auguste, 283
Limitations of hypnosis, 8
Long-term therapy, 175

Lorin, Will, 224
LSD, 42
Lyon, W., 216

Magic, Witchcraft, Animal Magnetism, Hypnotism and Electro-biology, 283
Man in a Trance, 224, 226
Malnutrition, 14
Marmer, Milton J., 161
Masochism, mechanism of, 118
Mastectomy, 160
Maxwell, William, 274
Medical applications, 12
Medico-legal aspects, 225, 238
Meditation, 42
Mellor, Norman H., 178
Memories, recovering, 21, 94, 150, 190-200
Menstrual difficulties, 13
Mental telepathy, 91
Mescaline, 42
Mesmer, Franz Anton, 275, 281
Metabolic problems, 89
"Midtown Study," 115
Miracle cures, 240
Mirror gazing, 91
Misconceptions about hypnosis, 5
Misuses of hypnosis, 5
Motivation
  effect of hypnosis on, 90
  enhancing, 139
  importance of, 204, 211, 218
Motor symptoms, hypnotically liberated, 220
Moya, Frank, 163
Mucous colitis, 13
Murphy, Bridey, 41-42, 239
Muscular phenomena, 80-81

Nail biting, 174, 177, 184
Nature of hypnosis, 257-271
"Neuro-linguistic programming," 294
Neurypnology, 283
Neurodermatitis, 13
Neurologic conditions, 167
Newman, Richard, 101
Night terrors, 178
"Normality," 114

Obesity, 14
Obsessions, induced, 95
Obsessive-compulsive neurosis, 173
Obstetrics, 15
Operant conditioning, 184
Orgone box, 131
Orne, Martin, 216, 293, 297
Orthopedic uses, 13, 15
Overeating, 174, 177

Pain
  control, 15, 156-168, 254
  syndrome, 90, 98, 166-168
Paracelsus, Philippis, 273
Paralytic phenomena, 18, 81, 174
Paranoid patients, hypnosis in, 246
Paranormal perception, 276
Paraprofessionals, 226-228
Paresthesias, diagnosis of, 18
Parker (magnetizer), 282
Paroxysmal tachycardia, 13
Pascal, Gerald R., 27
Pavlov, Ivan Petrovich, 263
Peptic ulcer, 13
Performance and hypnosis, 112-113, 253
Personality
  development of, 115-120
  hypnotizability and, 253
  reconstructive changes in, 123
Phenomena of hypnosis, 77-113
Phobias, 5, 181
Physical exhaustion (neurocirculatory asthenia), 13
Physiological
  reactions, 83-90
  theories, 262
Placebo influence, 129-134, 159, 254
Plastic surgery, 17

Posthypnotic suggestions, 19, 48, 71-72, 103-111
Postinduction reactions, 42
Primal Scream Therapy, 193
Prince, Morton, 290, 291
Proctoscopy, 17
Progress in therapy, enhancing, 151
Pseudoangina, 13
Psoriasis, 13
Psychiatric uses, 18
Psychoanalytic theories of hypnosis, 269
Psychological theories of hypnosis, 267
Psychosomatic symptoms, 12, 128, 174
Psychotherapy
  expediting, 19
  goals of, 129
  influence of hypnosis on, 18, 138-156
Psychotomimetic drugs, 42
Publicity about hypnosis, 4
Puységur, Armand de, 278

Radiation, hypnosis as adjunct to, 167
Rapport, 79, 136
Rationalization as defense, 95
Reaction(s)
  untoward, 219-221
  to induction, diagnostic value of, 43
"Reciprocal inhibition," 181
Reeducation, 97
Regression
  and revivification, 35, 98-103, 239
  theories of hypnosis, 269
Rehabilitative uses, 14
Reichenbach, Karl, 281
Reincarnation, 42, 239
Reiter, P. J., 215
Relationship
  influence of, 134-136, 243
  problems, 141
Religious healing, 240
Research in hypnosis, 84, 250, 251
Researcher bias, 250
Resistance, dealing with, 19, 20, 22-23, 32, 125, 138, 176, 190, 249, 258
Respiratory phenomena, 88
Reyher, Joseph, 29
Roberts, Oral, 275
Role playing, 152
  theories, 269
Rossi, Ernest L., 294, 296
Rowland, L. W., 216
Rubinstein, Robert, 101

Salzberg, Herman C., 27
Sanders, Raymond S., 29
Schneck, Jerome, 293
Schizophrenia, hypnosis in, 245
Scientology, 193
Search for Bridey Murphy, 41-42, 239
Self-hypnosis, 76, 153-154, 173, 178, 213, 223, 242, 243, 247
Self-image, devaluation of, 118
Sensory
  deprivation, 29, 259
  disturbances, 174
  phenomena, 90
  symptoms, hypnotically liberated, 220
Sexual
  arousal in hypnosis, 252
  dysfunction, diagnosis of, 18
  problems, hypnosis in, 89, 175, 247
  proclivities, 172
  seduction, 221-222, 238
Shaffer, G. Wilson, 31
"Shell hearing," 91-92
Short-term therapy, 136, 175, 212
Sidis, Boris, 290
Sigmoidoscopy, 17
Skin disease, 13, 85
Sleep
  and hypnosis, 37, 90
  theories of hypnosis, 262
Sleepwalking, 264
Smell, effect on, 91
Smoking, 174, 177, 253
Society for Clinical and Experimental Hypnosis, 292
Somatic symptoms, hypnotically liberated, 220
Somnambules, 218

Somnambulism 31, 66, 264
Spasms, 18, 174
Speech
  disorders, 41, 144, 174
  retraining, 15
Spiegel, Herbert, 293, 297
Spiritualists, 41, 238
Stage hypnotism, 48, 91, 228-230
Stages of hypnosis, 64-72
Stammering, 144
Starvation, 178
Stomach
  spasm (pylorospasm), 13
  ulcers, 89
Stress resolution, 12, 13
Susceptibility to hypnosis, factors in, 30
Suggestibility, 81-83
  and trance depth, 34
  tests for, 51-54
Suggestion, 241, 248, 254, 269
  theories, 167
Sumner, William G., 82
Supernormal phenomena, 276
Surgery, hypnosis in, 15, 159
Susceptibility to hypnosis, 22, 26
  in psychotics, 31
  increasing, 29
Sybil, 291
Symptom relief and removal, 140, 169-180, 245
  analytic techniques for, 186-189
  behavioral techniques for, 180-186
  limitations of, 180
Systematic desensitization, 181

Taste, effect on, 91
Tape recordings, 223, 253
Teaching uses of hypnosis, 8
Teeth-grinding, 166
Telekinesis, 276
Telepathy, 91
Tension control, 12, 14, 128-129
Theories of hypnosis, 261-271
  altered ego state, 270
  animal, 264
  behavioral, 266-267
  conditioned reflex, 266
  difficulty in defining, 271
  dissociation, 264
  physiological, 262
  psychoanalytic, 269
  psychological, 267
  regressive, 269
  role playing, 269
  sleep, 226
  suggestion, 267
Thermoanesthesia, 90
Three Faces of Eve, 291
Thumb sucking, 165
Tics, diagnosis of, 18
Time
  distortion, 168
  sense, 96-98
Trance
  depth, 24, 32, 35
  speaking, 41
Transference, 43, 45, 122, 147, 220, 270, 289
Traumatic memories, recovering, 210
Tuke, Daniel Hack, 285

Urinary problems, 13, 18, 89

Verbalization, facilitating, 144
Vision, effect on, 91-93
Visual disorders, 18, 174
Vomiting, 18

War neuroses, 194
Wart elimination, 85
Watkins, John, 293, 297
Weitzenhoffer, Andre, 26, 293, 297
Wells, W. R., 110
Werner, William E. F., 162
Wolberg, Lewis R., 297
Wolpe, Joseph, 181

Yoga, 242
Young, P. S., 216
Zen Buddhism, 242